ROUTLEDGE LIBRARY EDITIONS:
THE VICTORIAN WORLD

Volume 24

D1478688

THE LITERATURE OF STRUGGLE

THE LITERATURE OF STRUGGLE

An Anthology of Chartist Fiction

Edited by
IAN HAYWOOD

Routledge
Taylor & Francis Group

LONDON AND NEW YORK

First published in 1995 by SCOLAR PRESS

This edition first published in 2016
by Routledge
2 Park Square, Milton Park, Abingdon, Oxon OX14 4RN

and by Routledge
711 Third Avenue, New York, NY 10017

Routledge is an imprint of the Taylor & Francis Group, an informa business

British Library Cataloguing in Publication Data
A catalogue record for this book is available from the British Library

ISBN: 978-1-138-66565-1 (Set)
ISBN: 978-1-315-61965-1 (Set) (ebk)
ISBN: 978-1-138-64396-3 (Volume 24) (hbk)
ISBN: 978-1-138-64398-7 (Volume 24) (pbk)
ISBN: 978-1-315-62911-7 (Volume 24) (ebk)

Publisher's Note
The publisher has gone to great lengths to ensure the quality of this reprint but
points out that some imperfections in the original copies may be apparent.

Disclaimer
The publisher has made every effort to trace copyright holders and would welcome
correspondence from those they have been unable to trace.

The Literature of Struggle

An Anthology of Chartist Fiction

Ian Haywood

SCOLAR PRESS

Published by
SCOLAR PRESS
Gower House
Croft Road
Aldershot
Hants GU11 3HR
England

Ashgate Publishing Company
Old Post Road
Brookfield
Vermont 05036
USA

British Library Cataloguing in Publication Data

Literature of Struggle: Anthology of Chartist Fiction
(Nineteenth Century Series)
 I. Haywood, Ian II. Series
 823.809

ISBN 1–85928–032–3

Library of Congress Cataloging-in-Publication Data

The literature of struggle: an anthology of Chartist fiction/
 [edited by] Ian Haywood
     p.   cm.
   ISBN 1–85928–032–3 (hardback)
   1. Great Britain—Social conditions—19th century—Fiction.
 2. Social conflict—Great Britain—Fiction. 3. Labor movement—
 Great Britain—Fiction. 4. Working-class—Great Britain—Fiction.
 5. Working-class writings. 6. English fiction—19th century.
 7. Protest literature, English. 8. Chartism—Fiction.
 I. Haywood, Ian, 1958–
 PR1309.S63L58   1995
 823'.80358—dc20   95–687
                                                            CIP

ISBN 1 85928 032 3

Printed and bound in Great Britain by
Hartnolls Limited, Bodmin, Cornwall

Contents

5. Chartism

Acknowledgements

I would like to thank Alec Macaulay at Scolar Press for agreeing to take on this project. A semester of study leave and generous financial support with photocopying costs were gratefully received from Roehampton Institute London. The British Library and British Newspaper Library proved to be invaluable sources of material, though operating under severe pressures of cuts in public spending. Still on the production side, special thanks must go to Jane Harris for preparing camera-ready copy. The academic encouragement of my readers at Scolar Press was particularly welcome, as was the feedback and support of Stephen Roberts of the University of Birmingham. Colleagues running the Victorian Literature course at Roehampton Institute provided a valuable opportunity to talk about the book to undergraduates. Finally, for her unfailing support and enthusiasm, my thanks go to Theresa.

Introduction

As its name implies, Chartism was a movement whose vision centred on a literary document. The Charter was the expression and symbol of a disenfranchised working class claiming their membership of the body politic. In characteristic radical fashion, Chartism did not subscribe to the Burkean model of an organic, empirical political constitution founded in time-honoured institutions and slowly evolving customs. Nor did Chartists accept the brute theory that only the possession of property conferred citizenship. Both these bulwarks of tradition had been deployed in 1832 to exclude the 'swinish multitude' from the suffrage. Chartism saw the British constitution in Paineite terms as a form of mystified class power and a deformation of ancient rights. Drawing on the strong Saxonist tradition of English radicalism, Chartists saw themselves as the true constitutionalists, restoring to full liberty the 'free-born Englishmen'. They believed that political rights only had validity and meaning if they were written down and codified by law. The Charter was the Magna Carta of the working class.

The unprecedented mass campaign that spanned over 'ten remarkable years'[2] of Victorian history had one clear goal in mind: to transform the Charter from an ideal into a real document. The Charter was a unique product, generated out of the collective intelligence and will of a mass working-class movement. As G. D. H. Cole points out, it was not the Six Points themselves but Chartism's mass following that was new.[3]

The Charter was a massively over-determined document: it exposed the agonized growing pains of a rapidly industrializing, rationalizing society; highlighted the contradictions of *laissez-faire* reformers; and promoted the first great attempt by the working class to wield social and intellectual power. The Charter was the constitutive absence in the 1832 Reform Bill. The Whigs had tried to write the working class out of history, but only succeeded in impelling those not deemed worthy of a vote to write their own destiny. Even more, perhaps, than the directly repressive state apparatus of Poor Law 'bastilles', stamp duty, Irish coercion, rural police, trade union persecution and ineffectual factory regulation, it was the treacherous delegitimizing of the working class in 1832 that remained a powerful source of Chartist identity and resolve; as the first petition declared in 1839, 'they have been bitterly and basely deceived'.[4] The Charter combined Paineite political 'rights' with the radical belief that industriousness, not property, bequeathed value on the individual. While the Chartists employed the principles of classical political economy to validate their social identity, the Whigs did the exact opposite. To them, the working class only had an economic identity – in social and political terms the class were so marginalized as to be all but invisible. Chartism was therefore an attempt to restore the industrious subject to representation, to annunciate the working-class citizen as a fully-fledged citizen. This was surely one of the reasons Chartism was able to harness the energies of numerous popular protest movements around a single issue.

So writing was both a means and an end. Chartism was a remarkably literate movement, as shown by its scores of newspapers and periodicals.[5] These meshed together to form a local, regional and national discursive network. Of course: Chartism was also a campaign of mass meetings, rallies and conventions; but this activism was doubly mobilized through immediate reporting; agitation and representation were inseparable. Oratory could inspire from the page as well as the platform. Each Chartist publication was an act of self-representation, the signifier and signified of the disenfranchised. The prodigious Chartist consumption of print also reflected its foundation in the radical cultural traditions and social aspirations of the self-improving working class. It was no coincidence that Chartism's Jacobin precursor in the 1790s was called the London Corresponding Society.[6] As Dorothy Thompson has noted, 'It is an important part of the definition of Chartism to see it as a response of a literate and sophisticated working class'.[7] Chartist publications continued the radical counter-offensive against the state's attempt to control the reading habits of the working class. This process had begun in the revolutionary 1790s when the government took alarm at the huge demand for cheap editions of Paine's *The Rights of Man* (1791–92).[8] The first response of the state was direct repression. The edition was proscribed and radical publishers were imprisoned. As a result of these measures, freedom of the press and speech moved to the centre of the radical agenda for the next forty years.[9] The state's second response was more subtle. This was a campaign to pacify the working class by producing anti-Jacobin literature in a form that would appeal to a wide, self-educated readership. Hannah More's *Cheap Repository Tracts* (1795–98), for example, imitated the format and price of popular chap-books.[10] Altick claims these stories sold over two million copies.[11] This remarkable success heralded a new cultural battleground for English politics.[12]

As literacy levels continued to grow, the evangelicals realized that it was not only politics that threatened to corrupt the working class. Accelerated methods of mass literary production, based on increasing use of the steam press, made available to a mass audience the amoral pleasures of cheap, 'sensational' literature. The state's response to the twin evils of radicalism and commercialism was to redeploy the same measures of censorship and ideological control. In an attempt to price the radical press out of circulation, stamp duty on newspapers was raised to 4d in 1815, while the Six Acts of 1819 made the penalties for avoiding the tax more severe. The response of the radicals was to defy the duty and declare a.'war of the unstamped'. This conflict was a crucial formative influence on the Chartist consciousness. Some of the heroes of the 'pauper press', such as Hetherington, Cleave and Watson, joined the London Working Men's Association and took part in drawing up the Charter in 1837. The other plank of state policy was to invest in what Althusser calls the 'ideological state apparatus', those institutions like the family, education and the church that regulate morality and social values. New educational organizations such as the Mechanics Institutes and the Society for the Diffusion of Useful Knowledge (SDUK) were established with an obvious appeal for the autodidact.[13] Moreover, SDUK publications followed the example of Hannah More and exploited popular literary forms. To tempt the reader away from both dangerous politics and vulgar narratives the SDUK produced penny-issue magazines, more usually the source of cheap, sensational fiction.[14] Writers like Harriet Martineau were also hired to produce realistic,

2

pacifying tales of industrial working-class life which inculcated the virtues of *laissez-faire* economics.[15] The moral reformers were only too aware of the extent of the problem. As Louis James has shown, such was the appetite for literature among the working class that even the workshop became a place where pirated versions and poor imitations of Dickens would be read aloud. Though this situation was not new (the self-taught artisan had often managed to do some reading at work, and it was only the much-hated discipline of the factory system that made this increasingly impossible)[16] there was no doubting that the proletarian fiction market was rapidly expanding.

But radical literary networks and activities also continued to flourish. Radical publishers' and booksellers' premises doubled up as reading rooms and meeting places. There were even radical coffee-shops, such as the one run by Lovett in the mid 1830s.[17] Good education was a passionate and proud source of class identity. The title of Lovett's autobiography declared his lifelong pursuit of 'bread, knowledge and freedom'. The radical cultural credentials of Chartism were nowhere more evident than in the movement's demand for a national education system. This would be financed by the state but run by local communities to safeguard against ideological interference and erosion of self-determination.[18]

So it is not surprising that Chartism was a 'literate and sophisticated' mass movement. Nor that it invested in cultural production. To take its most famous publication, *The Northern Star* (1837–52) featured an 'arts' page which contained original and reprinted poetry, book reviews, extracts from British and international writings, and in the case of Thomas Martin Wheeler's *Sunshine and Shadows* (1849–50), a serialized novel. As Gustav Klaus has put it, there was 'an intimate relation between literature and politics' in the Chartist press.[19] While Klaus sees this 'intimacy' arising out of the traditions of the unstamped press, he underestimates the important influence of popular fiction. Chartism would have missed a golden opportunity if it had not mobilized the 'fiction department' of the movement, in Wheeler's words. As this anthology demonstrates, the 'fiction department's' response was at least as impressive as the prodigious output of Chartist poetry. Yet the fiction has been almost entirely ignored by literary historians and critics.[20] The implication of this neglect is that the poetry had the more direct role to play in Chartist political culture – poems could be recited or sung at rallies, and readily memorized – while the stories were merely ephemeral entertainment or callow attempts to break into a bourgeois art form and a commercial market. While poetry was undoubtedly highly regarded by Chartists, both in itself and as a signifier of civilized values, there is no evidence of a widespread disdain towards fiction.

It is partly in order to correct a deficient historical record that we need access to these stories. Of the numerous anthologies of Chartist writings,[21] only the pioneering 1956 volume by Kovalev has contained any fiction, and even he regarded the fictional excerpts as 'of a considerably lower literary level than the poetry'.[22] In fact, Chartist stories represent a unique moment in literary history, when the radical political energies of a mass movement were fused with popular narrative forms. The result was a vital, accessible, didactic and popular political fiction. As Klaus notes of this moment, 'the oppositional elements of proletarian culture began to acquire a literary dimension on an unprecedented, and even in later times rarely equalled, scale'.[23] This picture is different from that painted by Louis James in his seminal study *Fiction for the Working Man*

(1963). James acknowledges that the circumstances of a high working-class literacy 'linked as it was in a unique way to social and political factors' constituted 'a possible turning point in the emergence of the English working classes'. But before they could exploit the potential of 'cheap fiction' in their 'unique way', the working classes 'had largely abandoned their earlier aspirations'. So the collision of popular politics and fiction never occurred.[24] David Vincent, on the other hand, is more inclined to agree with Klaus. Vincent reckons that by the 1830s the state decided that commercialism rather than evangelical intervention would drive radical writing out of business. The working class would be pacified by an explosion of 'popular leisure', led by the sensation fiction of the penny weeklies. But Vincent points out the contradiction that the most successful publisher of penny fiction was George W. M. Reynolds, a Chartist and ferocious critic of the aristocracy. The state had miscalculated badly.[25] When we consider the subsequent development of radicalism in Britain, it is a pity that this 'turning point' was so rapidly forgotten.

This is not to suggest that Chartists valued fiction above other discourses. All writing shared the common goal of bringing about constitutional change. Fiction and poetry appeared alongside news, reports of conventions, rallies, and meetings, speeches, correspondence, public addresses, portraits of leaders and heroes and many other forms of writing. In this sense, any anthology which selects only one genre misrepresents the diversity and depth of Chartist political culture. This anthology needs to be read in conjunction with other collections of Chartist documents, and not be regarded as containing superior or aesthetically transcendent material. This does not mean the fiction has no literary qualities. As already noted, Chartists drew heavily on the techniques of popular fiction, particularly sensationalism and melodrama. But these popular forms were transformed by the political and social demands placed upon them. The 'unique' ways in which a new type of English fiction emerged can only be understood in the context of the relative autonomy of Chartist cultural production. Chartism was able to support a 'sort of working-class intelligentsia' – this is Vincent's phrase for writers like Thomas Cooper, Thomas Frost and Ernest Jones, who were able to make a living out of the movement by journalism, lecturing and teaching.[26] These factors generated an 'alternative public sphere', radically insulated from the norms of both high culture and bourgeois commercialism.[27] Chartist authors could elevate use value over exchange value, secure in the knowledge that their texts, which often appeared in Chartist newspapers or journals, participated directly in a national discursive network. This meant that political interventions into narratives were not perceived as incongruous, contradictory, or reductive. Chartist authors were fully aware that only a 'literature of your own', in Cooper's words, would be sufficient to represent their case.[28] To label Chartist stories 'propaganda' is entirely appropriate in that the remedy of specific social and political abuses defines the narratives more aggressively than in any other contemporary fiction. The stories were produced out of a countervailing radical aesthetic which wanted to correct the conventional misrepresentations of the lives of ordinary people.[29] Chartists understood very clearly the important ideological role of literature. To Chartists, art was an expression of the political condition, not its antithesis or its imaginary solution. Chartist literary aspirations were inseparable from their political and social ambitions: to elevate the marginalized and repressed majority of society. This clarity of aesthetic purpose enabled Chartists like Reynolds and Thomas Frost to work successfully within the commercial sector, harnessing the new modes of mass literary production to their own ends.[30]

I have divided the anthology thematically into five sections: The Condition of England; Ireland; Revolution; Women; Chartism. Other arrangements were possible, but this structure reflects some of the most prominent and most controversial causes which the movement embraced. Dividing the stories into themes helps us to see the range and variety of formal choices which Chartist authors were able to make, as well as highlighting continuities and recurrent features. Some of the conflicts and tensions within Chartism are also revealed by comparing differing narrative treatments of the same theme. With the rest of this introduction I want to demonstrate the kind of modern critical response I believe it is necessary to make in order to fully appreciate these tales.

The Condition of England

Two events in 1834 symbolized the class polarization of Britain; the transportation of the Tolpuddle martyrs and the passing of the Poor Law Amendment Bill. The treacherous Whigs were felt by the working class to be using 'class legislation' to the full. The reformed parliament had merely converted 'Old Corruption' into 'New' – as the first petition of 1839 put it, power had transferred 'from one domineering faction to another'.[31] The persecution of organized labour and the 'less eligible' workhouse Bastilles were prime examples of a contemptuous and callous regime glorying in its new power. As industrial capitalism wreaked terrible havoc on working-class communities and the old labour aristocracy, the new relief measures were perceived as punitive, impersonal, centralist, dehumanizing and immiserating. Far from alleviating the distress caused by Ricardian trade slumps, the workhouses were felt to be yet another tool of class discipline. The Whigs, it seemed, were determined to drive a modernizing juggernaut over all remnants of the old paternalist economy. It was not only the harshness of the workhouse system that met with such bitter and prolonged opposition. It was also what the workhouse stood for: the enforced transformation of social relations, naked proletarianization (the separation of poverty and pauperism) and loss of ancient rights.[32] The workhouse became a central symbol of the new oppression and figured prominently in Chartist demonology. John Knott points out that 'lurid stories' of workhouses were to be found regularly in the Chartist press.[33] So it should not come as any surprise to find the workhouses at or near the centre of many Chartist narratives.

The rural working class were the first victims of the new Poor Law. Their ability to resist its introduction had been severely weakened by the defeats of the Swing disturbances of 1830. The real battle began when the Commissioners tried to advance into the industrial regions of the North. It was to take many years to conquer this territory where the working class were more organized and experienced, having participated in campaigns to support the Reform Bill, factory legislation and trade union rights. The community basis of the anti-Poor Law campaign also attracted middle-class support. One of the movement's more fiery leaders was the renegade Lancashire Methodist Joseph Rayner Stephens. His inflammatory speeches to huge open-air audiences set an example for the mass mobilization of the northern working class which fed directly into

5

Chartism. When Stephens emerged from gaol in 1839 a chastened man, his oratorical mantle had passed on to Feargus O'Connor. He presented the Poor Law as straightforward 'class legislation' which the Charter would sweep away.

A confrontation with the workhouse lies at the centre of two anonymous stories which appeared in *Cleave's Gazette of Variety* in 1838. 'Will Harper – A Poor Law Tale' is seminal in the way it shapes its material. Harper personifies the destruction of the old paternalist economy and rural communities. For the first third of the tale his life story is a model of respectability and deference: he is sober, industrious, and completely fulfilled when he becomes a reliable breadwinner (we will return to the role of his wife in a moment). But after five prosperous years of marriage the family is plunged irreversibly into a spiralling decline of unemployment, poverty, demoralization and despair. The centrepiece of the story is Harper's clash with the workhouse overseer. There is little subtlety about the scene. The class enemy is a sneering caricature, and Harper suddenly emerges as a proto-radical, a mouthpiece for an anti-Poor Law tirade. The melodramatic sympathies are so strongly on Harper's side that it is difficult not to support his violent feelings. The tale comes very close to satisfying this desire for vengeance in the second, even more contrived, encounter with the overseer, though by now Harper has sunk terminally into the customary temptations of drink, neglect, and crime. Ironically, he poaches from the squire, who represents the old paternalism of the gentry. In this sense, the tale reflects the Poor Law's initial penetration of the rural regions. A Cobbetite nostalgia is signalled in the tale's ending. The fatherless family is saved from destitution by the community, and is not punished further. For all its crude and transparent construction, 'Will Harper' mapped out the fictional territory of much Chartist and subsequent working-class fiction. No tragedy was more poignant than the emasculation and demoralization of the respectable breadwinner. No story was more freighted with political significance than the slow destruction of family ties. The figure of the driven and desperate artisan was central to the Chartist literary imagination and its sense of social values. In 'The Convict' (*Chartist Circular*, 1839) Robert Wilson steals to feed his starving family and dies in gaol before he can be hanged. Arthur Morton in Thomas Martin Wheeler's *Sunshine and Shadows* also robs a stranger rather than surrender to the workhouse. John Haspen in Ernest Jones's 'The Working Man's Wife' (1852) declines into domestic violence and theft, and eventually murders his daughter's seducer. So 'Will Harper' established a powerful narrative formula for exposing the evils of *laissez-faire* reforms.[34] Echoes can be found in the more famous middle-class 'condition of England' novels. A version of the tragic artisan figure is to be seen in the character of John Barton in Elizabeth Gaskell's *Mary Barton* (1848) and Stephen Blackpool in Dickens's *Hard Times* (1854). In later working-class fiction the type recurs as Joseph Coney in Margaret Harkness's *Out of Work* (1888), Easton in Tressell's *The Ragged Trousered Philanthropists* (1914) and Mr Hardcastle in Greenwood's *Love on the Dole* (1933).

The companion piece to 'Will Harper' was 'The Widow and the Fatherless'. This takes up the story where the other left off: how would the wife survive? An encounter with the workhouse again dominates the action. This time the guardian is well-meaning but unable to provide relief. In desperation the widow resorts to begging. Luckily, she attracts the attention of a charitable gentleman who gives her sufficient money to tide her over until her second application to the guardians. The intervention of two chivalrous men is the *deus ex machina* that stops her being separated from her children. After a succession of insecure domestic jobs she finds a secure position. It is interesting to compare her 'decline' with Harper's. He accrues his masculine and class pride from 'supporting' his family. In fact, his wife Mary's domestic skills and management are crucial in sustaining his position. One reason unemployment was so devastating to respectable working-class families was that it undermined this masculinist sexual division of labour. The artisan's tragedy was predicated on this unequal economic identity. Even if the wife could obtain paid work, this was still ideologically unacceptable as it undermined the power relations between the male 'breadwinner' and the dependent, domesticated wife. To be a 'kept man' was just a further humiliation. Engels noted in *The Condition of the Working Class in England* (1844), that unemployment turned the family hierarchy 'upside down'.[35] So in 'The Widow and the Fatherless' there is no tragic loss of status, the heroine is not given a radical voice, and above all she is a passive victim, reliant on male intervention. She begs for money while the hero steals it. She can only offer her body to the male gaze. As the stories in the section on 'Women' show, a more common desperate remedy was prostitution.

'The Widow and the Fatherless' appeared on the front page of *Cleave's Gazette of Variety*. Above it were portraits of Fagin, the Artful Dodger and Charley Bates from Dickens's *Oliver Twist* (1837), a story which also exposed the corruption and exploitation of the workhouses. Some useful comparisons can be made between the narrative methods of Dickens and his radical counterparts.

Dickens bleaches the text of any specific political value by using the romance formula of the foundling – Oliver turns out to be of genteel birth. This decision was clearly influenced by a desire to make the book popular (as a journalist Dickens wrote a graphic account of workhouse conditons,[36] but Dickens's notion of 'popular' differs markedly from the naked class confrontation of the radical texts. While making Oliver the controlling point of view of the novel allows Dickens to show some of the abuses of child labour, Oliver does not stand for the suffering of a whole class. In the radical imagination, the tragic fall of the beleaguered working-class family marks a turning point in history.

One thing was crystal clear: the Poor Law was indeed a poor law. Another version of the workhouse confrontation scene occurs in Thomas Doubleday's *The Political Pilgrim's Progress* (1839) (this will appear in a subsequent volume of Chartist fiction), yet here the means of representation is a long way from realism, and is a measure of the range of generic choices available to Chartist writers. Doubleday heightens the horrors of the scene by exploiting the artistic freedoms of the allegory. The workhouse becomes the 'Castle of Despair' in which the hero, Radical, is accused by the guardians of Malthusian irresponsibility simply for marrying and having children. Once admitted to the 'castle', Radical's wife's head is shaved, and he is made to run up and down a hill carrying a heavy sandbag. The accompanying illustration depicts the Poor Law Commissioners as Cyclopean giants feasting on the smashed bodies of their victims. Fortunately, Radical and his family escape and continue their pilgrimage to the City of Reform. We might compare this mythologizing with the moment when a real workhouse was 'liberated' in the Plug riots of 1842. The *Illustrated London News* shows the victorious rioters distributing confiscated bread in a scene reminiscent of the Biblical parable of the loaves and the fishes.[37]

7

The shadow of the workhouse loomed largest during economic 'panics'. The terrible slump of 1841–42 is the setting for two stories which follow the attempts of the working class to cope with unemployment, starvation, and poverty. In 'A Simple Story' (*English Chartist Circular*, 1842), a young factory worker called Joe goes hungry so his family can eat. When his workmates discover this self-sacrifice they have a collection to help him out. Unfortunately, this is only a temporary relief, and we are told Joe eventually died 'in a decline'. Nevertheless, the tale celebrates working-class charitable deeds. The author attacks the misrepresentation of the working class in literary tradition, and declares that only someone from the working class can write truthfully about them: he 'has been for thirty years, from the time he was eight years of age, engaged in manufactures'.

The slump of 1842 is also the setting for Thomas Cooper's conspicuously titled story, "Merrie England" – No More! (1845). The cross-fertilization of literature and Chartist politics is particularly poignant in Cooper's career. In the 1842 insurrections Cooper made a speech to striking Staffordshire miners urging them to 'cease labour until the Charter became the law of the land'.[38] Cooper was charged with seditious conspiracy and imprisoned for two years. But while in Stafford jail he turned his hands to writing, producing his famous poem *The Purgatory of Suicides* and the short stories which became *Wise Saws and Modern Instances* (both were published in 1845). It was not unusual for imprisoned Chartists to continue their pursuit of knowledge while denied their bread and freedom. William Lovett and John Collins wrote their educational tract *Chartism: A New Organization for the People* (1840) while serving a prison sentence in Warwick jail (they had published a placard accusing the police of provoking the Birmingham Bull Ring riots of July 1839). Like many radicals before them, Chartists in jail managed to continue editing and journalistic work. Henry Vincent even wrote book reviews from inside Oakham prison.[39] It is also significant that Cooper's conversion to Chartism took place when he was asked to write about it. Working as a reporter for the *Leicestershire Mercury* he was sent to report on a local Chartist meeting. This did not particularly impress him as he saw nothing new in the demands. But after the meeting something unexpected happened. He was surprised to see nearby hosiery workers ('stockingers') still at work at this late hour. Anxious to learn more, he asked some of the workers what they earned, and was told 'four and sixpence'. His autobiography recalls what happened next:

> 'Four and sixpence,' I said, 'well, six fours are twenty-four, and six sixpences are three shillings; that's seven-and-twenty shillings a week. The wages are not so bad when you are in work.'
> 'What are you talking about?' said they. 'You mean four and sixpence a day; but we mean four and sixpence a week.
> 'Four and sixpence a week!' I exclaimed. 'You don't mean that men have to work in those stocking frames that I hear going now, a whole week for four and sixpence. How can they maintain their wives and children?'
> 'Ay, you may well ask that,' said one of them sadly.[40]

It 'seemed incredible' (p. 139) that the situation had deteriorated so badly since Cooper's days as a shoemaker. In close proximity to the Chartist meeting he had stumbled on 'the real state of suffering in which thousands in England were

8

living' (p. 138). He resolved to 'become the champion of the poor' (p. 146) and a dedicated Chartist. The misery Cooper had discovered was emblematic of the destruction of the old labour aristocracy. The suffering of the stockingers and handloom weavers in the transition to industrial capitalism was so extreme that it prompted parliamentary inquiries in 1840 and 1845.[41]

This is the bleak social territory that Cooper revisits in the two stories included here (both are taken from *Wise Saws and Modern Instances*). If England had become Disraeli's two nations of rich and poor, Cooper's starving workers are the epitome of the have-nots – 'martyrs of the economic system', in Mark Hovell's words.[42]

'"Merrie England" – No More!' develops its material in significant ways. The story is set mostly outdoors. This stems primarily from the artisans' unemployment but also shows their collective social identity (until the story follows one of the workers to his desolate home this approach also excludes women, of course). While on the streets, the workers debate and analyse their situation, displaying an impressive autodidactic erudition (a reflection of Cooper's own prodigious feats of self-education).[43] Their class-consciousness is so strong that it leads to a proto-insurrection. A recruiting sergeant, symbol of state oppression, is made to hand back John's son. Another positive outcome of this class solidarity is support for the Charter, which at the moment the story takes place (April 1842) was only a month away from its second presentation. But perhaps the most radical aspect of the story is at the formal level. Cooper refuses any narrative resolution:

> There is no "tale" to finish about John or his lad, or Jem and his wife. They went on starving, – begging, – receiving threats of imprisonment, – tried the "Bastille" for a few weeks, – came out and had a little work, – starved again; and they are still going the same miserable round, like thousands in "merrie England". What are your thoughts, reader?

This must be one of the most remarkable and original endings in Victorian fiction. Cooper challenges the conventions of fiction because they are incongruous and inappropriate. Having stressed the veracity of his story ('these conversations are *real*; they are no coinages') he cannot impose a resolution while the struggle was still taking place. His characters fade out into a lumpen, subsistence obscurity. The prose collapses into a string of disconnected fragments, a 'miserable round' of mere sequential events. Cooper pushes his realism to the limits of representation. Unless the reader is prepared to intervene in history, Cooper's language will fail totally and the 'thousands' will be left outside of history. Notice also the syntactical position of the workhouse. Far from being a demonic institution it is given the same, matter-of-fact status as the other 'miserable' processes that make up the texture of proletarian life. Instead of using melodramatic or sensational confrontations to embellish the class struggle, Cooper engages in a more subversive disruption of the rules of fictional representation. Cooper's achievement mirrored Chartism's political goal, which aimed at undermining the dominant means of political representation. It also echoes his characters' fervent disdain for the panacea of divine providence.

'Seth Thompson, the Stockinger', on the other hand, contains a flagrant *deus ex machina*. Seth is another struggling artisan-hero. His family are saved from destitution by the unexpected appearance of a wealthy, plantation-owning uncle. The uncle's 'fairy gold' allows Seth to achieve the traditional artisan goal of becoming a small master. He is widely respected in the community for his generosity and radical politics. Yet this is not enough to prevent the devastating effects of mechanization and trade slumps. Seth tells a meeting of 'starving framework-knitters' that he can no longer hold out against the 'tyrannies and extortions' of the large manufacturers. Rather than collude with their brand of capitalism, he decides to join his uncle in the West Indies. Seth's departure personifies the extinction of 'merrie England'. While Seth emigrates, the Hinckley stockingers 'remain in their misery still'. Yet the hero's salvation was only made possible by the uncle's intervention. Without his money Seth would have shared the fate of the starving stockingers. The *deus ex machina* is evidence that the old conditions for artisan mobility now only exist in fantasy.

The device serves a further function. The uncle's estrangement from England enables him to see how much the country has changed. In a scene reminiscent of Cooper's conversion to Chartism, the uncle is shocked that the 'happy England' he once knew has sunk to 'Irish' levels. In order to understand the significance of that indictment, we must now turn to Chartism's relations with England's oldest colony.

Ireland

If the Chartists wanted an example of the worst abuses of state power they only had to look across the Irish Sea. Ireland was a source of outrage, fear, and inspiration; outrage at the repression and exploitation; fear that such a fate awaited the English working class if the Charter failed; inspiration from the unceasing struggle for emancipation. Ireland also had a direct practical input into the Chartist movement, supplying two of its leaders (Feargus O'Connor and Bronterre O'Brien) and many of its rank-and-file members. According to Carlyle in his essay *Chartism* (1840), the 'crowds of miserable Irish [who] darken all our towns' were understandably attracted to the 'dismal wide-spread glare of Chartism'. Despite his racism and his appalling simianization of the Irish immigrant, Carlyle recognized where the ultimate blame for this subversive situation lay: 'England is guilty towards Ireland; and reaps at last, in full measure, the fruit of fifteen generations of wrong-doing.'[44]

Ireland was always a major component of the radical political agenda. As Lovett once put it, 'the cause of England and Ireland is one'. The London Working Men's Association issued an Address to the new Queen in 1837, demanding 'an immediate and radical remedy' to the Irish problem. The LWMA took the line that both nations suffered under the yoke of exclusive legislation. A 'community of feeling' between the Irish and English would deliver the Charter which in turn would deliver Repeal.[45] Chartists supported the Irish Repeal movement, despite clashing with its leader Daniel O'Connell. He was initially one of the MPs who endorsed the launch of the Charter in 1837. But the following year O'Connell showed his conservative class credentials by launching an attack on the Glasgow cotton spinners' strike. After a public reprimand he split from the movement and entered Chartist demonology as a traitor and Whig collaborator.[46] Such was the nervousness in the political establishment about Irish Home Rule that Thomas Attwood, who presented the first petition to Parliament in 1839, disowned this aspect of the

10

logic of universal suffrage.[47] Nevertheless, the 1842 petition made the demand for Repeal explicit (along with abolition of the Poor Law) and the 1848 petition was presented by O'Connor himself, now MP for Nottingham. During 1848 Ireland was once again in a revolutionary mood. It had suffered the recent catastrophe of the great famine. It had also seen the rise of a powerful new republican movement, 'Young Ireland', led by John Mitchel. He once declared 'Every Chartist is a Repealer, to begin with'.[48] Mitchel's trial for sedition in early 1848 was widely perceived as a politically motivated miscarriage of justice. Catholics were excluded from the jury, and Mitchel was transported. The Whigs, who had returned to power in 1847, were seen to act out of naked self-interest. Several members of the Cabinet were Irish landowners.[49] This did not prevent the Young Irelanders, inspired by the wave of revolutions sweeping through Europe, from eventually staging a small, ineffectual uprising near Limerick in July 1848. Although it was easily defeated and its leaders Meagher and Smith O'Brien transported, Ireland had yet again provided the revolutionary action lacking in English radicalism.[50] The rebellions of 1798 and 1803 were sources of inspiration and martyrology to Chartists. The trial speech of Robert Emmett was a popular Chartist gift.[51] As the son of a United Irishman, it should not surprise us that Feargus O'Connor named the *Northern Star* after that movement's newspaper.

The Irish revolutions of 1798 and 1803 figure in two stories published in the *Chartist Circular* in 1840. 'The Defender' is set in 1797 on the eve of the revolution, while 'The Rebel Chief' focuses on the aftermath of the 1803 rebellion. This chronology is interesting, as neither story deals with the main action but erects a frame around it. The emphasis is on putting the insurrections into perspective.

'The Defender' concerns the divided loyalties of the Defender rebel Martin Doyle. When his father is arrested by the authorities, Doyle is torn between fleeing with his family or giving himself up to save his father. He chooses the latter course, and is about to be executed when the British Commander, General Abercrombie, steps in with a last-minute reprieve. This *deus ex machina* stems from the fact that the general developed a friendship with Doyle's father when first stationed in Ireland in less troubled times. That the two old men do not initially recognize each other personifies the deterioration in the Irish situation. A substantial amount of historical information is loaded onto this plot. The narrator expects these details to be 'interesting to our present reader'. So there is no incongruity in switching from fiction to fact. The story's thesis is that the severity of the White Terror precipitated the revolution (a critique also developed in 'The Rebel Chief'). The Defender insurgents (the Catholic equivalent of the Protestant Peep-o-day Boys) were spurred on by the savage British campaign of incendiarism, floggings (the punishment of 500 lashes inflicted on rebels is accurate) and ignominious executions. A further air of authenticity is given to the tale by the appearance of Gaelic words in the characters' speech. So the ending of the story feels almost deliberately unsatisfactory. Doyle and his family are restored to pastoral isolation as if 1798 or 1803 never existed. Narrative closure and historical process are antithetical.

A more glaring ambivalence affects 'The Rebel Chief'. Most of the story is a straightforward account of a young British officer's pursuit of Holt, the last remaining 'fallen chieftain', in the wake of the 1803 uprising. The officer is captured, but released for being kind to Holt's wife. Holt then risks his life by giving himself up to a liberal magistrate. The gamble pays off, and Holt

11

emigrates to America. The story demonstrates a post-Romantic ambivalence towards the figure of the revolutionary hero. The narrator condemns insurrection as futile and costly, but Holt is chivalrous and noble, the moral superior of the vengeful British authorities who are determined to have his blood. Until his belated appearance in the story, Holt is the Romantic Other: enigmatic, elusive, associated with the seductive, feminized wilderness (both desired and feared), posing a threat only as mythic force. By the end of the tale he has become a spokesman for reconciliation and paternalist government (represented in 'The Defender' by General Abercrombie). Holt colludes in the destruction of his signifying potential. His part of the clemency deal is to lead the military to his secret lair, the 'last wretched retreat' of Irishness. The state's new roads will open 'a ready access to the very heart of the mountain recesses'. The feminine Irish wilderness must succumb to the penetrative state infrastructure. To the captive British officer the land was alien and sublime (an atmosphere enhanced by the fact that the rebels speak in Gaelic). Now it is exposed to the gaze of the 'all powerful' masculine state. The conquest of the wilderness is an act of political clearance, the closure of the revolutionary dream.

The other two stories in this section of the anthology reflect the contemporary social misery in Ireland, most notably the Great Hunger of 1846–48. Consecutive failures of the potato crop left millions of Irish to starve or emigrate. The British government refused to intervene in the Irish economy, fearing this would undermine food prices. Meanwhile the Irish peasants were expected to pay their rent and were evicted if they defaulted. The Irish landlord system had always been a glaring example of colonialist exploitation and injustice. So the subtitle of 'The Desmonds: A Tale of Landlordism in Ireland' (*Reynolds's Miscellany*, 1846) would have struck a radical chord. Though the tale is not explicitly about the famine, it is clearly about parallel issues of deprivation and dispossession. The illustration which accompanies the story could easily have been mistaken for an image of the famine. It shows a destitute and desolated family, the men ragged and harrowed, the women and children huddled and forlorn. In fact, the Desmonds are grieving for the loss of Gerald Desmond, who has been executed for murdering their new landlord. There is a clear connection here with the 'tragic artisan' plot. Yet the Desmonds' fall is much greater than the English labour aristocracy, for the Desmonds were once actual gentry. Their loss of social status is the result of the colonial mechanisms of dispossession, confiscation, rack-renting, and finally, eviction. The spiral of decline is complete when a new English landlord clears their land to make way for his 'beautifying park'. The tale ends with characteristic ambivalence towards violent remedies: the murder is condemned but the system of landlordism is identified as ultimately to blame.

The tone of 'The Meal-Mongers: Or, Food Riots in Ireland' (1848) is more upbeat. The story shows a successful mini-insurrection in the shape of a famine-stricken village community who ambush a party of 'Meal-Mongers'. These are small farmers who hoard grain to keep its price high (which is a possible comment on the government's non-intervention policy). Further villainy is located in the figure of the canting, bombastic Anglican schoolmaster, Fogarty, who prefers to convert rather than feed the locals. Yet the radical message of the story is weakened by the mock-epic touches in the battle scene: a 'storm' of bellowing donkeys, a 'leprechaun' urchin defending the meal-cart. This tone jars with the grim historical context of 'Famine, Monopoly and

Revenge'. It is as though there had to be a trade-off between a social victory and a trivialized politics. As the next section will show, Chartism was not a revolutionary movement in the sense of recommending or celebrating armed insurrection. There may have been historical moments that seemed more favourable to an armed response, but as 'The Meal-Mongers' demonstrates, a reluctance to glorify violence outweighs even the revolutionary fervour of 1848. The leader of the ambush is actually a Young Irelander, but this theme is not developed. It is possible that beneath the Irish setting lay an even more vital theme: the reclaiming of the land. The tale appeared in *The Labourer*, a periodical set up by O'Connor and Ernest Jones to publicize the Chartist Land Plan. This was an attempt to resettle urban labour in agricultural communities, and reverse the tide of history by peaceful means.

Revolution

We should not be too surprised to discover an ambivalence towards revolution in the Irish stories. Chartism was never a fully-fledged insurrectionary movement. It was a constitutional movement with revolutionary social implications. At times the 'physical force' arguments were edged into prominence by prevailing historical conditions. This was certainly the case in 1839, 1842 and 1848. Like any large movement, Chartism spanned a range of positions from the militant to the moderate. On the other hand, the famous polarization between 'physical' and 'moral' force has been exaggerated. The right to arm and drill was based on an appeal to ancient constitutional rights. Even William Lovett saw the justice of arming as a last resort against state aggression – 'peacefully if we may, forcibly if we must'.[52] If necessary, Chartists would defend their communities and their rights by establishing militias. The extent to which such defensive preparations converted into active insurrectionary plans is still hard to judge. Arming was only one of the 'ulterior measures' drawn up in 1839 in anticipation of the Charter's rejection by Parliament. The others were a consumer boycott, creating a run on the banks by withdrawing savings, and the 'national holiday' or general strike. Even this programme was felt by the majority of the leadership to be ultimately too radical, and the decision to call a general strike was reversed only one week before it was due to commence on 12 August. Dissenters pointed out with bitter irony that the middle classes had threatened armed action at the time of the Reform Bill crisis.[53]

When Chartism finally got its 'insurrection' at Newport in November 1839 there was no widespread jubilation. John Frost and the other leaders only narrowly avoided being executed for treason. On the other hand, this act of apparent leniency could well have been a calculated move by the government to avoid creating martyrs (it was politically acceptable for Chartists to die in squalid prisons but not on the scaffold). With its network of spies and informers the state was in a good position to gauge the revolutionary temperature. Newport was not an isolated incident. In the summer of 1839 there were violent outbreaks at Newcastle and Birmingham, and shortly after Frost's trial ended in early 1840 further disturbances occurred in Dewsbury, Sheffield and Bradford. So there is evidence to support the view that a revolutionary consciousness permeated the movement at this time, but without any national or official co-ordination.

13

The pattern of events in the summer of 1842 resembled 1839. The Charter was rejected in May, and the movement was again pressing for 'ulterior' tactics. When the factory-owners in the north began locking out workers who refused wage cuts, a 'national holiday' fell into the Chartist lap. This time there was no backsliding. Chartist orators, including Thomas Cooper, were quickly despatched to the manufacturing regions to proselytize the strikers. A special conference was held in Manchester at which a decision was taken to support the strikers until the Charter was granted. Chartists were spurred on by the belief that Whig manufacturers had provoked the strike to lever the Tory government into repealing the Corn Laws. The strikes fizzled out after a few weeks, but the alliance between Chartism and industrial militancy was a pivotal moment. Eric Hobsbawn believes this was the closest England came to revolution; 1842 was Chartism's 1848.[54]

Hobsbawn refers, of course, to that spectacular year of revolutions which swept across Europe from France to Hungary. Just as the French revolution of 1830 inspired the Reform Bill movement, so the deposing of Louis Phillipe in February 1848 re-invigorated Chartism's spirit: 'for us, too, the tocsin sounds' declared the *Northern Star*.[55] The climax of this renewed energy was a third petition and a mass rally on Kennington Common on 10 April. This event, poignantly captured in a very early daguerreotype,[56] is usually interpreted as Chartism's last, abortive moment. According to this version of Chartism's collapse, the authorities crushed any chance of an uprising by putting London under martial law (an astonishing 85,000 special constables were sworn in).[57] To quash the nation-wide disturbances that erupted in subsequent months, the state employed the same strategy of mass arrests it had used in 1839–40 and 1842. Exhausted and demoralized after ten years of constant campaigning, Chartism went into terminal decline as a mass movement.

This account of the rapid disintegration of Chartism is misleading. For a start, Chartism became more not less revolutionary after 10 April. As David Goodway and John Saville have shown, there were plans for an insurrection in August 1848. An underground army of around 5,000 Chartists and Irish Confederates may have been in existence. But before any action could begin, the conspiracy was betrayed by government agents and its leaders, including the black Chartist William Cuffay, were transported.[58] So 10 April marked the beginning, not the end, of a revolutionary phase of Chartist activity. The misrepresentation of events in popular memory is a testimony to the success of counter-revolutionary mythology. According to Saville, there was a concerted effort by the establishment to 'bury' the significance of 1848, to write it out of history.[59] Hence the construction of 10 April as the closure of the Chartist narrative. Kingsley's *Alton Locke* (1850) is a prime example of this. An entire chapter devoted to 'The Tenth of April' shows Alton's final disillusionment with the movement. There is no mention, for example, of 'August 1848', or of continuing state repression.

But it is wrong in any case to see 1848 as the first occasion on which Chartism developed an internationalist, revolutionary perspective. A rich vein of republicanism had entered English radicalism in the Jacobin 1790s. Liberation movements in Ireland and on the Continent were monitored closely by radicals. The spirit of the Jacobin Corresponding Societies was preserved and handed on. In 1836 the London Working Men's Association issued an 'Address to the Polish and European Working Classes' in which it argued powerfully for

14

'national prejudices and bigoted feelings' to be jettisoned.[60] Chartists were prominent members of several support organizations for European republican struggles, such as the Peoples' International League (founded in 1847) and the Society of Fraternal Democrats (founded in 1845). The former group was closely allied to Joseph Mazzini, exponent of 'Young Europe', while the latter gravitated more towards German political philosophy, notably the ideas of Marx and Engels. In February 1848 both these groups sent delegates to Paris to congratulate the transitional government. The Peoples' International League delegation included Mazzini and W. J. Linton, the Chartist engraver, editor, and republican theorist. Ernest Jones, George Julian Harney, and Philip McGrath represented the Society of Fraternal Democrats. Jones was imprisoned later that year for making a speech in which he predicted that a green flag would soon be flying over Downing Street. So the republican character of Chartism after 1848 (when the Executive of the National Charter Association was under the influence of Jones, Harney, Linton and Reynolds) was more of a culmination and consolidation than a new beginning. There had always been popular support for the Poles and other 'patriots' fighting the old imperial oppressors Russia, Austria and Prussia. The importance of these struggles was reflected in Chartist political vocabulary. Henry Hetherington, for instance, believed the Whigs had 'Polandized' Ireland.[61]

But even the most ardent admirer of romantic 'patriotism' had to admit that despotic Europe was not, Ireland excepted, industrial Britain. Admiration did not mean emulation. To copy the methods of insurrection on the continental model would mean a bloody battle to control the urban centres of power. Many Chartists believed the state machine was simply too powerful: armed with lethal weaponry, highly centralized, serviced by the new railways, and solidly supported by the middle class. As Reynolds put it, '*Here*, we can achieve all we require by moral means: *there*, oceans of blood must be waded through by the sons of Freedom'.[62] This was a compelling case, but those still enamoured of seizing power believed they had an ace up their sleeves: Macerone's *Defensive Instructions for the People on Street Warfare*, first published in 1832. The book is a beginner's manual in the art of insurrection, a handbook on urban warfare inspired by the French and Belgian revolutions of 1830. In modern parlance, it became a Chartist 'underground classic'. As the commander of the northern security forces reported, Macerone was in circulation in the tense days of 1839 when the 'ulterior measures' were being drafted.[63] The first two stories in this section of the anthology were written to steer the movement either away from, or further towards, the Maceronian option.

Alexander Somerville (who is better known for his autobiography) issued his *Warnings to the People on Street Warfare* in six weekly letters from May to July 1839. The context of their composition is the relocation of the National Convention from London to Birmingham. The Convention moved in May to be further away from the centre of state power. According to Lovett, Birmingham was in 'a very excited state'.[64] Somerville obviously wanted to make an immediate impact on Chartist policy, so it is all the more interesting that he should choose to combine polemic with fiction. In order to demonstrate the folly of undertaking a Maceronian uprising, Somerville constructs a realistic account of 'street warfare supposed to be raging in the town of Birmingham' (he was particularly well qualified to imagine this possibility, as he had served in the regiment sent to put down the Birmingham Political Union in the Reform Bill disturbances).[65] To create maximum authenticity and excitement he uses

15

the devices of eye witness and newspaper accounts. These enable him to provide graphic detail, suspense and immediacy, and to juxtapose conflicting responses to the unfolding events. They also allow Somerville to demonstrate his radical credentials. In order to expose the culpability of the social system, he places the bloodthirsty rhetoric of the Tory press alongside the callous response of the financial markets – this is where the real power now resides. Somerville declares his affiliation with Chartism at the outset. He does not believe physical-force Chartists are treacherous, merely misguided. But in trying to guide his peers away from Macerone, one wonders if Somerville is not infected by the power and *frisson* of his vision. He shows the rebellion spreading to Glasgow, recently the scene of the cotton spinners' strike (Carlyle's 'Glasgow Thuggery'.)[66] He foregrounds a few individual Chartist heroes. Above all, the narrative is not resolved. Though the superiority of state weaponry has begun to assert itself (this was Somerville's main rebuttal of Macerone), the cities are left in partial rebel control. This lack of closure can be compared with Ernest Jones's account of an abortive proletarian revolution in *De Brassier* (1851–52). Though the uprising is crushed, there is still an underlying ambivalence. The rebel leader, 'Hotwing', is an impetuous drunkard who nevertheless becomes genuinely valiant (compare the short portrait of 'The Insurgent Leader' taken from the *Chartist Circular*, 1840), and the manipulable volatility of the people is as nothing compared to the premeditated ferocity of the state. Despite the counter-revolutionary hegemony in the years after 1848, Jones could not paint a wholly negative picture.

The pro-Maceronian lobby found a voice in 'The Revolutionist', a short story published in the *Chartist Circular* in 1840. Where Somerville extrapolates from the present, this story embellishes the past. The tale is a flagrant manipulation of the early stages of the French revolution of 1789. The battle for Paris is turned into a proletarian and Maceronian victory. The author claims to be correcting the bias of 'government-paid' historians, but the real intention is surely to galvanize 'our poor Chartist brethren'. A young 'operative' becomes a spontaneous revolutionary leader after watching the execution of a republican nobleman. With remarkable swiftness and dexterity the new hero exposes the villainy of the nobleman's arch-enemy, organizes a revolutionary council and defeats government troops by unleashing on them an irresistible 'Maceronian chariot'. During this action the hero is suddenly joined by none other than Napoleon Bonaparte, who clearly owes all subsequent success to this 'lower class' victory. Where Somerville imagines a 'Parisian' Birmingham, 'The Revolutionist' creates a 'physical force' Paris.

A battle for a capital city also provides the culminating scenes of Ernest Jones's *The Romance of a People* (1847). Jones turned to the Polish uprising of 1830 after being outraged at the Austrian annexation of the Polish republic of Cracow in 1846. In order to show the emotive attraction of Polish nationalism Jones develops a hero who is wrenched away from his patriotic roots and press-ganged into the imperial army. Once there, Wladimir Scyrma does well and is promoted, yet despite his success he never loses his nationalist instincts. The 1830 revolution brings him to his senses. He defects and returns to his own people and his first love, his adoptive sister Zaleska. She is a 'daughter of the people', a personification of the beauty and passion of the Polish nation. Wladimir and Zaleska join the retreat of the Polish army to Warsaw and participate in the refusal to surrender. The concluding scene in a Warsaw church shows Jones's skill at wringing maximum sentimental and symbolic value out of defeat. The other impressive feature of this long and often consuming narrative is that, despite Jones's obvious admiration for the Polish cause, he contrives a scene to open up nationalism to critical scrutiny. At the peak of his 'Russian' career Wladimir is wooed by the 'glittering sophistry' of a Russian princess. She argues that nationalism is socially backward – in Poland Vladimir would still be a peasant.[67] Her beauty is the 'glittering' allure of power, privilege, and 'progress'. She is the antithesis of Zaleska, and only the intervention of history prevents Wladimir succumbing to her attractions. She has found his weak spot: nationalism is indeed weakened by class distinctions.

Women

There seems to be no greater confirmation of the patriarchal basis of Chartism than the exclusion of women from 'universal' suffrage. However, the situation behind the scenes was contradictory and unresolved. Lovett claimed in his autobiography that the first draft of the Charter included women's enfranchisement. This was 'unfortunately left out' after members of the London Working Men's Association feared it would 'retard the suffrage of men' and alienate potential political support.[68] So it may have been pragmatism, not mere dogmatism, that led to the dropping of women from the Charter. There was certainly no hostility to women being active campaigners and organizers. The fact that Chartism had strong roots in the Reform Bill and anti-Poor Law campaigns meant it could draw on a dedicated tradition of organized female politics. Chartist women established Radical Associations, became lecturers, and suffered prison sentences.[69] In the domestic sphere, women were vital in arranging consumer boycotts as well as fulfilling the conventional duties of supporting the activities of husbands, and educating children. There is no evidence that Chartist women lobbied for political equality – they saw the Charter predominantly as a victory for their class. Despite this apparent unanimity, published expressions of dissent came from several male Chartists. Essays by R. J. Richardson (1840) and John Watkins (1841) argued for extending the suffrage to unmarried and widowed women (married women did not require their own vote as they 'are one' with their husbands).[70] In its final years, under a more socialist leadership, the case for truly universal suffrage seemed even more compelling.[71] So the denial of women's political rights was not as stable as might first appear. Dorothy Thompson states: 'the idea of women's votes was always widespread among the Chartists.'[72] Moreover, argues Thompson, the defeat of Chartism led to a consolidation of sexist attitudes and practices in the subsequent development of the labour movement. Yet again, it seems, Chartism was a watershed. There is certainly strong evidence of Chartist writers possessing a feminist consciousness, as the stories in this anthology (and subsequent volumes) will show.[73]

Most Chartist writers were, predictably, male. I have only been able to locate one named woman author of Chartist fiction, though women poets were more numerous. There is also a dearth of representations of Chartist women in Chartist (or any other) writing. Hence the character of Mary Graham in *Sunshine and Shadows* is unique in both Chartist and Victorian fiction.

The focus of Chartist fiction is not on Chartist women but on women's social and sexual exploitation. This was not an exclusively Chartist concern, but I

17

would claim that Chartist fiction is a unique and valuable response. Public anxiety about the plight of working women gathered momentum in the Chartist period. In 1842 a Royal Commission Report into children's and women's labour shocked the nation. One of the great contradictions of capitalism had been exposed: women were needed as a reserve army of cheap labour, but their working conditions (particularly in mining, where they often dragged heavy tubs half-naked) offended both common standards of decency and dominant notions of feminine purity. It was not only that women workers routinely suffered sexual harassment by peers and superiors. The real irony was that the factory and mine seemed guaranteed to promote promiscuity by bringing the sexes into close physical proximity. The industrial revolution's separation of work and home had also given young women workers a 'dangerous' degree of independence. So the workplace became sexualized, a site of illicit female desire. It is difficult not to believe that voyeuristic titillation contributed to the scandalous *frisson* of official reports.[74]

No occupation represented 'female slavery' more clearly than 'sweated' needlework. The dressmaker, milliner or seamstress epitomized exploitation. The numbers of women employed in London alone were vast: Reynolds put the figure at 30,000. Their appallingly low pay was notorious: 'No craftswomen are more industrious, yet none are worse paid than dressmakers' claimed the essay 'Female Slavery' in the *Labourer*.[75] As Henry Mayhew's investigations into the life of the London poor revealed, low pay drove high numbers of 'female operatives' into casual prostitution.[76] These circumstances may explain the prominence of needlewomen in Chartist stories. Another reason could have been the narrative opportunities presented by the complex social character of the work. It embraced both working-class and downwardly mobile genteel women. Women were often customers or employers, which added to the situation a further conflict between class and gender identities. Sweating labour also offered an insight into the contradictions of the production of luxury. To quote 'Female Slavery':

> These poor creatures, suffering from the extreme of indigence, and often want, are brought into contact with the most exaggerated luxury which riches can invent. They live upon the frontiers of fashionable society, and become imbued with all its taste for show, and dress, and gentility, without the means of gratifying it (p. 251).

It is not surprising that the lives of women workers on class 'frontiers' should attract the imagination of Chartist writers.

One such group was servants. The two short sketches from W. J. Linton's periodical the *National* (1839) mount a furious attack on the servant system. The numbers of women in domestic service grew throughout the nineteenth century. No self-respecting middle-class household could afford to be without servants. Servants were crucial signifiers of their own and their employers' class. Their labour enabled middle-class women to become signifiers of a leisured lifestyle. In 'The Free-Servant' Jane Stephens is a casualty of the cash nexus. Her employers are not vindictive, merely careless. Jane is overworked, falls ill and disappears into urban obscurity. As 'Female Slavery' puts it, maids-of-all-work 'are treated, for the most part, as servants or serfs, the only bond between them and their employers being money wages' (p. 252). Linton offers

18

a robust solution to 'domestic slavery' – 'fine ladies' should look after their own homes.

Linton's other sketch, 'The Outcast', focuses on sexual exploitation. Rose Clifford is a working-class fallen woman, victim of an elopement, desertion, and lack of social protection. Her decline into prostitution leads Linton into a passionate attack on the hypocrisy of religious and sexual morality. While the victim is blamed and punished, the class system protects her abuser. Society's real prostitutes are the women of arranged marriages. A measure of Linton's progressive sexual politics is that the whole issue of the *National* in which the sketch appeared is devoted to feminism. The story is followed by extracts from Godwin, Wollstonecraft, and Shelley, all reinforcing the view that conventional bourgeois marriage is superficial, materialist, and ruinous to women.

The first of our stories to deal with sweated labour shows the particular burdens of daughters when hard times afflict the family fortunes. In 'The Young Seamstress' (*Reynolds's Miscellany*, 1847), Caroline Melford's slop work has to support her insane father and two siblings. The father used to be a small farmer until a lawsuit pitched him into downward mobility and madness (for the respectable breadwinner emasculation and proletarianization go hand-in-hand). Caroline shows a greater adaptability than her father by taking on low-paid needlework which she can combine with household duties. But as the demands on her become too great she tries to skimp on her work, only to be turned away empty-handed by her employer. On the verge of collapse, her family starving, she finds reserves of energy to finish the work and earn her two shillings for fifty hours of labour. The story then takes an interesting turn. The narrator teases the reader with alternative endings. The first is an unresolved, realistic continuation of subsistence living which is reminiscent of Cooper's '"Merrie England" – No More!': 'still she laboured, still she hoped, and still she struggled on'. But not wishing to offend literary decorum, the narrator summons up a *deus ex machina*. The old lawsuit is miraculously annulled, and the family can return to their former life.

At least Caroline did not suffer sexual depredation. A series of increasingly gruesome fates awaits her fictional successors. Annie Lee, the 'fragile' heroine of 'The Slave of the Needle' (which appeared in Reynolds's *London Journal* in 1850) is 'slain in the murderous war of avarice and brutal passion'. The villain of the story is her employer Mr Watkins. He is the new, bourgeois class enemy, and has appropriately all the cunning of a 'police spy'. Annie has been 'booked' into his sexual empire since her arrival. Once her mother dies she is no match for his persistence and 'refined villainy'. She falls into self-destructive prostitution, drink, and an obscure death. The narrator makes clear that the story is designed to modernize the social territory of melodrama. Annie's fate is contrasted to the heroines of 'wire-drawn romances' who are coated in 'sickly sentiment'. The new battleground for melodrama is the workplace and the social relations that flow from it.[77] So the story moves, without apology, from tabulated details of Annie's daily budget to prolonged seduction scenes. The incorporation of economic discourse is not incongruous because the sexual encounter is defined by the larger social structure. To Chartists, the individual was always a social subject. Annie's sexual enslavement is a condition, almost a precondition, of her employment. It is the social power wielded by her employer which creates the pornographic male gaze, not the reverse: 'Presently the great man arrived; and the trembling slaves of the needle opened their little bundles for his inspection'.

Taken together with Ernest Jones's *Woman's Wrongs* (1852) and G. W. M. Reynold's penny novel *The Seamstress: Or, the White Slave of England* (1850) (to be included in forthcoming volumes), these stories about independent, urban, and vulnerable working women opened up new social territory to English fiction. What is more, their radical form and message, combined with their popular appeal, make them unique cultural responses to the 'woman question'.

Chartism

The major achievements under this heading are undoubtedly Thomas Doubleday's *The Political Pilgrim's Progress* (1839) and Thomas Martin Wheeler's *Sunshine and Shadows* (1849–50). In order to publish them in their entirety these stories have been given a separate volume. Both narratives depart in substantial and significant ways from dominant notions of realism. Though the same cannot be said of the short pieces gathered in this section of the anthology, they are still of particular interest as fictional representations of Chartism, produced by and for the movement.

Though she is the only named female author of Chartist fiction, Mary Hutton chose an exclusively male perspective for 'The Poor Man's Wrongs' (1839). The central character is a pilgrim-like working-class bard fleeing from England to Scotland to escape the Poor Law. He is also mourning the death of his sons in the Carlist wars (there is an echo here of the first version of Wordsworth's 'Old Man Travelling'). He is given refuge by the allegorically named Albert Freeland, a Scottish smallholder. Despite the prevailing national distress, both men are inspired by the 'beacon-star' of Chartism. The story's ending reflects the optimism of the movement leading up to the Charter's first presentation. A similar buoyancy is to be found in 'The Charter and the Land' (1847), a story written to promote the National Land Company. A Stockport weaver is on the slippery downward slope until he is converted to O'Connor's Land Scheme.[78] William Wright and his family are fortunate enough to be awarded a cottage at O'Connorville. In another version of the pilgrimage motif, we see the family take up their Utopian new life in the 'Holy Land' (notice also that the *deus ex machina* is now provided by Chartism itself). A more tragic tone colours Ernest Jones's 'The London Doorstep' (1848), written in the aftermath of 10 April. Jones shares the narrative equally between a Midlands artisan and his wife. While the artisan stumbles into the Blackfriars Bridge disturbances and converts spontaneously to Chartism (he can then die a martyr's death), his wife dies a passive victim of 'Social Murder'.

The remaining text to comment on is Ernest Jones's *De Brassier: A Democratic Romance* (1851–52). Along with *Sunshine and Shadows* this is one of the best-known Chartist narratives, probably because it has been read from the beginning as a satirical portrait of Feargus O'Connor. The story shows the rise of an unscrupulous aristocrat to absolute control of a mass radical movement. His motives are merely to revenge himself on his own class who refused to support his wastrel lifestyle. Jones denied basing De Brassier on any Chartist leader, and claimed he was trying to inoculate the still active membership from demagoguery. He wanted the tale read, not as a memorial, but as an intervention. To give a flavour of this long, multiplotted story, I have chosen a scene in which De Brassier summons a National Convention merely to further his megalomania. The scene shows a marked contrast in style to Wheeler's reportage used in *Sunshine and Shadows*. Jones was prepared to burlesque Chartism's history to attack its political naivety. The scene is best read alongside accounts of actual Chartist Conventions, where it is apparent that no speaker dominated in this way.

Where do we go from here? This book will be faithful to the spirit of Chartism if it opens up rather than forecloses debate. I have tried to restore to the modern eye an important aspect of Chartism's struggle for representation.The picture is still incomplete. More work is needed on both production and reception, and we need to continue the search for women authors. Hopefully, these stories will show our incomplete understanding of nineteenth-century radical and popular cultural history. This collection can also be used for comparison with the canonical 'condition of England' novelists. If the 'fiction department' of Chartism can achieve even some of these ends, this book will have served its purpose.

Notes

The place of publication is London unless otherwise noted.

1. In a note to *The Purgatory of Suicides* Thomas Cooper likens the Newport rising of 1839 to the Magna Carta or the Glorious Revolution of 1688. See *The Purgatory of Suicides: A Prison-Rhyme in 10 Books* (Jeremiah How, 1845), p. 180.
2. The phrase comes from Frank Peel, *The Risings of the Luddites, Chartists and Plugdrawers* (Heckmondwike: Senior and Co., 1888), p. 320.
3. See G. D. H. Cole, *Chartist Portraits* (Macmillan, 1941), pp. 18–19.
4. See William Lovett, *The Life and Struggles of William Lovett in his Pursuit of Bread, Knowledge and Freedom* (London and New York: Garland Publishing, 1984), p. 470 (first published in 1876).
5. Gustav Klaus reckons there were 'nearly a hundred' Chartist papers and journals. See *The Literature of Labour: Two Hundred Years of Working-Class Writing* (Brighton: Harvester Press, 1985), p. 48.
6. Jennifer Bennett makes the point that the connection with the 1790s was particularly strong in the East London Democratic Association, which became one of the tributary bodies of London Chartism. See 'The London Democratic Association 1837–41' in James Epstein and Dorothy Thompson, eds, *The Chartist Experience* (Macmillan, 1982).
7. See J. F. C. Harrison and Dorothy Thompson, *Bibliography of the Chartist Movement, 1837–1976* (Brighton: Harvester Press, 1978), p. xi.
8. According to Louis James, the cheap 6d reprint of Part Two of *The Rights of Man* (1792) sold 32,000 copies in a month. E. P. Thompson puts the total sales for the first year at 200,000 – sufficient to make Paine a household name. See Louis James, *Print and the People 1819–1851* (Harmondsworth: Allen Lane, 1976), p. 33; E. P. Thompson, *The Making of the English Working Class* (Harmondsworth: Pelican, 1977), p. 117 (first published in 1963).

9. See A. Aspinall, *Politics and the Press c. 1780–1850* (Home and Van Thel, 1949); Patricia Hollis, *The Pauper Press: A Study in Working Class Radicalism of the 1830s* (Oxford: Oxford University Press, 1970).

10. See R. K. Webb, *The British Working Class Reader 1790–1848. Literacy and Social Tension* (George Allen and Unwin, 1955), p. 42; Richard D. Altick, *The English Common Reader. A Social History of the Mass Reading Public 1800–1900* (Chicago and London: University of Chicago Press, 1967), pp. 73–76 (first published in 1957).

11. Altick claims (p. 76) that *Cheap Repository Tracts* had sold over two million copies by 1796.

12. In addition to the books already mentioned by Altick, Webb, James and Hollis, see Louis James, *Fiction for the Working Man 1830–1850* (Penguin University Books, 1974) (first published in 1963); Victor Neuberg, *Popular Literature: A History and Guide from the Beginning of Printing to the Year 1897* (The Woburn Press, 1977); David Vincent, *Literacy and Popular Culture in England 1750–1914* (Cambridge: Cambridge University Press, 1989).

13. For an example of the attraction of Working Men's Institutes, see Malcolm Chase, ed., *The Life and Literary Pursuits of Allen Davenport* (Aldershot: Scolar Press, 1994), p.57.

14. Louis James (1976, p. 36) puts the maximum circulation figures of *The Penny Magazine* at 200,000.

15. Harriet Martineau, *Poor Laws and Paupers Illustrated*, 4 vols (published under the superintendence of the Society for the Diffusion of Useful Knowledge, 1833–34). See also *The Rioters, or, A Tale of Bad Times* (1827).

16. See David Vincent, *Bread, Knowledge and Freedom: A Study of Nineteenth Century Working Class Autobiography* (Methuen, 1981), p. 124.

17. The Cornish Coffee House in Bunhill Row was a 'second home' to Allen Davenport (Chase, 1994, p. 27).

18. See William Lovett and John Collins, *Chartism: A New Organisation for the People* (James Watson, Henry Hetherington, John Cleave, 1840); Thomas Cooper, *The Purgatory of Suicides* (Jeremiah How, 1845), Book X.

19. Klaus (1985), p. 49.

20. A recent example of this neglect is Christopher Harvie, *The Centre of Things: Political Fiction in Britain from Disraeli to the Present* (Unwin Hyman, 1991), pp. 16–18. While Harvie is to be credited for including Chartist fiction in his survey, all his references are from secondary sources, and the author of *Sunshine and Shadows* is called 'Thomas William Wheeler'.

21. Garland Publishing has issued two lengthy series of facsimile reprints of nineteenth-century radical and working-class texts. See F. M. Lenthal, ed., *The World of Labour: English Workers 1850–1890* (1984–), 29 titles; Dorothy Thompson, ed., *Chartism: Working Class Politics in the Industrial Revolution*, (1986–), 22 volumes. Louis James, *Print and the People* (1976) is an anthology of facsimile reprints of popular literature 1819–1851. James explains, unaccountably, that 'it proved impossible to deal adequately with the major political and social movements, such as

Chartism or the Corn law agitation, so these have been largely omitted' (p. 13).

22. Y. V. Kovalev, 'The Literature of Chartism', *Victorian Studies*, volume 2, number 2 (1958), p. 137. The article is a translation of the Introduction to Kovalev's *An Anthology of Chartist Literature* (Moscow: Foreign Languages Publishing House, 1956).

23. Klaus (1985), p. 60.

24. James (1974), p. 25.

25. Vincent (1989), *passim*; see also Anne Humphreys, 'Popular Narrative and Political Discourse in *Reynolds's Weekly Newspaper*', in Laurel Brake, ed., *Investigating Victorian Journalism* (Macmillan, 1990). Humphreys claims (p. 35) that Reynolds was 'the most popular writer in Victorian England'.

26. Vincent (1981), p. 51.

27. Vincent (1989), p. 251.

28. See *Cooper's Journal*, volume 1, number 9 (2 March 1850), p. 129.

29. See, for instance, the opening paragraphs of 'A Simple Story' (included in this anthology).

30. Thomas Frost's account of his days with the 'Salisbury Square School' of fiction is to be found in 'Popular Literature Forty Years Ago', chapter VI of *Forty Years Recollections: Literary and Political* (Sampson and Low, 1880). See also discussions of Reynolds in Neuberg (1977), James (1974) and Vincent (1989).

31. Lovett (1984), p. 430.

32. See John Knott, *Popular Opposition to the 1834 Poor Law* (Croom Helm, 1986), p. 275.

33. Knott (1986), p. 136.

34. It is possible that Harriet Martineau produced the first fictional portrayal of the desperate artisan in *The Rioters* (1827). In terms of Chartist poetry, an important example of the figure is to be found in W. J. Linton's *Bob Thin, or the Poorhouse Fugitive* (privately printed, 1845) – the first section of this long poem has been reprinted in Brian Maidment, ed., *The Poorhouse Fugitives: Self-taught Poets and Poetry in Victorian Britain* (Manchester: Carcanet, 1992) (first published in 1987). The most famous real-life example is Richard Pilling, the powerloom weaver arrested for his part in the 'Plug' riots of 1842. Pilling's trial speech, which had the court in tears and resulted in an acquittal, can be found in F. C. Mather, *Chartism and Society: An Anthology of Documents* (Bell and Hyman, 1980), pp. 188–91.

35. See Frederick Engels, *The Condition of the Working Class in England* (Panther Books, 1984), p. 173 (first published in German in 1845; in English in 1892).

36. Charles Dicken, 'A Walk in the Workhouse', in Andrew Lang, ed., *The Works of Charles Dickens*, 34 volumes, (Chapman and Hall, 1899), volume 34, pp. 202–11 (reprint of edition of 1867–68).

37. The *Illustrated London News* (1842), p. 236.

38. See Cooper (1845), p. vii.

39. Henry Vincent reviewed Capel Lloft's epic poem *Ernest, or Political Regeneration* in *Cleave's Gazette of Variety* (12 December 1840), p. 2.

40. See *The Life of Thomas Cooper. Written by Himself* (Hodder and Stoughton, 1872), pp. 138–39. Further page references are cited after quotation.

41. Details can be found in Mark Hovell, *The Chartist Movement* (Manchester: Manchester University Press, 1918), pp. 316–17.
42. Hovell (1918), p. 21.
43. Cooper claimed to have learnt by heart the whole of *Paradise Lost* and seven Shakespeare plays by the age of 24. Local people regarded him as a 'prodigy of learning'. See *Life* (1872), p. 73.
44. Thomas Carlyle, *Chartism* (1840) in *Thomas Carlyle: Selected Writings* (Harmondsworth: Penguin, 1988), pp. 173, 176, 170.
45. See Lovett (1984), p. 149, p. 129, pp. 182–90; see also the *Charter* (24 February 1839), p. 76.
46. See Lovett (1984), p. 182, and David Goodway, *London Chartism 1836–1848* (Cambridge: Cambridge University Press, 1982), p. 62.
47. An account of Attwood's actions can be read in the *Charter* (12 May 1839), p. 253.
48. Cited in Dorothy Thompson, 'Ireland and the Irish in English Radicalism before 1850', in Epstein and Thompson (1982), p. 142.
49. Both Palmerston (Foreign Secretary) and Lansdowne (Lord President of the Council) were Irish landlords. See John Saville, *1848: The British State and the Chartist Movement* (Cambridge: Cambridge University Press, 1987), p. 2.
50. Reynolds likens Ireland to revolutionary France in *Reynolds's Political Instructor,* number 26 (4 May 1850), p. 203: 'good reader, do not, for heaven's sake, suppose that we find fault with Hungarians battling for nationality, Romans shedding their blood for freedom, or John Mitchel invoking "the god of battles" on the side of his peace-ridden, starved, or deceived countrymen'.
51. The extent of the demand for such gifts can be estimated by the fact that an advertisement appears in *Reynolds's Political Instructor*, number 9 (5 January 1850).
52. Lovett (1984), p. 213.
53. Lovett (1984) claims the middle classes commanded 10,000 armed men (p. 77); the Scottish Chartist John McAdam puts the figure at 70,000 – see Janet Fyfe, ed., *Autobiography of John McAdam* (Edinburgh: Clarke Constable, 1980), p. 10.
54. Eric Hobsbawm, Introduction to Engels (1984), p. 14
55. Cited in Saville (1987), p. 79.
56. Ironically, this daguerreotype is now part of the Royal Photographic Collection.
57. Saville (1987), p. 109.
58. The best accounts of the events of 1848 are to be found in Goodway (1982) and Saville (1987).
59. See Saville (1987), chapter 7.
60. See Lovett (1984), p. 151.
61. Hetherington is cited in James Epstein, *The Lion of Freedom: Feargus O'Connor and the Chartist Movement, 1832–1842* (Croom Helm, 1982), p. 13. Engels (1984) thought Chartism was republican in spirit (p. 255).
62. *Reynold's Political Instructor,* number 4 (1 December 1850), p. 27.
63. Napier is cited in Hovell (1918), p. 137; see also Charles Kingsley, *Alton Locke,Tailor and Poet: An Autobiography* (1850), chapter XXXIII.
64. Lovett (1984), p. 220.

65. Somerville recalls how the Scots Greys were told to 'rough-sharpen' their swords in anticipation of offensive action. For his part in the regiment's refusal to attack defenceless civilians, Somerville was brutally flogged. See Alexander Somerville, *The Autobiography of a Working Man* (MacGibbon and Kee, 1967), p. 164 (first published in 1848).
66. Carlyle (1988), p. 152
67. See Lovett (1984), p. 154.
68. Lovett (1984), p. 170.
69. See Dorothy Thompson, *The Chartists: Popular Politics in the Industrial Revolution* (Aldershot: Wildwood House, 1986), chapter 7 (first published in 1984).
70. R. J. Richardson, *The Rights of Woman* (1840) is reprinted in Dorothy Thompson, *The Early Chartists* (Columbia, South Carolina: University of South Carolina Press, 1971). John Watkins, *Address to the Women of England* appeared in the *English Chartist Circular* (April 1841), p. 49.
71 See W.J. Linton's argument for women's suffrage in C. G. Harding's periodical *The Republican* (1848), pp. 165–68.
72. Thompson (1986), p. 124.
73. See, for example, Cooper, *The Purgatory of Suicides*, Book IX, stanza 16.
74. See E. Royston Pike, *Human Documents of the Industrial Revolution in Britain* (George Allen and Unwin, 1970) (first published in 1966).
75. 'Female Slavery' by 'S.' appeared in the *Labourer*, volume 2 (1847), pp. 241–53. Further page references are cited in the text. According to Ivy Pinchbeck in *Women Workers and the Industrial Revolution 1750–1850* (Virago, 1981) (first published in 1930), needleworkers' pay could be as low as four shillings a week (p. 289).
76. See Henry Mayhew, *London Labour and the London Poor* (Frank Cass and Co., 1967), 4 volumes, volume 4, p. 255 (first published 1861–62). Judith Walkowitz regards these statistics as exaggerated; see *Prostitution and Victorian Society: Women, Class and the State* (Cambridge: Cambridge University Press, 1980), pp. 14–15.
77. A more extended discussion of Chartist writers' use of melodrama will be found in the Introduction to volume 3 (forthcoming).
78. See Alice Mary Hadfield, *The Chartist Land Company* (Newton Abbot: David and Charles, 1970); Joy Maskill, 'The Land Plan', in Asa Briggs, ed., *Chartist Studies* (Macmillan, 1958).

Will Harper: A Poor-Law Tale (1838)

Will Harper was, at one time of his life, the pride and boast of the village in which he lived. He was an honest, hard-working man, kept his situation as a farm servant under one master, for many years, with credit to himself, and, though frugal and care-taking, had at all times a hand ready to relieve the necessities of those upon whom Fortune frowned. Then at the country sports, too, Will was almost sure to come off victorious; at cricket he was a first-rate player, and at quoits none could venture to compete with him – at least with any chance of winning. Nor was Will Harper deficient in the more refined accomplishment of dancing, for the girls, who are the best judges after all in these matters, declared that he was the very best hand at a reel or a country dance in the whole parish. In fact, as a proof that they really thought so, the rustic maidens were ready to pull caps for him whenever at country fair or wake an opportunity occurred for enjoying their favourite pastime.

Having thus enumerated a few of the accomplishments and good qualities of honest Will Harper, it will not be wondered at that he was, as we have observed before, respected and beloved by all who knew him. Even the excellent vicar was proud of one whom he regarded as a most worthy member of his flock, and the squire, whenever he met him, would stop and chat with as much familiarity as though he had been an equal. Many a bright eye sparkled with delight upon him as he passed, and Will knew well enough, both from personal observation and the hints of various friends, that half the unmarried girls in the village would willingly resign their liberty into his hands.

On a Sunday when he attended church, – and he was a constant attendant there, – many a bosom heaved as he passed down the aisle to take his seat in the pew near the reading desk. On these occasions his dress was always attended to with the most scrupulous nicety; – not, however, that he was ridiculously attached to finery, – but there was a neatness and care about his personal appearance that might well be copied by many others in his humble sphere of life. After the service was over, he would return home to the cottage of his aged parents, and their frugal meal being concluded, he would stroll out to enjoy the beauties of nature, or, perhaps, visit some friend with whom he could pass away a rational hour or two.

Bye and bye, however, the heart of Will Harper became entangled in the meshes of love. The image of pretty Mary Dalton, had long haunted him in his visions; but somehow or other he had never had the courage to pop the question, and thus learn whether she really loved him in return or not. It is certain that he flattered himself into the belief that he was not disregarded by her; but then he was naturally timid, and feared to learn from her own lips that though she might esteem him very highly as a friend, yet could she never love him as a husband. Poor Will! Little need had he for this timidity – the maiden did love him; – nay, did not disguise the fact, and her only surprise was that he had never yet found courage to utter half with his lips what his eyes had so often expressed. At last, however, Will did muster the necessary resolution, the question was popped, and he became the accepted lover of Mary Dalton. From this time Will passed every moment he could spare from daily toil in the society of her who had thus reciprocated his affection. Each meeting, indeed, tended but to prove more satisfactorily the deep and unalterable attachment that existed between them, and both looked forward with unmingled pleasure to the moment that was to unite them in those bonds that were to be severed only by death. At length the day was named, and then began the bustle of preparation which even in humble life attend the nuptial ceremony. Will and Mary had both contrived to lay by some of their earnings, and part of these savings were of course to be laid out in furnishing a little cottage with those articles of useful furniture that were absolutely necessary. Nothing, however, was bought which their station needed not, and in this particular, among many others, Will saw with pleasure the care and prudence that ever marked the conduct of his beloved Mary.

The day at last arrived, and Will led his bride to church, accompanied by a host of rustic friends. On their return the squire met the nuptial party, and having congratulated the bride and bridegroom upon their union, presented them with a small gift to assist, as he expressed it, towards defraying the expenses of the day. Will's heart glowed with rapture at this manifestation of esteem on the part of one so much his superior in life, and thanking him fervently, he turned away to hide the tear of gratitude that dimmed his eye. As the good squire left them, the bridal party resumed their way, and returning to the cottage of the bride and bridegroom, the remainder of the day was passed in that joyous merriment which usually accompanies celebrations of a similar kind.

We will now pass over the next five years, during which period neither Will nor his wife had even the most trivial cause to regret the choice each had made of a partner. Two children, – a boy and a girl, – had served to rivet yet more firmly the bonds of affection in which their hearts were linked. Care had never for an instant haunted their bosoms; they passed peacefully onwards from day to day, and were in fact, the envy and example of all who knew them.

But alas! happiness, though apparently based upon the securest foundation, seldom lasts for ever, and a period came when all Will Harper's firmness was to be put to the test. Hard times came; farmers were reduced from prosperity to a state little better than beggary, and the price of labour consequently fell to a standard which afforded a bare subsistence even to those who toiled incessantly from sun-rise to sunset. Poor Will soon felt the severity of the times; yet he complained not, but lived in the fond hope that ere long matters would again change for the better. Even in this, however, he was doomed to be disappointed; instead of getting better, things got worse and worse every day, until at last, on his master becoming a bankrupt, Will Harper lost his situation, and was then thrown upon the world to starve or obtain a scanty livelihood in the best manner he could. But the pressure of distress was now everywhere felt alike; it was impossible for labourers to obtain employment, and though Will Harper would cheerfully have undertaken any work that might be offered, he wandered about day after day, and week after week, without being able to earn so much as would provide a single meal for his suffering wife and family.

Under these afflictions he found in Mary a constant source of consolation. If he returned home at night depressed in spirits she would endeavour to make him forget his disappointments by forced cheerfulness of her own demeanour, and by turning the tide of his melancholy recollections would – though but for a time – kindle in his heart a ray of hope that the period of their miseries would not be of long duration. It is true that Will, for his own part, was not over sanguine upon the matter, yet he would not lacerate the heart of his kind wife by refusing to listen to her gentle consolations, and taking her hand, he would

27

assure her that under any circumstances his love for her must remain unchanged.

Months passed away, but still no brighter prospects appeared to relieve their gloom; indeed, matters grew worse and worse, the little money they had saved was all spent, and nothing but starvation stared them in the face. Then, for the first time, Will Harper felt the full force of the miseries that were crowding upon him. Destitution they had already suffered enough from; but while their little stock of money lasted, they had been enabled to provide food for their young family. Now, however, even that hope failed them, and the much-dreaded workhouse was the last terrible resource that presented itself. To those who have honourably striven by toil to avoid this species of degradation, nothing can be more horrible than to be driven to apply for parochial relief. Harper and his wife shrunk even at the bare reflection, but the certainty of the misery to which their children would be subjected, at last compelled him to this sad alternative, and it was determined that on the next day Will should apply at the workhouse for the miserable pittance that the parochial officers might be pleased to dole out.

Will Harper passed a restless night, for his heart sickened at the bare thought of the step he was thus compelled to take. Mary, too, participated in his feeling; she wept in silence, for she feared to augment that grief that she had not the means to alleviate. Throughout that day their children had been without food, save a small piece of dry bread which had been divided between them. This was a severe blow to the parents; they could have endured any privations themselves, but to see their helpless offspring suffering the sharp pains of hunger, was more than they could bear. This, indeed, it was that had strengthened Will's resolution to apply to the parish, and for this he was resolved to endure the degradation to which he was about to submit. That night, they slept not; their hearts were too full of their own griefs, and in the morning they arose dejected and oppressed.

Dreading to hear his children cry for food, which he had it not in his power to give them, Will Harper left the cottage, and proceeded towards the town where the workhouse was situated. He was too early, however, to find the overseer, and he therefore strolled about until the time should arrive when he might obtain admittance. At last, the clock warned him that he might seek the interview, and, retracing his steps, he once more stood at the door of the workhouse. It was in vain that he tried to overcome his repugnance to appear as a pauper before those of whom he had never before asked even the most trifling favour.

He paused irresolutely at the portal, and it was not till after he had made two or three ineffectual efforts that he at last ventured to knock at the door. In a few seconds he was answered by a surly porter who having learned his business admitted him into the gloomy passage, where he was desired to wait till it should be the pleasure of the relieving officer to see him.

To Will Harper this seemed an age; he was anxious to return to his despairing wife and family, but as the great man could not be disturbed till he thought proper, the supplicant for parochial aid was e'en compelled to wait with what patience he could, till he could obtain the required audience. After remaining till his patience was nearly worn out, the porter again appeared, and desired that he would follow to the room occupied by the overseer, who was now ready to hear his case. Will proceeded in silence through a long vaulted corridor, dimly lighted at intervals by small barred windows which scarcely answered the

28

purpose for which they were intended. Having reached the end of this, his conductor knocked at a door which, being thrown open, Will soon found himself within a small apartment, which being handsomely furnished, afforded a sad contrast to the other parts of this wretched abode of poverty. Before a good fire, and surrounded with the luxuries of life, sat the man who was intrusted with the duty of administering to the necessities of his less fortunate fellow creatures. He was engaged, when Will entered, in looking over a newspaper, and deigned not to raise his head, although well aware that a poor creature in the most abject state of distress was waiting to lay his case before him. Presently, however, he threw down the paper on the table, yawned, and falling back in his chair, inquired of the poor applicant what he wanted with him.

"I have come to ask relief from the parish sir," answered Will, hesitating and casting his eyes abashed upon the ground.

"Relief!" exclaimed Mr. Wasp, pushing the table violently from him, "and pray what claim have you to ask assistance out of the parish funds?"

"I have lived in the neighbourhood many years," answered the supplicant, "and have never before asked this from mortal man."

"Hum! I should suppose not," returned the other; "you are young and strong enough to earn your own living without burdening other people with the expense of keeping you."

"I am young and strong enough it is true," answered Will, venturing for the first time to look in the face of the overseer; "but if all refuse to employ me, how am I to support those that look up to me for their daily bread?"

"Don't question me in this way, you insolent fellow!" exclaimed Wasp, reddening with passion, "but confine yourself to answering what I ask of you. How is it, sirrah, that you can get no employment? Your character, I suppose, is forfeited."

"My character is unsullied," cried Will, "and nought but the misery of my poor children could have forced me to take this step."

"Aye, children, that's always the excuse," said Wasp; "but I owe a duty to the parish, and I will not see its funds wasted to support a parcel of idle fellows."

"You also owe a duty to the poor," replied Will, with a firmness that somewhat surprised the insolent overseer.

"You may send your wife and family to the Union workhouse, fellow: we'll find her employment – but understand me, she will be separated from her children."

"What, part a mother from her infants, whom she has cherished through every difficulty?" exclaimed Will indignantly; "and what law do you call that which would countenance you in such a fiendish proceeding?"

"Don't question me, man, as to my right of proceeding as I please," returned Wasp, with cool indifference. "I have law on my side, and that is enough. There is an Act of Parliament just passed, and upon that I shall take the course I have just mentioned."

"An Act of Parliament!" exclaimed Will; "then you will obey a law made by man against one that has been declared by God himself?"

"Of course," replied the overseer, "so you can decide at once whether you will agree to the conditions, or save the parish the expense of keeping your family in idleness."

"I have already decided," answered the other, "and rather than suffer them to exist upon the miserable pittance thus unwillingly offered to them, they shall starve to death one by one before my eyes. Aye, Master Wasp, you may laugh at my miseries; you may deride the sufferings of the poor, while your own appetite is pampered at the expense of the parish; but mark my words – a day will come, and that too, ere long, when you shall be made to feel that poverty may have its hour of triumph over the heartless oppressor."

An insulting laugh of scorn was the only answer returned by Mr. Wasp. The poor supplicant for relief eyed the heartless official with a look of rage he could not suppress. He clenched his hands, and was about to rush upon the overseer, when suddenly his better feelings overmastered the impulse, and fleeing from the apartment he stopped not until he found himself at some distance from the town. By this time the fever which had maddened his brain, began in some degree, to abate, and then again came the horrible recollection of all the deprivations to which his wife and children were subjected. To see those he loved pining in absolute want; to hear their piteous cries for food which he had it not in his power to give them, was more than he could endure, and already a thought of committing suicide had crossed his phrenzied brain.

At this period a well-known voice met his ear, and turning round he beheld the squire, who was closely regarding him with a look of kindness and compassion. Will would have turned away, but the other advancing towards him, insisted upon knowing the cause of his present melancholy. This after some hesitation was explained, when the good hearted squire putting into his hands a few shillings to answer the immediate exigencies of his case, promised to interfere in his behalf, and desired him to call at his mansion on the following morning to learn the result of his mediation. It was in vain that Will hesitated to accept the trifle that had been given him; the squire urged him to accept it for the sake of his starving family, and hastening away, he left the poor fellow imploring a thousand blessings upon his head for the timely relief he had thus benevolently administered.

Will paused for some time, watching the retiring form of his kind friend, and then recollecting the destitute condition of his family, he once more continued his way homewards with a heart lightened of half its grief.

As he passed onwards, however, he was hailed by a man, who had formerly been a fellow-labourer with him, but who was said to have become one of the most desperate poachers in the country. Will would have shunned the companionship of this man, and he continued his way for this purpose; but the other hastened after him, and finally prevailed upon him to enter a public-house, merely, as he said, to have a sup of ale together. Yielding as his disposition was, Will was unfortunately easily persuaded to have another. Another quickly succeeded that. His head became dizzy. A game at skittles was then proposed; Will had not resolution enough to resist it – he played, – several games were lost in succession, nor did he reflect upon the horrors that awaited him at home, until he had lost all the money that had been given him by the squire, except a single shilling. This fact startled him; and abruptly quitting the society of his betrayer, he returned to his cottage, nearly overpowered with the quantity he had been drinking.

On entering the room he encountered the tearful gaze of his sorrowing wife, who had long been anxiously waiting his return. Will expected to hear her reproaches, yet not one word of complaint escaped her lips. Will felt the force of this silent admonition more keenly than if she had assailed him with a volley of reproaches, and putting into her hands the solitary coin that remained, bade her get some food to satisfy the children's craving for bread. This was soon done, and Will, stupefied with the effects of the liquor he had drank, reeled off to bed – not to sleep – but to reflect upon the folly of which he had that day been guilty.

Early on the following morning Will arose, fevered and nervous through the effects of the last night's excesses. In vain the breakfast was placed before him – he felt too ill to eat or drink, and rising from his seat he left the house for the purpose of proceeding at once to the squire's mansion, according to the appointment he had made the day preceding. Reproaching himself for having so thoughtlessly squandered away the money that had been given him, he proceeded onwards for the place of his destination. At last he reached the gates that opened into the park, but conscious of the folly he had committed, he stood for some time irresolute whether to enter or return home. Whilst Will stood leaning in melancholy abstraction over the gate, he was again accosted by the same man who had tempted him astray the day before. Will started, and would have hurried forward, but the other catching him by the arm, demanded whither he was going?

This was soon explained; but the other, instead of tendering friendly advice, laughed deridingly at him for looking to others for support, when he had it in his power to assist himself. Will inquired how that was to be done, and received for an answer that if he chose to join with him in his poaching expeditions he would never again have to complain of poverty or ask assistance of those who would not give it except under the most galling conditions. Will listened, and the prospect of raising his family from their present state of wretched poverty almost tempted him to embrace the proposition. The other saw him waver; he urged him yet more earnestly, and the result was that Will promised to accompany him that very night on a poaching expedition in the squire's grounds.

We will not describe the scenes which followed, and in which the unfortunate hero of our tale took a prominent part. It is true that his family no longer suffered under the cruel pressure of poverty and famine, but Will became altogether an altered man. He was no longer the kind husband and father that he had been; evil companions had contaminated him, and his lawless course of life soon made him morose and arbitrary to those he had till now loved. His wife saw the change that had taken place in her husband's conduct: she wept, but her tears flowed in secret; and if ever, by any chance, she was seen to cry, she was scolded by her husband for repining, now that their circumstances had been so much improved.

One evening in the autumn, when Will was preparing to go out on his unlawful occupation, a sudden and violent storm arose, which seemed to threaten their crazy cottage with instant annihilation. Prevailed upon by his wife's entreaties Will consented to remain under the shelter until the violence of the tempest had passed off. This, however, he did unwillingly, for he had been drinking hard that day, and was more than usually morose in consequence. Mary endeavoured by her own good nature to dispel the gloom that hung about him, but all was in vain; he occasionally paused at the window to watch the forked lightening as it darted athwart the heavens.

At this juncture a loud knocking was heard at the door; Mary flew to open it, and Wasp, the overseer, entered craving a shelter from the raging storm. Will heard the voice, and terrible emotions immediately took possession of his heart.

31

He remembered the interviews he had lately had with the man who stood before him; vengeance filled his soul, and, excited as he was with liquor, he resolved upon instant reparation. A knife happened to lie upon the table before him; with eager haste he grasped the fatal instrument of death, and he prepared to rush upon the object he hated. Mary, however, had observed the terrible working of her husband's mind, and uttering a loud scream, she threw herself between him and his defenceless victim. The children, too, awakened from their slumbers, jumped from their bed and threw themselves at their father's feet. Fortunately this saved the life of the intended victim, but they were too late to prevent all the evil consequences; the weapon entered the arm of the overseer, and he fell to the ground bleeding, though not mortally wounded.

The sequel is soon told; Will Harper was immediately afterwards arrested and lodged in the county jail, to answer for the crime of which he had been guilty. But, a prey to grief and despair, he soon sank under his accumulated sufferings and died a few days before the assizes at which he was to have been arraigned. Mary was at first inconsolable, but at length the recollection of her children's wants roused her to exertion. Pitied by her neighbours, she became the object of their especial regard, and through their means she was enabled to rear her children in a path of honest industry, which rendered them respected even in spite of the remembrance of their father's faults.

The Widow and the Fatherless (1838)

"Can it be in merry England," – SCOTT
"Ah! little think the gay, licentious proud." – POPE

"I can do nothing for you, my good woman," said the magistrate, in reply to the timid appeal of a poor woman for parochial relief for herself and helpless family. "The law, as it now stands, has deprived us of all power of affording such assistance. As, however, I believe your statement to be true, I will strongly recommend your case to the consideration of the board of guardians, who will, I have no doubt, take immediate measures for your relief."

"Twill be too late, I fear," said the poor woman, turning aside to conceal her emotion from the magistrate. "My children and myself have passed two entire days without food; and nothing but their famishing state would have induced me to have implored your worship's interference."

The magistrate's eyes glistened at the unhappy woman's extreme emotion, and turning to the clerk, he bade him hand her a small sum from the poor-box, to which he added a trifle from his own pocket, for her immediate necessities; then giving her a letter to take to the overseer, he quitted the bench, loaded with the blessings of the poor creature he had thus humanely assisted.

The expense of bringing up this small family, added to some pecuniary losses, was heavily felt by the poor couple, who strove with unwearied industry to maintain them in a plain and decent way. This, however, shortly after the birth of their fifth child, they found themselves utterly unable to accomplish, the father having met with an accident which deprived him of the use of his limbs, and which, after a tedious illness, put a period to his existence.

The poor widow, if possible, doubly exerted herself to support herself and children, her neighbours kindly assisting her to the utmost of their humble means; her eldest daughter, too, relieved her of much of the drudgery of the younger children, and became a valuable helpmate to her in her little business. The latter, however, gradually fell off; and, to increase the misfortunes of the family, the eldest daughter was attacked with a violent fever, which confined her to her bed.

Hastily did she quit the office, and, as fast as her weakness would permit, returned to her desolate home. The small sum she had received she sparingly expended on her way, cheered with the hope that the benevolent magistrate's letter would have the effect of procuring her a small weekly sum to enable her to support her family, with the aid of her own exertions.

Her husband and herself had resided in the same house in the parish in which she lived for about sixteen years, carrying on the business of a green-grocer, and had been the parents of five children, the eldest of whom, a female, at the period our tale commences, had just entered her fourteenth year.

The poor widow struggled hard against those accumulated misfortunes. The little necessaries requisite for her daughter's situation speedily exhausted their humble means, and though the strictest economy was observed, want, absolute want, began to stare them in the face. To add to their difficulties, the shop (on which they had hitherto depended for support) could not be properly stocked, their exhausted means preventing them supplying it in the usual way. Customers rapidly fell off – new and well-filled shops in the same line opened – tax-gatherers and creditors for petty sums became clamorous – the landlord distrained – and the unhappy woman was driven from her once happy home, with but a handful of goods, and her pockets filled with duplicates of articles which had been pledged for their support. She took refuge at the house of a friend, as he styled himself, by whom she had been strongly urged to occupy, till better times, two unoccupied apartments in his house. Here she remained for a period, seeking for some employment; but, in consequence of the embarrassed state of her affairs, she was unable publicly to apply for any situation. At length a person (who in the lifetime of her husband had been his assistant) offered her the care of his house in the country, assuring her the situation would be permanent, and that he would liberally remunerate her for her services, and also give employment to some of her children. Gladly did she avail herself of his offer, and made immediate preparations for the journey, and the expense of conveying herself and family, by disposing of several articles of furniture – leaving the rest in the care of her friend. She reached her situation in safety, and took a cheap lodging in its neighbourhood for her little family, trusting in a few days to see her two elder children in some trifling employment. Again was she doomed to disappointment – her employer, on one pretence and another, delaying the engagement of her children; and in a few weeks after, stating his intention to get married, declared he should no longer require her services. In vain did she remind him of the promise he had made to her previous to her quitting town, and the expense she had been put to. He coldly expressed his regret, declaring he had but recently determined upon marriage; then handing her a small balance due to her, he retired.

Thus once more without resource, the poor widow began actively to arrange for her return to London, humbly trusting that Providence would raise up some friend to procure for her a situation by which she might be enabled to earn the common necessaries of life.

They arrived in town in safety, and after paying the expenses of their journey, the widow hastened to procure for herself and family a cheap apartment, which, after some difficulty, she succeeded in obtaining. She then sent to the house of her friend for the return of the few articles she had left in his charge; but received for answer, "that he should detain them until she had paid him the rent of the apartments she had occupied in his house." This unexpected answer extremely shocked the poor creature, who, however, for the sake of her family, rallied her broken spirits, and arranged the few things they had as decently as possible. Then leaving her children in charge of her eldest daughter, she quitted the place to seek for employment. This, however, was easier sought than obtained. Day after day did she traverse the streets, and return disconsolate to her almost famished family, whose only food consisted of a few potatoes, and to procure even these their very clothing had been disposed of.

At length every disposable article had been parted with, and they had been without food an entire day. The unhappy parent could no longer endure the agony of witnessing the famishing looks of her children; but hastily covering her neck with an old silk handkerchief, she rushed from the place and proceeded to the house of the overseer. Overcoming the reluctant feeling which ever attends honest poverty, she timidly knocked at the door, which was opened by a female servant, of whom she inquired if the overseer was at home, and was answered in the affirmative.

On learning her business the servant said, it would be of no service to speak to him, as it was not board-day. On beholding the widow's agony at this intelligence, she said she would deliver the message, but she feared that it would be useless. Bidding the widow wait a few moments, she went to the parlour, the door of which she opened, and the widow heard her relate her statement, when she was interrupted with:

"How often have I told you, Betty, I would not be annoyed in my own house by these creatures. Tell her to go to the union workhouse, and on board-day, mind, which is next Thursday, and if her story is true, she will then be relieved."

Betty: "She seems in great distress, sir."

Overseer: "Ah! they all seem so. But it won't do. If I were to give her a trifle, it would all be spent at the next gin-shop."

Betty: "Oh, sir, she appears to be quite a different sort of person. The poor of that sort you may easily tell – they are always dirty sluts – this poor woman is clean and tidy."

Overseer: "Ah! one of those that accompany some hulking fellow through the streets, with seven or eight tidily dressed children, with clean pinafores, and all that sort of thing. It won't do. There, go, Betty, and tell her to come next board-day, if she really wants relief."

In vain did Betty try to induce him to change his determination. Growing angry, he peremptorily ordered her to quit the room – an order she reluctantly complied with.

Returning to the widow, she stated how ineffectual had been her endeavours to induce the overseer to see her, but suggested to her to apply at the union workhouse immediately, as they were bound to give relief in urgent cases.

The widow thanked her, and sighing deeply, quitted the door, and proceeded to the union workhouse. Ringing the bell, a porter appeared, who demanded her business. She related her case, but the only answer she received was, "Board-day's next Thursday."

Unable to get a further answer, as the fellow immediately closed the door, she returned despairingly to her miserable home. Her younger children were crying for something to eat around their eldest sister when she entered. Seating herself on a small box (for chairs they had none) the unhappy woman gave way to her feelings in a paroxysm of tears. Then bidding them to be quiet for a few minutes and she would speedily return with food, she once more quitted her room.

They had now been nearly two days without food of any kind. Maddened to desperation, the poor widow, on leaving her children, had determined upon soliciting charity from the first person she should meet. She passed several, however, before she could muster courage to address them: and had wandered perceptibly near to the union workhouse. At length she gently laid her finger on the sleeve of a passer-by, and endeavoured but ineffectually, to implore his pity. Big scalding tears coursed each other down her pallid cheeks – her mouth became parched – her tongue, glued to its roof, refused its office, and for a moment or two she stood ineffectually endeavouring to speak. The agitation of her mind at last so entirely overcame her, that she fell to the ground insensible, from which, however, the stranger speedily raised her. On her recovery she briefly stated the fact of her children being literally perishing for want of food,

35

and that despair on their account, had led her to the humiliating step of imploring pity of the passers-by. The gentleman immediately handed her a shilling, and quitted the spot, bidding her not to despair, for if what she had related was true, no doubt but that she would receive speedy and effectual relief.

With a fervent blessing on the head of the generous stranger she turned to retrace her steps, when at that instant a policemen, who had witnessed the transaction, approached and took her into custody on the charge of begging in the public streets. In vain did she state the real circumstances of the case – the starving situation of her children, &c. To all her remonstrances he turned a deaf ear, telling her she must state it all to the magistrate before whom she must appear.

Luckily for the poor half-distracted creature, the magistrates were then sitting, and the case being stated, was at once dismissed, to the satisfaction of all present. On turning to quit the office, a person who was near her, advised her to request the magistrate to grant her an order for the relief of herself and children, and the conversation already detailed at the commencement of our tale took place.

Of the few necessaries she had been enabled to procure through the benevolence of the stranger and the magistrate, the poor family sparingly partook, with the consolation that at least provision for another day was in the house, and a hope that the following day would be productive of further good. Animated with this conviction she cheerfully proceeded to the union workhouse (it being board-day). On ringing the bell, and giving her name, residence, &c., she was directed to wait with others in a large stone-paved room, until she should be called.

Here she waited patiently for about two hours, eye-witness to scenes she had been unused to. At length her name was called, and she was ushered into a large boarded room, in which the "guardians" were accustomed to meet. To the several interrogatories she replied modestly and firmly, detailing minutely the benevolence she had experienced from the magistrate and the stranger with a warmth of gratitude which appeared satisfactory to her hearers.

She was asked whether her late husband was a native of London, to which she replied, "No; but of Beverley, in Yorkshire." This announcement occasioned a little surprise to one of the guardians, and several questions were put to her, all of which she answered satisfactorily. She was then directed to withdraw.

On her re-admission, the chairman informed that the board had carefully weighed her statement, and had, with two exceptions, unanimously agreed to send her children into Yorkshire, to the parish of their father – and that she herself would be provided for in the union workhouse.

This cruel determination (for such it appeared to her) for a few moments overpowered her. She begged most fervently to be allowed to accompany her children. This, however, could not be acceded to; and she was about departing, when she was recalled by a voice she thought she had heard before, and raising her eyes she beheld the magistrate who had relieved her on the preceding day.

"Your feelings, poor woman, shall be no further wounded. I have caused the most minute inquiries to be made into the truth of your statement, and so well satisfied am I with all that I have heard respecting you, that you shall have immediately a vacancy in my establishment under an excellent woman – my housekeeper – that is, if you will accept it."

36

"With humble gratitude and joy, sir," exclaimed the widow. "And my children –"

"Shall be my care," exclaimed another voice. It was the stranger who had presented her with the shilling. "I, too, have made inquiries, and fully satisfied with the result, no longer hesitate to join heartily with the magistrate in his benevolent intentions."

The sequel is soon told – the widow fulfilled the duties of her office so much to the magistrate's satisfaction, that he gave her the situation of housekeeper (which became shortly after vacant) and her eldest daughter her mother's situation. The stranger, too, amply redeemed his promise – by placing the other children at school, and sinking a sum of money to defray the expenses of the apprenticeship of her other children.

The Convict (1839)

Robert Wilson was a market-gardener. Early in life he married a deserving young woman, whom he loved with entire tenderness, and by whom he had several children. No man on earth could be fonder of his little off-spring than Wilson; and they, on the other hand, almost worshipped their father, taking great delight in nothing so much as in doing what he wished. Wilson was not very wise, nor was he at all learned; but his heart, which, as I have said, was full of tenderness, told him, with unerring instinct, that his children would be governed more perfectly, and with more wholesome effect, under the dominion of love, than under that of fear; and *his* was indeed a happy family where affection, pleasure, obedience, and faith, (faith in each other,) went hand in hand. Wilson was well situated for passing his life comfortably and rationally – his garden being just far enough out of London to render inconvenient his mixing in the squalid profligacies of town (had he been so inclined); and yet he was not so entirely in the country as to harden him into the robust callousness and ignorant vices of village life. He could just hear enough of the "stir of the great Babel," to interest him in it, and to keep his faculties alive and awake to the value of his own quiet, and to the unaffected caresses of his dear wife and children, which always appeared more and more precious after he had been hearing, in his weekly visits to town, some instance of mercenary hypocrisy and false heartedness.

I lodged two years in his house, and have often seen him, on a summer's evening, sitting in an open part of his garden, surrounded by his family in unconscious enjoyment of the still and rich sunset. I was his guest the last time I saw him, poor fellow, in this placid happiness. We drank tea in the open air, and amused ourselves afterwards I recollect, with reading the preceding day's newspaper, which Wilson used to hire for the evening. We sat out of doors later than usual, owing to the deliciousness of the night, which, instead of deepening into darkness, kept up a mellow golden radiance, sweeter than the searching daylight: for before the colours of the sun had entirely faded in the west, the moon came up over the eastern horizon – and the effect was divine. My poor host, however, did not seem so happy as usual. He had been thoughtful the whole evening, and now became more pensive: and nothing roused him even into momentary cheer, except the playfulness of his eldest daughter – a merry little girl of four or five years of age. It was sad to see him, with his dejected face, striving to laugh and romp with the child, who, in a short time, began to perceive the alteration in her father's manner, and to reflect in her smooth face the uneasiness of his. But their pastime was of short continuance. It was melancholy pretence. There was nothing hearty in it, except the dance of the child's forehead locks, tossed to and fro in the clear moonshine.

I soon found out the cause of this depression. He was beginning to be pinched under an ugly coalition – an increasing family, decreasing business, and times taxed to the uttermost. The gentlefolks living about the great squares did not spend so much money as formerly in decking their windows and balconies with early flowers and rare exotics; and this was an important source of Wilson's revenue. He bore up, however, with sad patience, for a long time; till hunger thinned and stretched the round faces of his children, and his wife's endearments, instead of coming with hope and encouragement, seemed like tokens of love growing more spiritual and devoted under despair; they were embraces hallowed and made sublime by famine. All this was more than the poor man could bear. The failing voices of his unconscious children were like madness bringing sounds in his ears: and one night, losing in the tumult of his thoughts all distinction between right and wrong, he rushed forth and committed a robbery.

I shall never forget, as long as I live, the hour when he was apprehended by the officers of justice.

A knock was heard at the outer gate, and on Mrs. Wilson's going to open it, two men rushed by her into the house, and seized her pale and trembling husband; who although he expected and dreaded such an event, was so staggered by it, as to lose for a few moments his consciousness of all about him. The first thing he saw, on coming to himself, was his wife stretched at his feet in a fearful swoon, and as he was hurried off, he turned his eyes towards her with a heart-broken expression, calling out, in a tone half-raving and half-imploring, – "Look there, look there!"

It would be in vain to attempt a description of the wretched hours passed between him and his wife in the interval which elapsed between this period and the time of his trial. The madness of his utter despair, perhaps, was less intolerable than the sickening agitation produced in her mind by the air-built hopes she dared to entertain in weary succession, and were only born to be soon stricken back into nothing. This was indeed a ghastly and withering conflict. The poor woman, after enduring it for three weeks, could not be easily recognized by her old acquaintances. There was no trace of the happy, bustling wife. She moved silently among her children; her face was emaciated and hectic; and her eyes were red with the constant swell of tears. It was a mighty change.

The day of trial at length came on. Wilson was found guilty, and sentence of death was passed on him. The laws, in their justice, condemned him to be hanged, and the laws, in their justice, had enforced the taxation, the hard pressure of which so mainly assisted to drive him into the crime. But the world is inexplicable.

His wife did not survive his news many hours. She died in the night without a struggle. It was no use to let the condemned man know this. I knew he would never ask to see her again: for their meeting in the prison had already been torturing beyond endurance.

I visited him in his cell two days before the time appointed for his execution. He was silent for many minutes after I entered, and I did not attempt to rouse him. At length, with a voice quivering under an effort to be composed, he said, "Although, Mr. Saville, I do not request (I was going to say I did not *wish*, but God knows how false that would be) to behold my wife again in this bitter, bitter world, because such a dreary meeting would drive her mad; yet I think it would do me good if I could see my child, my eldest girl, my little Betsy. I know not why it is, but I have an idea that her soft prattle, ignorant as she is of my fate, would take something away from the dismal suffering I am to undergo on Wednesday. Therefore bring her – will you? – this afternoon; and frame some postponing excuse for my poor wife. These, dear sir, are melancholy troubles; but I know you are very good."

39

In the afternoon, accordingly, I took the child, who asked me several times on the road why her father did not come home. As we walked along the gloomy passages to his cell, she clung close to me, and did not say a word. It was very different, poor thing, to the open and gay garden about which she used to run.

The door of her father's miserable dungeon was soon opened, and the child rushed into his arms. "I do not like you to live in this dark place, father," she cried; "come home with me and Mr. Saville, and see mother who is in bed."

"I cannot come just now, my child," he answered; "you must stay a little with me, and throw your arms round my neck, and lean your face on mine."

The child did as she was bidden, and the poor man, straining her to him, sobbed bitterly and convulsively. After a few minutes, he looked with yearning eyes in her face, saying, "Come, my dear, sing your poor father that pretty song which you know you used to sing to him when he was tired on an evening. I am not well now. Look at me, my child, and sing."

How sad it was to hear the child's voice warbled in that dolorous place! I could scarcely bear it; but it seemed to have a contrary effect on the father. His eyes were lighted up, and a smile appeared upon his countenance. The song was of love, and woody retirement, and domestic repose, and the baffled frowns of fortune. While the child was singing, I left the cell to make some arrangements with the gaoler, who was walking close to the door. I had not, however, been thus engaged five minutes, before we heard something fall heavily, accompanied by a violent scream, and rushing into the cell, I saw the unhappy convict lying on the floor, and his little girl clinging around his neck. The gaoler and I lifted him up, and, alarmed at the hue of his face, called in the medical attendant of the prison, who soon told us the poor man was dead.

The account given by the child was, that, after she had done singing, her father started, then looked sharply in her face, and, with a strange and short laugh, fell from his chair. I suppose she had sung him into a temporary forgetfulness of his situation; that she had conjured into his mind, with her innocent voice, a blessed dream of past days and enjoyments, and that, the spell ceasing when her melody ceased, the truth of things had beat upon his heart with too stunning a contrast, and it had burst.

A Simple Story (1840)

How little of the patient endurance of misery, the real benevolence of heart, and generosity of action, of the toil-worn portion of the community, is known by the more favoured children of fortune, or the votaries of pleasure.

Nor shall we be surprised at this ignorance or this inattention of the virtues of the poor, when we consider that the literary works of the day, are mostly produced and conducted by individuals classically educated, and are written expressly for that class who alone are able to purchase them.

Without any disrespectful feelings towards the talented writers of the present day, it is our humble opinion that the well-known fable of the statue of which man was the carver, representing man as standing triumphant over the prostrate lion, with its natural and appropriate moral, will not be inapplicable to partly account for this. Another and probably a more satisfactory reason, will be found in the recollection that, while through the medium of assize courts, and magisterial examinations, publicity is necessarily and properly given to the crimes of the depraved, the vices of the idlers and the follies of the ignorant, it is to be lamented, that there exists in the minds of the superficial observer, a strong propensity to associate the ideas of crime, folly and ignorance, with those of labour, manufactories, mills, and working population, and scarcely ever do many think of the one without the other rushing into the mind.

Nor is this the only disadvantage the sons of industry lie under; while the crimes they abhor are indiscriminately attributed to them, the virtues they possess are unobtrusive, and practised in circles that men of letters but seldom enter, and if at all visited, for a period far too short for an acquaintance with the actions or discovery of the traits that dignify the character of man however humble, and prove that real generosity is not confined to rank or station, creed or caste.

While we read occasionally of the vanities and follies of the wealthy, we have also their benevolent actions proclaimed with trumpets and tongues. Their annual subscriptions to the hospitals and dispensaries, and their donations for the erection of churches are advertised in the newspapers, and their remembrance perpetuated, by the amount of the gift being blazoned in letters of gold most conspicuously in the interior of the building subscribed for.

These observations are not by any means intended to disparage the liberality of the rich, but merely to show, that although the kind and noble acts of the operative most unfrequently obtain similar publicity, it does not therefore follow that there exists but few if any virtues among the millions termed the "lower classes."

But whenever sketches are given of the poor in any literary periodical, it is generally the composition of some clever, irresistible humorist, seeking to raise, it may be, a good natured smile, or even a broad grin at provincialisms, the peculiar habits and usage of trade, the eccentricities of individuals remarkable in some other mode than their poverty; but how rarely do we hear of the benevolence, the active sympathy, or charities for the poor.

O! let not those who enjoy in rich profusion the comforts and luxuries of life, smile disdainfully at the idea of the charities of the poor, but remember, that the widow in giving but her mite, gave more than the rich out of all their abundance.

To eradicate the erroneous notions formed by those who have no other opportunities of contemplating the characters of artizans than such are afforded by the publicity given to the voices of a fraction of their number, and from a correct and more extensive knowledge of their intellectual attainments, their moral capabilities, and kind feelings, to enable those high in fortune's scale to form a true and proper estimate of humble but real worth, it is necessary that some of the artizans' own class should devote a portion of time and talent in detailing a few of the occurrences daily taking place in every large manufacturing district throughout the country. Occurrences that may with propriety be published and contrasted with the darker pictures that have hitherto been laid before the public, and which may bear comparison with the brightest actions of any class or age, without fear of suffering in consequence.

These remarks are suggested by the reminiscences of one who has been for thirty years, from the time he was eight years of age, engaged in manufactories, and from these reminiscences the following may be published:–

During one of those seasons of general distress and anguish usually known by the name of panics, and which (many thanks to our sapient legislators) have been of such frequent recurrence in the course of my short life as to bring with astonishing rapidity many wealthy and enterprising merchants, many skilful and assiduous manufacturers to a state of bankruptcy and many more to its very verge, and has brought (with few exceptions) millions of the working population to know by bitter experience what it is to exist months together deeply suffering from scantiness of food, fire and clothing and much more from continual dread lest their means of procuring that small quantity should presently fail, and that their families with themselves should perish for want; instances of persons having so perished being alas! but too common of late years in this highly favoured and Christian land.

During one of those periods of wretchedness and woe, between two and three o'clock, on a certain Saturday afternoon, a youth – an apprentice – about eighteen years of age, was standing at the "muffle" door outside the shop in which he was engaged, waiting for the heating of a pan of work in the process of being annealed. "I wish it was seven o'clock, Joe," said he to a lad, not yet fourteen, who was by his side, and with whom he had toiled, when their branch of the trade was brisk, for sixteen and sometimes eighteen hours per day without a murmur at their laborious employment, – that being the hour at which they discontinued work and received their wages; "I wish it was seven o'clock, Joe, for I am quite tired of this week."

"Ah! my eye, John, so do I wish it was."

"Why what is the matter, Joe? you look as if you'd been crying."

"There is nothing the matter with me," was the answer, in a tone in which sorrow and pride were evidently struggling for the mastery.

"But there is something the matter with you, for your eyes are quite red; has your mother been thrashing you?"

"No."

"Your father has then?"

"No – he has not."

"There is something the matter with you, I am sure," again said John, looking his companion earnestly in the face, "for your eyes are full of tears now," which as he spoke gushed down the poor lad's cheek. "Tell me," added John, "if there is anything that I can do for you and I will do it; but don't cry."

"I am very hungry," said Joe; his voice growing tremulous, and strongly indicative of his emotion.

"Hungry! why, have you had no dinner?"

"No, and I did not have any yesterday, and I had but half a round off a quartern loaf for my breakfast this morning."

"Why, how ever is that? I knew your father was short of work, but I did not think that it was that bad with you."

"Oh, father has not had above a day and a half – or two days work a week for above twelvemonth, and very often not at all; but it was not so bad with us till this last fortnight, as my brother Bill has been very bad, and not able to work, or else he got eight shillings a week; now, there's nothing coming in but what I get, and Mary's shilling."

"And how many brothers and sisters have you got?"

"Seven; but Mary goes out to nurse a child and gets a shilling a week, and her victuals, – she's rarely off," said Joe, drawing the sleeve of his shirt across his eyes as he spoke, his heart evidently lightened by talking of their misery.

"And have none of them had any more victuals than you to-day?"

"No, for mother gave me the biggest piece because I go to work; and I don't think that my father or mother had any today, for mother was crying when I came out."

"Stop a minute," said John, his apron streaming in the wind as he turned round the corner of the muffle into the shop; from which he soon returned, bringing in his hand a handkerchief, out of which he was taking a piece of bread and some cheese. "Here, Joe; here is my four o'clock; why did you not tell me you had no dinner before? I would have given you a part of mine cheerfully."

"Thank you, John; but I did not like for any body to know how bad we were off; don't say anything about it."

"Very well; make haste and eat it," said John, as he carried his pan of work into the shop, leaving the poor lad with the bread and cheese in his hand, and the tears in his eyes.

In about five minutes after this, the voice of one of the men was heard shouting, 'Joe! Joe!' to which no answer was returned.

"I wonder what that lad is up to, as he don't speak?"

"Perhaps he's putting some coal upon the fire; he'll be here in a minute or two, I dare say,' replied John, thinking the lad was so intent upon his bit of victual, as not to have heard the call.

"He's not putting coal on the fire, or we should hear him; Joe! Joe!" with stentorian lungs, again shouted the workman, "I want him to place up my work, and put it in the pan to anneal, or shall not be able to finish it tonight; Joe!" again cried he, as he walked into the yard in search of him.

"He's off, that's certain, and this fire wants attending to; but I'll warm his ear for him, when he does come back."

Panning his work himself, which he had just finished, and placed in the muffle, the workman saw poor Joe coming down the entry, panting for breath, as though he had been running fast.

"I'll make you remember running off, kicking up your heels, when you are wanted, young fellow," said the man, bestowing on Joe, as he entered the shop, a box on the ear, that made him reel several paces; no complaint was made although the blow was a severe one.

In half an hour John was again at the muffle door, by the side of poor Joe.

"Did M – hurt you much, when he hit you?"

"He made my head ring a bit, but I did not mind that."

"You should not run to play, particularly of a Saturday afternoon."

"I did not go to play."

"Where did you go then?"

"I ran across to give my brothers and sisters some of the bread and cheese you gave me for they wanted it as bad as I did."

While the request to spare the feelings of honest though mistaken pride, by keeping silent upon the subject of the distress of the family had been complied with, it was not to be endured; that punishment should have been inflicted upon and silently borne by the unhappy lad, who, notwithstanding the extremity of his own hunger, impelled by his fraternal love, had tried to share his morsel, with equally suffering brothers and sisters; much less, could it be either just or right, that a groundless suspicion of his being idle or negligent should be allowed to exist, through that very act which displayed a spirit and feeling so noble and so generous.

An opportunity was therefore soon taken to communicate to the giver of poor Joe's unmerited punishment, the real cause of his absence.

"God bless the lad!" emphatically exclaimed M –, "where is he? I am sorry I hit him," and, in a few minutes, one handkerchief contained the whole of the provisions, brought by both men and boys for their refreshment at four o'clock, with which Joe was quickly despatched to his miserable home.

> "The poorest poor,
> Long for some moments in a weary life,
> When they can know, and feel that they have been
> Themselves the fathers and the dealers out
> Of some small blessings, have been kind to such
> As needed kindness."

"I have known," continued M –, "what it is to be out of work myself, and I can feel for his poor father and mother; many times must their hearts have ached, before it came to letting those poor children be with-out a morsel at dinner time: many a bitter sigh have they heaved as one thing after another has been disposed of out of the house, I've no doubt."

This was the strain of the conversation till seven o'clock, when after the men and boys received their wages, a trifling amount was voluntarily, aye, cheerfully contributed by each individual, and carried to the wretched family, when it was ascertained that M – was quite right in his conjecture – there had been sighing bosoms and aching hearts indeed, for one article of wearing apparel after another had been disposed of till none were left, except those upon their persons; and then, one piece of furniture after another had been pledged or sold, till the very last thing a virtuous woman parts with – that emblem of her plighted love, the indication of her virtue, and a memento of peculiar and interesting sensations – the wedding ring from her finger, all had been given up for the loan of a paltry sum to purchase food; and yet, amidst all this protracted mental and physical suffering, not one of the family had ever ever been suspected of a dishonest act.

Should any of the readers of the CIRCULAR desire to know where poor Joe now is, or what has become of him, we regret to add that he died about three years after the incident occurred, which is related above, from a want of sufficient nourishment, the condition of too many of the working classes. It was said by the neighbours that he died in a decline.

Seth Thompson, the Stockinger

or,

"When Things are at the Worst They Begin to Mend" (1845)

Thomas Cooper

Leicestershire stockingers call that a false proverb. "People have said so all our lives," say they; "but, although we have each and all agreed, every day, that things were at the worst, they never begun to mend yet!" This was not their language sixty years ago, but it is their daily language *now*; and the story that follows is but, as it were, of yesterday.

Seth Thompson was the only child of a widow, by the time that he was six years old, and became a "winding boy," in a shop of half-starved framework-knitters at Hinckley, – a kindred lot with hundreds of children of the same age, in Leicestershire. Seth's mother was a tender mother to her child; but he met tenderness in no other quarter. He was weakly, and since that rendered him unable to get on with his winding of the yarn as fast as stronger children, he was abused and beaten by the journeymen, while the master stockinger, for every slight flaw in his work, – though it always resulted from a failure of strength rather than carelessness, – unfeelingly took the opportunity to "dock" his paltry wages.

Since her child could seldom add more than a shilling or fifteen-pence to the three, or, at most, four shillings, she was able to earn herself, – and she had to pay a heavy weekly rent for their humble home, – it will readily be understood that neither widow Thompson nor Seth were acquainted with the meaning of the word "luxury," either in food or habits. A scanty allowance of oatmeal and water formed their breakfast, potatoes and salt their dinner, and a limited portion of bread, with a wretchedly diluted something called "tea" as an accompaniment, constituted their late afternoon, or evening meal; and they knew no variety for years, winter or summer. The widow's child went shoeless in the warm season, and the cast-off substitutes he wore in winter, together with lack of warmth in his poor mother's home, and repulses from the shop fire by the master and men while at work, subjected him, through nearly the whole of every winter, to chilblains and other diseases of the feet. Rags were his familiar acquaintances, and, boy-like, he felt none of the aching shame and sorrow experienced by his mother when she beheld his destitute covering, and reflected that her regrets would not enable her to amend his tattered condition.

Seth's mother died when he reached fifteen, and expressed thankfulness, on her death-bed, that she was about to quit a world of misery, after being permitted to live till her child was in some measure able to struggle for himself. In spite of hard usage and starvation, Seth grew up a strong lad, compared with puny youngsters that form the majority of the junior population in manufacturing districts. He was quick-witted, too, and had gathered a knowledge of letters and syllables, amidst the references to cheap newspapers and hourly conversation on politics by starving and naturally discontented stockingers. From a winding-boy, Seth was advanced to the frame, and, by the time he had reached seventeen, was not only able to earn as much as any other stockinger in Hinckley, when he could get work, but, with the usually improvident haste of the miserable and degraded, married a poor "seamer," who was two years younger than himself.

Seth Thompson at twenty-one, with a wife who was but nineteen, had become the parent of four children; and since he had never been able to bring home to his family more than seven shillings in one week, when the usual villainous deductions were made by master and manufacturer, in the shape of "frame-rent" and other "charges," – since he had often had but *half*-work, with the usual deduction of *whole* charges, and had been utterly without work for six several periods, of from five to nine weeks each, during the four years of his married life, – the following hasty sketch of the picture which this "home of an Englishman" presented one noon, when a stranger knocked at the door, and it was opened by Seth himself, will scarcely be thought overdrawn:–

Except a grey deal table, there was not a single article within the walls which could be called "furniture," by the least propriety of language. This stood at the farther side of the room, and held a few soiled books and papers, Seth's torn and embrowned hat, and the mother's tattered straw bonnet. The mother sat on a three-legged stool, beside an osier cradle, and was suckling her youngest child while she was eating potatoes and salt from an earthen dish upon her knee. Seth's dish of the same food stood on a seat formed of a board nailed roughly across the frame of a broken chair; while, in the centre of the floor, where the broken bricks had disappeared and left the earth bare, the three elder babes sat squatted round a board whereon boiled potatoes in their skins were piled, – a meal they were devouring greedily, squeezing the inside of the root into their mouths with their tiny hands, after the mode said to be practised in an Irish cabin. An empty iron pot stood near the low expiring fire, and three rude logs of wood lay near it, – the children's usual seats when they had partaken their meal. A description of the children's filthy and bedaubed appearance with the potato starch, and of the "looped and windowed" rags that formed their covering, could only produce pain to the reader. Seth's clothing was not much superior to that of his offspring; but the clean cap and coloured cotton handkerchief of the mother, with her own really beautiful but delicate face and form, gave some relief to the melancholy picture.

Seth blushed, as he took up his dish of potatoes, and offered the stranger his fragment of a seat. And the stranger blushed, too, but refused the seat with a look of so much benevolence that Seth's heart glowed to behold it; and his wife set down her porringer, and hushed the children that the stranger might deliver his errand with the greater ease.

"Your name is Thompson, I understand," said the stranger; "pray, do you know what was your mother's maiden name?"

"Greenwood, – Martha Greenwood was my poor mother's maiden name, sir," replied Seth, with the tears starting to his eyes.

The stranger seemed to have some difficulty in restraining similar feelings; and gazed, sadly, round upon the room and its squalid appearance, for a few moments, in silence.

Seth looked hard at his visitor, and thought of one whom his mother had often talked of; but did not like to put an abrupt question, though he imagined the stranger's features strongly resembled his parent's.

47

"Are working people in Leicestershire usually so uncomfortably situated as you appear to be?" asked the stranger, in a tone of deep commiseration which he appeared to be unable to control.

Seth Thompson and his wife looked uneasily at each other, and then fixed their gaze on the floor.

"Why, sir," replied Seth, blushing more deeply than before, "we married very betime, and our family, you see, has grown very fast; we hope things will mend a little with us when some o' the children are old enough to earn a little. We've only been badly off as yet, but you'd find a many not much better off, sir, I assure you, in Hinckley and elsewhere."

The stranger paused again, and the working of his features manifested strong inward feeling.

"I see nothing but potatoes," he resumed; "I hope your meal is unusually poor to-day, and that you and your family generally have a little meat at dinner."

"Meat, sir!" exclaimed Seth; "we have not known what it is to set a bit of meat before our children more than three times since the first was born; we usually had a little for our Sunday dinner when we were first married, but we can't afford it now!"

"Good God!" cried the stranger, with a look that demonstrated his agony of grief and indignation, "is this England, – the happy England, that I have heard the blacks in the West Indies talk of as a Paradise?"

"Are you my mother's brother? Is your name Elijah Greenwood?" asked Seth Thompson, unable longer to restrain the question.

"Yes," replied the visitor, and sat down upon Seth's rude seat, to recover his self-possession.

That was a happy visit for poor Seth Thompson and his wife and children. His mother had often talked of her only brother who went for a sailor when a boy, and was reported to be settled in some respectable situation in the West Indies, but concerning whom she never received any certain information. Elijah Greenwood had suddenly become rich, by the death of a childless old planter, whom he had faithfully served, and who had left him his entire estate. England was Elijah's first thought, when this circumstance took place; and, as soon as he could settle his new possession under some careful and trusty superintendent till his return, he had taken ship, and come to his native country and shire. By inquiry at the inn, he had learnt the afflictive fact of his sister's death, but had been guided to the poverty-stricken habitation of her son.

That was the last night that Seth Thompson and his children slept on their hard straw sacks on the floor, – the last day that they wore rags and tatters, and dined upon potatoes and salt. Seth's uncle placed him in a comfortable cottage, bought him suitable furniture, gave him a purse of 50l. for ready money, and promised him a half-yearly remittance from Jamaica, for the remainder of his, the uncle's life, with a certainty of a considerable sum at his death.

Seth and his wife could not listen, for a moment, to a proposal for leaving England, although they had experienced little but misery in it, their whole lives. The uncle, however, obtained from them a promise that they would not restrain any of their children from going out to Jamaica; and did not leave them till he had seen them fairly and comfortably settled, and beheld what he thought a prospect of comfort for them, in the future. Indeed, on the very morning succeeding that in which Seth's new fortune became known, the hitherto despised stockinger was sent for by the principal manufacturer of hosen, in Hinckley, and offered "a shop of frames," in the language of the working men;

that is, he was invited to become a "master," or one who receives the "stuff" from the capitalist or manufacturer, and holds of him, likewise, a given number of frames, – varying from half-a-dozen to a score or thirty, or even more; and thus becomes a profit-sharing middleman between the manufacturer and the labouring framework-knitters. Seth accepted the offer, for it seemed most natural to him to continue in the line of manufacture to which he had been brought up; and his uncle, with pleasurable hopes for his prosperity, bade him farewell! –

"Well, my dear," said Seth to his wife, as they sat down to a plentiful dinner, surrounded with their neatly-dressed and happy children, the day after the uncle's departure, "we used to say we should never prove the truth of the old proverb, but we have proved it at last: times came to the worst with us, and began to mend."

"Thank God! we have proved it, my love," replied the wife; "and I wish our poor neighbours could prove it as well."

Seth sighed, – and was silent. –

Some years rolled over, and Seth Thompson had become a well-informed, and deep-thinking man, but one in whom was no longer to be found that passionate attachment to his native country which he once felt. The manufacturer under whom he exercised the office of "master," had borrowed the greater part of Seth's uncle's remittances, as regularly as they arrived; and as Seth received due interest for these loans, and confided that the manufacturer's wealth was real, he believed he was taking a prudent way of laying up enough for the maintenance of his old age, or for meeting the misfortunes of sickness, should they come. But the manufacturer broke; and away went all that Seth had placed in his hands. Every week failures became more frequent, – employ grew scantier, for trade was said to decrease, though machinery increased, – discontent glowered on every brow, – and the following sketch of what was said at a meeting of starving framework-knitters held in Seth Thompson's shop but a month before he quitted England for ever, may serve to show what were his own reflections, and those of the suffering beings around him.

About twenty working men had assembled, and stood in three or four groups, – no "chairman" having been, as yet, chosen, since a greater number of attendants was expected.

"I wish thou would throw that ugly thing away, Timothy!" said a pale, intellectual looking workman, to one whose appearance was rendered filthy, in addition to his ragged destitution, by a dirty pipe stuck in his teeth, and so short that the head scarcely projected beyond his nose.

"I know it's ugly, Robert," replied the other, in a tone between self-accusation and despair, – "but it helps to pass away time. I've thrown it away twice, – but I couldn't help taking to it again last week, when I had nought to do. I think I should have hanged myself if I had not smoked a bit o' 'bacco."

"Well, I'm resolute that I'll neither smoke nor drink any more," said a third; "the tyrants can do what they like with us, as long as we feed their vices by paying taxes. If all men would be o' my mind there would soon be an end of their extravagance, – for they would have nothing to support it."

"Indeed, James," replied the smoker, "I don't feel so sure about your plan as you seem to be, yourself: you'll never persuade all working-men to give up a sup of ale or a pipe, if they can get hold of either; but, not to talk of that, what's to hinder the great rascals from inventing other taxes if these fail?"

"They couldn't easily be hindered, unless we had all votes," said the first speaker, "we're all well aware of that; but it would put 'em about, and render the party more unpopular that wanted to put on a new tax."

"I don't think that's so certain, either," replied the smoker; "depend on't, neither Whigs nor Tories will run back from the support of taxes. D'ye ever read of either party agreeing to 'stop the supplies,' as they call it, or join in any measure to prevent taxes from being collected till grievances are redressed?"

"No, indeed, not we," chimed another, lighting his short pipe by the help of his neighbour's, and folding his arms, with a look of something like mock bravery; "and, for my part, I don't think they ever will be redressed till we redress 'em ourselves!"

"Ah, Joseph!" said the pale-looking man, shaking his head, "depend upon it that's all a dream! How are poor starvelings like us, who have neither the means of buying a musket, nor strength to march and use it, if he had it, – how are we to overthrow thousands of disciplined troops with all their endless resources of ammunition? – It's all a dream, Joseph! depend on't."

"Then what are we to do, – lie down and die?" asked the other; but looked as if he were aware he had spoken foolishly, under the impulse of despair.

"I'm sure I often wish to die," said another, joining the conversation in a doleful tone; "I've buried my two youngest, and the oldest lad's going fast after his poor mother; one can't get bread enough to keep body and soul together!"

"Well, if it hadn't been for Seth Thompson's kindness," said another, "I believe I should have been dead by this time. I never felt so near putting an end to my life as I did last Sunday morning. I've been out o' work, now, nine weeks; and last Saturday I never put a crumb in my mouth, for I couldn't get it, and I caught up a raw potato in the street last Sunday morning, and ate it for sheer hunger. Seth Thompson saw me, and – God bless his heart! – he called me in and gave me a cup of warm coffee and some toast, and slipped a shilling into my hand." And the man turned aside to dash away his tears.

"Ay, depend upon it, we shall miss Seth, when he leaves us," said several voices together.

"It's many a year since there was a master in Hinckley like him," said the man with the short black pipe, "and, I fear, when he is gone, the whole grinding crew will be more barefaced than ever with their extortions and oppressions of poor men. Seth knew what it was to be nipped himself when he was younger; that's the reason that he can feel for others that suffer."

"It isn't always the case, though," said another; "look at skin-flint Jimps, the glove-master; I remember him when he was as ragged as an ass's colt: and where is there such another grinding villain as Jimps, now he is so well off?"

"The more's the shame for a man that preaches and professes to be religious," said the smoker.

"It was but last Saturday forenoon," resumed the man who had mentioned Jimps, the glove-master, "that he docked us two-pence a dozen, again: and when I asked him if his conscience wouldn't reproach him when he went to chapel, he looked like a fiend, and said, 'Bob! I knew what it was to be ground once; but its my turn to grind now!'"

"And they call that religion, do they?" said the smoker, with an imprecation.

"It won't mend it to swear, my lad," said the intellectual-looking man; "we know one thing – that whatever such a fellow as this may do that professes religion, he doesn't imitate the conduct of his Master."

50

"I believe religion's all a bag of moonshine," said the smoker, "or else they that profess it would not act as they do."

"Don't talk so rashly, Tim," rejoined the other; "we always repent when we speak in ill-temper. Religion can't cure hypocrites, man, though it can turn drunkards and thieves into sober and honest men: it does not prove that religion is all a bag of moonshine, because some scoundrels make a handle of it. Truth's truth, in spite of all the scandal that falsehood and deceit brings upon it."

"Isn't it time we got to business?" said one of the group.

"I don't think it will be of any use to wait longer," said another; "there will not be more with us, if we wait another hour; the truth is, that men dare not attend a meeting like this, for fear of being turned off, and so being starved outright; – there's scarcely any spirit left in Hinckley."

"I propose that Seth Thompson takes the chair," said another, taking off his ragged hat, and speaking aloud.

A faint clapping of hands followed, and Seth took a seat upon a raised part of one of the frames at the end of the shop, and opened the meeting according to the simple but business-like form, which working men are wont to observe in similar meetings, in the manufacturing districts.

"I feel it would scarcely become me to say much, my friends," he said, "since I am about to leave you. I thought, at one time, that nothing could have ever inclined me to leave old England; but it seems like folly to me, now, to harbour an attachment to a country where one sees nothing but misery, nor any chance of improvement. I would not wish to damp your spirits; but if I were to tell you how much uneasiness I have endured for some years past, even while you have seen me apparently well off and comfortable, you would not wonder that I am resolved to quit this country, since I have the offer of ease and plenty, though in a foreign clime. I tell you, working men, that I had power over Mr. –, by the moneys I had lent him, or I should have been turned out of this shop years ago. Week by week have we quarrelled, because I would not practise the tyrannies and extortions upon working men that he recommended and urged. It is but a hateful employ to a man of any feeling, – is that of a master-stockinger under an avaricious and inhuman hosier. But, if the master's situation be so far from being a happy one, I need not tell you that I know well, by experience, how much more miserable is that of the starved and degraded working man. Indeed, indeed, – I see no hope for you, my friends, – yet, I repeat, I would not wish to damp your spirits. Perhaps things may mend yet; but I confess I see no likelihood of it, till the poor are represented as well as the rich."

It might produce weariness to go through all the topics that were touched upon by Seth and others. They were such as are familiarly handled, daily, in the manufacturing districts; ay, and with a degree of mental force and sound reasoning, – if not with polish of words, – that would make some gentlefolk stare, if they were to hear the sounds proceeding from the haggard figures in rags who often utter them. The "deceit" of the Reform Bill, as it is usually termed by manufacturing "operatives;" the trickery of the Whigs; the corruption and tyranny of the Tories; the heartlessness of the manufacturers and "the League;" and the right of every sane Englishman of one and twenty years of age to a vote in the election of those who have to govern him, were each and all broadly, and unshrinkingly, and yet not intemperately, asserted.

One or two, in an under-tone, ventured to suggest that it might be advantageous to try, once more, to act with the Anti-Corn Law men, since many of the members of the League professed democracy; and, if that were done, working men would not fear to attend a meeting such as that they were then holding. But this was scouted by the majority; and a proposal was, at length, made, in a written form, and seconded, – "That a branch of an association of working men, similar to one that was stated to have been just established at Leicester, should be formed." The motion was put and carried, – a committee, and secretary, and treasurer, were chosen, – and the men seemed to put off their dejection, and grow energetic in their resolution to attempt their own deliverance from misery, in the only way that they conceived it could ever be substantially effected: but their purpose came to the ears of the manufacturers on the following day, threats of loss of work were issued, and no association was established!

Seth Thompson took his family to the West Indies, pursuant to the many and urgent requests contained in his uncle's letters, and soon entered upon the enjoyment of the plenty in store for him. Hinckley stockingers remain in their misery still; and, perhaps, there is scarcely a place in England where starving working men have so little hope, – although "things," they say, "have come to the worst," – that "they" will ever "begin to mend."

"Merrie England" – No More! (1845)

Thomas Cooper

On an April morning in forty-two – scarcely four years bygone, – a group of five or six destitute-looking men were standing on a well-known space in Leicester, where the frustrum of a Roman milestone (surmounted, in true Gothic style, with a fantastic cross) was preserved with an iron palisade, and where the long narrow avenue of Barkby Lane, enters the wide trading street called Belgrave Gate. The paleness and dejection of the men's faces, as well as the ragged condition of their clothing, would have told how fearfully they were struggling with poverty and want, if their words had not been overheard.

"Never mind the lad, John," said the tallest and somewhat the hardest-featured man of the party; "he can't be worse off than he would have been at home, let him be where he will. What's the use of grieving about him? He was tired of pining at home, no doubt, and has gone to try if he can't mend his luck. You'll hear from him again, soon, from some quarter or other."

"But I can't satisfy myself about him, in that way, George," replied the man to whom this rough exhortation was addressed; "if the foolish lad be drawn into company that tempts him to steal, I may have to hear him sentenced to transportation, and that would be no joke, George."

"I see nothing so very serious, even in that," observed another of the group; "I would as lief be transported to-morrow as stay here to starve, as I've done for the last six months."

"It would seem serious to me, though," rejoined John, "to see my own child transported."

"Why, John, to men that scorn to steal, in spite of starvation," resumed George, "it's painful to see any child, or man either, transported: but where's the real disgrace of it? The man that pronounces the sentence is, in nine cases out of ten, a bigger villain than him that's called 'the criminal.' Disgrace is only a name – a mere name, you know, John."

"I'm aware there's a good deal o' truth in that," replied John; "the names of things would be altered a good deal, if the world was set right: but, as wrong as things are now, yet I hope my lad will never steal, and have to be sentenced to transportation. I've often had to hear him cry for bread, since he was born, and had none to give him; but I would sooner see him perish with hunger than live to hear him transported, for I think it would break my heart; – and God Almighty forbid I ever should have to hear it!"

"Goddle Mitey!" said George, pronouncing the syllables in a mocking manner, and setting up a bitter laugh, which was joined by every member of the group, except the mournful man who had just spoken; "who told thee there was one? Thy grandmother and the parsons? Don't talk such nonsense any more, John! it's time we all gave it over: they've managed to grind men to the dust with their priestcraft, and we shall never be righted till we throw it off!"

"No, no," chimed in another, immediately; "they may cant and prate about it: but, if their God existed, he would never permit us to suffer as we do!"

"Well, I'm come seriously to the same conclusion," said one who had not spoken before, and was the palest and thinnest of the group: "I think all their talk about a Providence that disposes the lot of men differently here, 'for His Own great mysterious purposes,' as they phrase it, is mere mysterious humbug, to keep us quiet. What purpose could a being have, who, they say, is as infinitely good as he is infinitely powerful, in placing me where I must undergo insult and starvation, while He places that man, – the oppressor and grinder, who is riding past now, in his gig, – in plenty and abundance?"

"Right, Benjamin," said George; "they can't get quit of their difficulty, quibble as they may: if they bedaub us with such nicknames as 'Atheistical Socialists,' we can defy them to make the riddle plainer by their own Jonathan Edwards, that they say good Robert Hall read over thirteen times, and pronounced 'irrefragable.'"

"Just so," resumed Benjamin, "whether man be called a 'Creature of Circumstance,' or a 'Creature of Necessity,' it amounts to the same thing. And, then, none of the Arminan sects can make out a case: they only prove the same thing as the Calvinist and the Socialist, when their blundering argument is sifted to the bottom."

"So that, if there be a Providence," continued George, "it has appointed, or permitted, – which they like, for it comes to the same, – that old — should fling the three dozen hose in your face last November, and that you should be out of work, and pine ever since; it appointed that I should get a few potatoes or a herring, by begging, or go without food altogether, some days since Christmas; and that each of us here, though we are willing to work, should have to starve; while it appointed that the mayor should live in a fine house, and swell his riches, by charging *whole* frame-rents, month after month, to scores of poor starving stockingers that had from him but half week's work."

"And, with all their talk about piety," rejoined Benjamin, "I think there is no piety at all in believing in the existence of such a Providence: and since, it appears, it can't be proved that Providence is of any other character if there be One at all, I think it less impious to believe in None."

John stood by while this conversation was going on; but he heard little of it, – for his heart was too heavy with concern for his child, – and, in a little time, he took his way, silently and slowly, towards other groups of unemployed and equally destitute men, who were standing on the wider space of ground, at the junction of several streets, – a locality known by the names of "the Coal-hill," and "the Haymarket," from the nature of the merchandise sold there, at different periods, in the open air.

"Have you found the lad yet?" said one of John's acquaintances, when he reached the outermost group.

"No, William," replied the downcast father; "and I begin to have some very troublesome fears about him, I'll assure you."

"But why should you, John?" expostulated the other; "he's only gone to try if he can't mend himself – Look you, John!" he said, pointing excitedly at what he suddenly saw; "there he goes, with the recruiting serjeant!"

The father ran towards the soldier and his child; and every group on the Coal-hill was speedily in motion when they saw and heard the father endeavouring to drag off the lad from the soldier, who seized the arm of his prize, and endeavoured to detain him. An increasing crowd soon hemmed in the party, – a great tumult arose, – and three policemen were speedily on the spot.

54

"Stick to your resolution, my boy!" cried the soldier, grasping the lad's arm with all his might; "you'll never want bread nor clothes in the army."

"But he'll be a sold slave, and must be shot at, like a dog!" cried the father, striving to rescue his child, a pale, tall stripling, who seemed to be but sixteen or seventeen years of age.

"Man-butcher! – Blood-hound!" shouted several voices in the crowd: whereat the policemen raised their staves, and called aloud to the crowd to "stand back!" "I demand, in the Queen's name, that you make this fellow loose his hold of my recruit!" said the soldier, in a loud, angry tone, to the policemen; two of whom seemed to be about obeying him, when a dark, stern-browed man among the crowd, of much more strong and sinewy appearance than the majority of the working multitude who composed it, stepped forward, and said,

"Let any policemen touch him that dare! If they do they shall repent it! There's no law to prevent a father from taking hold of his own child's arm to hinder him from playing the fool!"

The men in blue slunk back at these words; and the soldier himself seemed intimidated at perceiving the father's cause taken up by an individual of such determination.

"Tom," said the determined man to the lad, "have you taken the soldier's money?"

"Not yet," answered the lad, after a few moments' hesitation.

"Then he shall have my life before he has thee!" said the father, whose heart leaped at the answer, and infused so much strength into his arm, that with another pull he brought off his lad, entirely, from the soldier's hold. The crowd now burst into a shout of triumph; and when the soldier would have followed, to recapture his victim, the stern-browed man confronted him with a look of silent defiance; and the red-coat, after uttering a volley of oaths, walked off amidst the derision of the multitude.

"Don't you think you were a fool, Tom, to be juggled with that cut-throat?" said the stern-browed man to the lad, while the crowd gathered around him and his father.

"I wasn't so soon juggled," replied the lad; "he's been at me this three months; but I never yielded till this morning, when I felt almost pined to death, and he made me have some breakfast with him, – but he'll not get hold of me again!"

"That's right, my lad!" said one of the crowd; "the bloody rascals have not had two Leicester recruits these two years; and I hope they'll never have another."

"No, no, our eyes are getting opened," said another working man; "they may be able to kill us off by starvation, at home; but I hope young and old will have too much sense, in future, to give or sell their bodies to be shot at, for tyrants." "Ay, ay, we should soon set the lordlings fast, if all working men refused to go for soldiers," said another.

"So we should, Smith," said a sedate-looking elderly man; "that's more sensible than talking of fighting when we've no weapons, nor money to buy 'em, nor strength to use 'em."

"Then we shall wait a long while for the Charter, if we wait till we get it by leaving 'em no soldiers to keep us down," said a young, bold-looking man, with a fiery look; "for they'll always find plenty of Johnny Raws ready to list in the farming districts."

"And we shall wait a longer while still if we try to get it by fighting, under our present circumstances," answered the elderly man, in a firm tone; "that could only make things worse, as all such fool's tricks have ended, before."

"You're right, Randal, you're right!" cried several voices in the crowd; and the advocate of the bug-bear "physical force" said not another word on the subject.

"No, no, lads!" continued the "moral force" man, "let us go on, telling 'em our minds, without whispering, – and let us throw off their cursed priest craft, – and the system will come to an end, – and before long. But fighting tricks would be sure to fail; because they're the strongest, – and they know it."

"Yes, it must end, – and very soon," observed another working man; "the shopkeepers won't be long before they join us; for they begin to squeak, most woefully."

"The shopkeepers, lad!" said the dark-looking man, who had confronted the soldier; "never let us look for their help: there is not a spark of independence in any of 'em: they have had it in their power, by their votes, to have ended misrule, before now, if they had had the will."

"Poor devils! they're all fast at their bankers', and dare no more vote against their tyrants than they dare attempt to fly," said another.

"There is no dependence on any of the middle class," said the dark-looking man; "they are as bad as the aristocrats. You see this last winter has passed over, entirely, without any subscription for the poor, again, – as severe a winter as it has been."

"Ay, and work scarcer and scarcer, every day," said another.

"They say there are eight hundred out o' work now, in Leicester," said the elderly, sedate man, who had spoken before; and I heard a manufacturer say there would be twice as many before the summer went over: but he added, that the people deserved to be pinched, since they would not join the Corn Law Repealers."

A burst of indignation, and some curses and imprecations, followed "Does he go to chapel?" asked one.

"Yes; and he's a member of the Charles Street meeting," said the elderly man.

"There's your religion, again!" – "There's your saintship!" –"There's your Christianity!" – "There's their Providence and their Goddle Mitey!" – were the varied indignant exclamations among the starved crowd, as soon as the answer was heard.

"I should think they invented the Bastile Mill, while they were at chapel!" said one.

"Is it smashed again?" asked another. "No, but it soon will be," answered the man who confronted the soldier.

These, and similar observations, were uttered aloud, in the open street, at broad day, by hundreds of starved, oppressed, and insulted framework-knitters, who thus gave vent to their despair. Such conversations were customary sounds in John's ears, and, having recovered his son he took him by the arm, after this brief delay, and, walking slowly back towards the Roman milestone, the two bent their steps down the narrow street called Barkby Lane. After threading an alley, they reached a small wretchedly furnished habitation; and the lad burst into tears, as his mother sprung from her laborious employ at the wash-tub, and threw her arms round his neck, and kissed him. Two or three neighbours came in, in another minute, and congratulating the father and

56

mother, on their having found their son, a conversation followed on the hatefulness of becoming "a paid cut-throat for tyrants," the substance of which would have been as unpleasing to "the powers that be" as the conversation in the street, had they heard the two. The entry, into the squalid-looking house, of another neighbour, pale and dejected beyond description, gave a new turn to the homely discourse.

"Your son has come back, I see, John," said the new-comer, in a very faint voice: "I wish my husband would come home."

"Thy husband, Mary!" said John; "why, where's he gone? Bless me, woman, how ill you look! – What's the matter?"

The woman's infant had begun to cry while she spoke; and she had bared her breast, and given it to the child: but – Nature was exhausted! there was no milk; – and, while the infant struggled and screamed, the woman fainted. She recovered, under the kindly and sympathetic attention of the neighbours; and the scanty resources of the group were laid under contribution for restoring some degree of strength, by means of food, to the woman and her child. One furnished a cup of milk, another a few spoonfuls of milk of oatmeal, another brought a little bread; and when the child was quieted, and the mother was able, she commenced her sad narrative. She had not, she said, tasted food of any kind for a day and two nights: and she had pawned or sold every article of clothing, except what she had on, and she was without a bonnet entirely: nor had her husband any other clothes than the rags in which he had gone out, two hours before, with the intent to try the relieving officer, once more, for a loaf, or a trifle of money: to complete their misery, they owed six weeks' rent for the room in which lay the bag of shavings that formed their bed; and, if they could not pay the next week's rent, they must turn out into the street, or go into the Bastile.

Her recital was scarcely concluded, when the sorrowful husband returned. He had been driven away by the relieving officer, and threatened with the gaol, if he came again, unless it was to bring his wife and child with him to enter the Union Bastile! – and the man sat down, and wept.

And then the children of misery mingled their consolations, – if reflections drawn from despair could be so called, – and endeavoured to fortify the heart of the yielding man, by reminding him that they would not have to starve long, for life, with all its miseries, would soon be over.

"I wonder why it ever begun!" exclaimed the man who had been yielding to tears, but now suddenly burst out into bitter language: "I think it's a pity but that God had found something better to do than to make such poor miserable wretches as we are!"

"Lord! what queer thoughts thou hast, Jim!" said the woman who had previously fainted, and she burst into a half-convulsive laugh.

"Indeed, it's altogether a mystery to me," said the man who had so recently found his son; "we seem to be born for nothing but trouble. And then the queerest thing is that we are to go to hell, at last, if we don't do every thing exactly square. My poor father always taught me to reverence religion; and I don't like to say any thing against it, but I'm hard put to it, at times, Jim, I'll assure ye. It sounds strange, that we are to be burnt for ever after pining and starving here; for how can a man keep his temper, and be thankful, as they say we ought to be, when we ought to be, when he would work and can't get it, and, while he starves, sees oppressors ride in their gigs, and build their great warehouses?"

"It's mere humbug, John, to keep us down: that's what it is!" said Jim: "one of these piety-mongers left us a tract last week; and what should it contain but that old tale of Bishop Burnet, about the widow that somebody who peeped through the chinks of the window-shutters saw kneeling by a table with a crust of bread before her, and crying out in rapture, 'All this and Christ!' I tell thee what, John, if old Burnet had been brought down from his gold and fat living, and had tried it himself, I could better have believed him. It's a tale told like many others to make fools and slaves of us: that's what I think. Ay, and I told the long-faced fellow so that fetched the tract. He looked very sourly at me, and said the poor did not use to trouble themselves about politics in his father's time, and everybody was more comfortable then than they are now. 'The more fools were they,' said I: 'if the poor had begun to think of their rights sooner, instead of listening to religious cant, we should not have been so badly off now:' and away he went, and never said another word."

"But I don't like to give way to bad thoughts about religion, after all, Jim," said John: "it's very mysterious – the present state of things: but we may find it all explained in the next life."

"Prythee, John," exclaimed the other, interrupting him, impatiently, "don't talk so weakly. That's the way they all wrap it up; and if a guess in the dark and a 'maybe' will do for an argument, why any thing will do. Until somebody can prove to me that there *is* another life after this, I shall think it my duty to think about this only. Now just look at this, John! If there be another life after this, why the present is worth nothing: every moment here ought to be spent in caring for eternity; and every man who really believes in such a life would not care how he passed this, so that he could but be making a preparation for the next time: isn't that true, John?"

"To be sure it is, Jim; and what o' that?"

"Why, then, tell me which of 'em believes in such a life. Do you see any of the canting tribe less eager than others to get better houses, finer chairs and tables, larger shops, and more trade? Is old Sour-Godliness in the north, there, more easily brought to give up a penny in the dozen to save a starving stockinger than the grinders that don't profess religion? I tell thee, John, it's all fudge: they don't believe it themselves, or else they would imitate Christ before they tell us to be like him!"

Reader! the conversation shall not be prolonged, lest the object of this sketch should be mistaken. These conversations are *real:* they are no coinages. Go to Leicester, or any other of the suffering towns of depressed manufacture, where men compete with each other in machinery till human hands are of little use, and rival each other in wicked zeal to reduce man to the merest minimum of subsistence.

If the missionary people – and this is not said with a view to question the true greatness and utility of their efforts – if they would be consistent, let them send their heralds into the manufacturing districts, and first convert the "infidels" there, ere they send their expensive messengers to India. But let it be understood that the heralds must be furnished with brains, as well as tongues; for whoever enters Leicester, or any other of the populous starving hives of England, must expect to find the deepest subjects of theology, and government, and political economy, taken up with a subtlety that would often puzzle a graduate of Oxford or Cambridge. Whoever supposes the starving "manufacturing masses" know no more, and can use no better language, than the peasantry in the agricultural counties, will find himself egregiously mistaken. 'Tis ten to one but he will learn more of a profound subject in one hour's conversation of starving stockingers than he would do in ten lectures of a university professor. Let the missionary people try these quarters, then; but let their heralds "know their business" ere they go, or they will make as slow progress as Egede and the Moravians among the Greenlanders. One hint may be given. Let them begin with the manufacturers; and, if they succeed in making *real* converts to Christianity in that quarter, their success will be tolerably certain among the working men, and tolerably easy in its achievement.

There is no "tale" to finish about John or his lad, or Jem and his wife. They went on starving, – begging, – receiving threats of imprisonment, – tried the "Bastile" for a few weeks, – came out and had a little work, – starved again; and they are still going the same miserable round, like thousands in "merrie England." What are your thoughts, reader?

The Defender: An Irish Tale of 1797 (1840)

Upon an evening towards the close of the summer of 1797, a gentleman, advanced in years, and of a striking appearance, issued from a country town, in the east of Ireland, and sauntered along the pathway that led from it, by its river's edge, into the open country.

For a few hours that he had been a guest, along with two younger companions, dressed in half-military attire, at the principal inn of the town, he proved an object of much curiosity to the good folk of the community around him; but, as yet, all their attempts to ascertain his name, quality, or occupation in the world, were unsuccessful.

Unlike his young friends, he was habited in what is sometimes called, in Ireland at least, "plain clothes;" but in fashion and material, they bespoke a gentleman of the time, and of the higher order of gentlemen; and his features, air and manner bore out the pretension. He seemed to be betwixt sixty and seventy; his stature was tall, his step firm and noble; and his face, showing the remains of youthful beauty, expressed a peculiar mixture of mental habits of blandness and command, urbanity and determination, condescension and self-respect.

At the very commencement of his rural excursion, he was observed to pause and look about him; turn and glance back the way he had come; turn and gaze steadfastly along the way he was about to go. And so he continued on his saunter, stopping, and turning, and looking again and again; his handsomely-shaped lips, sometimes in motion, as if unconsciously they gave utterance in words to thoughts connected with the objects he contemplated.

It was plain, indeed, that he enjoyed the scenery, either under the excitement of a first impression from it, or in consequence of his renewal of an old acquaintance with it, after a long separation. Even a casual observer, arguing from the earnestness and vivacity of his regards and his manner, such as we have described both, during his walk, would have declared as much; but we can draw the necessary distinction for the reader. It was indeed an old friendship that the visitor of our country town was claiming with the mute features of nature. Years – many years – more than half the term usually allotted to human life – had elapsed since the summer's evening when he last trod the little pathway over which he now wandered; and the hills, the trees, the water, the meadows, the houses, the distant mountains, everything he gazed upon, re-appeared to his eye as indeed familiar objects, and yet seemingly with a kind of strangeness upon them, as to form, or size, or colour, or relative position, which rendered them unsatisfactory to the overwhelming pretensions of memory, and which long absence, among scenery widely different in character from them, had treacherously produced.

No events in the spectator's life of very great interest were connected with the present landscape; yet it served to call up before his mind the great changes of fortune, of feeling and of opinion, which he had experienced during his distant and devious separation from it; and by reminding him of the simple and every-day tenor of the portion of his youth whiled away in its presence, the subsequent passages of his manhood and of his age, to the present hour, became more contrastedly important."Aye," he would say, "when I used to lie in the shade, under that granite rock, to coquet with my pocket volume of poetry, or when I used to cross-fish for salmon with young Martin Doyle, the miller's son, on the banks of this pretty stream, little did I foresee the swelling circumstances, the exertions, and the dangers which, in other climates, among a strangely different people, were to form my future and my present character and place in the world."

His thoughts took another and a sadder turn. "Little, too, did I then calculate the changes that time has since wrought within me and upon me: the cooling-down of the fine breezy freshness of those morning-days; the stilling of the delightful pulsating of hope, in the certainty of experience – nay, even of achievement and of fame; the sense of age, and its near fellowship with death; ay, and even this changed person, these furrowed features, this staid step, these sinewy hands, this snowy hair – ah, yes, I grant ye, youth is delusion, or else carelessness; but even, for that very reason, it is happier than age."

And again his reflections, as connected with the place, diverged in their nature. Though not a native of the little valley, nor even of the country which contained it, he had formed a passing intimacy, during the early part of his life alluded to, with some of its inhabitants; and upon this intimacy arose, in his kindly heart, good wishes towards them, which time, absence, and, above all, coming back to their vicinity, served but to strengthen. But circumstances had lately visited with misfortune the district inhabited by his old, humble friends, and a cloud of danger hung threateningly over their heads; while he had returned amongst them, a stern man, endowed with much of the power which was to direct the fine workings of the storm, for their weal or their woe. And now he paused a moment to ponder the wondrous changes which take place in personal responsibility, and in an individual's relation towards his fellow-creatures: and then arose a benevolent sigh for the human misery he had witnessed upon earth, and which he was doomed still to witness – nay, perhaps instrumentally to cause; and, as one of the minor chords of memory became generously touched at the thought, he began to feel interest for the present and future fate even of some of the former lowly dwellings on the banks of the gentle river by which he walked.

Quickening his pace, he advanced up towards its source. Two or three men passed him: he looked critically into their features, but memory found in the survey nothing she could own. Still he proceeded onward, until he came in view of another man, who, with a fishing-rod in his hand, was sitting over the water under a huge fantastically-limbed ash-tree. This person seemed very intent upon his solitary sport. He was old, and not hale for his years; on the contrary, it seemed, if one might judge from his sitting position, that his tall and gaunt figure was somewhat bent and prematurely enfeebled. He wore a whitish hat, made whiter by flour dust, which also plentifully covered his whole person, and even his face; and, in fact, it was plain to be seen that he was a miller; nay, a look up the river at the little mill, in the eddies of the broken stream from whose weir his fishing flies were floating, intimated that he was the miller of the valley.

The strange gentleman regarded him with attention, but, it would seem, not with satisfaction to his object in doing so. He stepped nearer and nearer to him, and appeared still at fault.

"It must be a new proprietor of the mill," he said to himself, "or else Martin's father, whom I have never before seen – for still I half fancy there is a kind of family likeness. Good evening, friend," he continued to the sportsman, suddenly coming close to his side.

The old man, his attention previously absorbed by his fishing-rod, and his ears thrown off their guard by the near noise of the rushing weir, and of the rippling and dancing water that ran to him from its base, had not till this moment noticed the stranger; now he started at the sudden salutation, and having glanced at the person who gave it, looked earnest and respectful, took off his hat, and inclined his head – we had almost said politely, as, with a smile, he answered – "A kind good evening, sir." But the other observed that there was no recognition in his bow, nor in his smile, nor in his glance.

"Don't let me interrupt your sport: there ought to be some good trout-fishing about this part of the river."

"Thank you then, sir; and I will throw out again."

Suiting the action to the word, he wound, with the hand of a master, his angle and fishing-line above and around his head, cleverly steering them clear of entanglement with the branches of the ash-tree, and then caused the line to fall lightly and without a curve in it upon the water. "And indeed it is a good spot to find a trout in, sir, as you say – or, to speak the thruth, it used to be long ago, when I was a boy; but – dickens in 'em for throuts! – I believe it's gettin' bad an' scarce they are wid the times, like all the rest of the world. But look, sir, there's a fine rise at me! Is he hooked? No! – bad manners to him, he's off!"

"From what you say, my friend, you and the trouts hereabout seem to be a long while acquainted."

"And so we are, sir, sure enough – all our lives long; born and bred together, your Honour.'

"You live in the mill, I suppose?"

"I own the mill, your Honour – that is, little Martin and I between us; we owns it aquallike."

"And how is Martin – little Martin, as you call him?"

The fisher half stopped in his sport, and looked with curiosity at the speaker, as he answered – "Why, then, brave and hearty, sir; an' will your Honour let me ask you where you met Martin afore to-night, to know or care about him."

"Oh, no matter for that; we are old friends – I was right," resumed the stranger, in his own mind; "this is indeed Martin's father, by the twinkle of his eye." Then he went on aloud – "Can I see him? Is he at home?"

The old man laid his rod on the bank, and, with a changed countenance, in which some alarm mingled with scrutiny, again fixed his eyes on his catechist, as he hesitatingly replied – "At home, sir? an' you'd want to see him? Why, I believe – I'm almost sure – he is at home wid 'em at the hopper; only I'd make bould to be asking again, sir, who is it that wants him?"

"Oh, don't be afraid of me," said the gentleman smiling; "I mean him no harm; let him come out from the hopper, and, when he knows who I am – which he will be sure to do at the first look – Martin will tell you so himself."

"Why then, sir, I'm inclined to think you mean him no harm, sure enough; for, now I look at you myself the second time, it isn't the likes of your Honour, with that smile on your face, and your Honour all alone, too," he continued, glancing watchfully around, "that he or I need be afeard of. But here he comes, at any rate, to make us all sure one way or another."

A man in the undress of a miller, carrying a chubby child in his arms, with which he talked and laughed cheerily, approached them from the mill; and this

62

"little Martin" was about thirty years of age, and about six feet two inches high, and tall, athletic, and seemingly almost riotous in his spirit of activity, for he came jumping and bounding along, over every obstacle, great or small, in his way.

"Come here, Maurtheen, you *gommeral*," cried his father, "here's a strange gentleman – and a gentleman he is every inch of him – that knows you well, and that you know well, and that wants to be speaking to you."

Little Martin, stopping short at a civil distance, looked more disturbed than his father had just done. "*Me*, father? Want to spake to me? I never saw *him* afore in my life then."

The stranger saw, indeed, that he had been quite mistaken in his anticipations of the identity of this individual, who, perhaps deriving all his features from the mother, bore not the slightest resemblance, except in the loftiness of his stature, to the old angler under the tree; and a new light began to break in upon the observer's mind.

"I beg your pardon," he resumed; "I certainly must have been in error. Of this little Martin of yours I have, indeed, no recollection; but let me ask you another question or two: your own name is Martin, I suppose?"

"It is, your honour; and so was my father's afore me."

"Martin Doyle?"

"Martin Doyle, sir, an' nothing else."

"Is this possible?" asked the gentleman of himself. "Is that old man before me the real Martin Doyle I want? – the former obliging companion of my fishing sports on the banks of this river? Well, time has dealt harder with him than with me; and yet I am not recognised by *him* either," he added, with by no means a pleasing argument, philosophically-minded as he was, built there upon in his own thoughts; perhaps he had never before so fully admitted to himself *that he was old.* The looking-glass, with its every day familiarity, may flatter us into a comfortable idea that, as years pass on, our features do not change *much* ; but when we meet, after a long absence, an early associate of about our own age, and find his features changed *very much*, then we just begin to suspect our own liability to human accidents of the same kind.

"And maybe it's about myself, and not about my son you'd be asking, afther all, sir?"

"Do you recollect the – regiment, that was quartered, some time ago, in the town yonder?"

"Blood an' ages! an' sure I do, sir. Sometime ago? – haith, an' its a good long time ago; let me see, its nigh hand to forty – forty-one – forty-two years ago, every day of it; but I remember the – th regiment for all that."

"And why do you remember it so well?"

"Because I loved and liked every man in it – common men, officers, and all; an' all in regard of the officers – five, or six, or seven of them, that used to run from the town to the river side here, two or three at a time, an' call me from the hopper to go fishing' with them; hearty, pleasant cratures they were. An' many many a summer's night they'd bespake a loand o' the kitchen fire, in the mill; and we'd fry the throuts we used to ketch together on it, and have to say that we eat 'em out o' the river, afther a manner. An' there was one or two o' the whole clan o' the officers that I liked above the rest; an' good reason I had: I fell sick o' the faver that was in the place, and it's kind friends they showed themselves while it had me down – bad manners to it! – kind friends to me an' my poor ould mother – God bless 'em for the same, wherever they are, alive or dead, this evenin'!"

"I believe you earned the goodwill of the two gentlemen you speak of by a good action of your own towards one of them?"

"Blessed hour, your Honour! how do you know that?" The old miller started up as nimbly as he could, now wholly abandoning his fishing-rod.

"I knew your old friends abroad."

"Praise be to God! Strange things 'ill always be comin' to pass in this world. Musha, sir, maybe" – He drew quite close to the stranger, peering at him in the coming twilight, as if he hoped to make a gratifying discovery; but added, with a disappointed expression of face – "Avoch, no! – your honour is neither the one nor the other of them. But you met 'em abroad, you say, sir? An' they spoke to you of one poor Martin Doyle it seems? They thought of him, an' of ould innocent times; an' of the poor little ould mill, an' the throuts, an' the ould river's side, in Ireland – an' they far away? It was like them, the cratures."

"Indeed, they did; and they would have been ungrateful if they had not done so – one of them, at least – the young gentleman you saved from drowning, at the risk of your own life – at almost the certainty of losing it, indeed – very near this spot, the spring when there was such a tearing flood in the river."

"Huth, sir! that little matter is not worth spakin about; what did I do, but what we're all bound to do for ache other? – An' they're alive, sir, an' well and happy, I hope, this blessed day?"

"They are alive, and well, and as happy as, I believe, the generality of their fellow-creatures."

"Musha, then, the Lord be praised! and more o' that to them; but there is one of the two I'd be asking afther, your Honour, wid all the veins of my heart – young Masther Ensign Abercromby – how is *he*?"

Before the strange gentleman could answer, little Martin, who had been listening with great interest, said in a tone of great excitement – "You're spakin' of a great man now, father; the great General Abercromby; him that the whole world is talkin' about; an' a man as good as he is great, they say; an', more nor that, the very general that has come over to Ireland from England, about a month ago, to review the King's throops an' see if they are in fit ordher to finish their work on the people."

"The Lord be praised, again!" ejaculated the old man; "sure it was thrue for me when I said, a while agone, that strange things id never stop happenin'; an' is what little Martin says thrue, sir?"

"I cannot vouch for the truth of the compliments he has paid to General Abercromby," answered the gentleman, smiling; "but the principal facts he has mentioned are true."

"They are, your Honour, an' what I am goin' to say is thrue, besides: the general has been reviewing the throops, in different parts o' the counthry; an' so bad did he find 'em, in regard o' their bein' so long let loose to murther and plunder the poor people, that he tould themselves to their faces, that they 'were in a state of discipline that made them formidable to any one but an enemy." And little Martin related this anecdote with increased vivacity – with a vehemence, indeed, which was not lost upon the most observant of his hearers.

"Well, Martin," resumed this individual, addressing the father; "so far so good, as regards your own good-natured inquiries after your old friends; but they will, doubtless, be asking, in their turn, after your welfare in the world, when I happen to see them again; I want to know, therefore, all about you, for their satisfaction – how you are in health, in wealth, and in expectations."

"Thankee kindly, sir. The health is nothin' to brag of, praise be to God! There's an ould rhumatiz on me this many a year, an' I had a heavy pleuracy the last spring – but we mustn't complain. As to the other things, why, the hopper clucks merrily, praise be to God over again! an' I'm alive to see little Martin, there, ind another little Martin intirely, in his arms, growin' fat on it; and while there's wather in the river to keep it goin' for them, an' for the little girl of a wife he has – an' good little creature she is – never throuble comes into my mind about the hereafter in this ugly world; that is, if the Peep-o'-day Boys, and the Defendher-boys, an' the sogers, 'ud only let us alone, your Honour, an' lave us in pace an' quietness."

The son fidgeted, and seemed about to speak again, very earnestly, but checked himself.

"And no doubt they will let you alone, Martin; for I am quite sure you have had too much good sense to give any one cause to inconvenience you, in these unsettled times."

"I'm obleeged to your Honour for your good thought – an', deed-an'-deed, I desarve it from you, sir; never a meddle nor make can any one bring agin ould Martin Doyle, on the head of a single disturbance that's in the counthry."

And you can say the same for your son?" half questioned the stranger – much doubting the fact, however; and little Martin fidgeted more and more.

"I can, your Honour – I hope and pray to God that I can; ever an' always 'twas my word to him, and my advice, and my command, to keep clear of oath-takin', an' everything o' the kind; an' if he hasn't hearkened to the words o' my mouth, he's a worse boy and a worse son than I took him for."

"I'll do nothing to shame you, father," said the person spoken of, still vehemently; "an' I hope an' pray, like yourself, that we may be left to rest in pace; only how can we expect to escape, in the long run, our share of what a'most every other man, woman and child in the land of Ireland, is sufferin, or has suffered? In our own poor country alone, I could reckon four hundred cabins, an' snugger houses, burnt down within the last two months; there's six smokin' yet, on the very next lawnland; and where are them that, last May-day, lived under their roof-threes? – I'll tell your Honour," continued the young "Defender," his eyes still kindling, and his voice and manner becoming still more marked with excitement, as he clasped closer, with one sinewy arm, the urchin that nestled on his breast, and began to wave the other round his head – "I'll tell your Honour – if your Honour will take the answer from the greatest-spoken Irishman that Ireland ever saw, instid of from my own foolish words – I'll tell your Honour?"

Little Martin meant, indeed, Ireland's immortal Curran; even then, in the very exercise of his oratory, well known among the humbler politicians of his country; and the young miller went on with a quotation, truly learnt by heart, from a speech recently delivered, upon an important trial in Dublin, by the orator. We subjoin the passage, without adding little Martin's brogue to it.

"Where shall you find the wretched inhabitant of this land? You may find him perhaps in jail, the only place of security – I had almost said of habitation; you may see him flying from the flames of his own dwelling, or you may find his bones bleaching on the green fields of his country; or he may be found tossing upon the surface of the ocean, and mingling his groans with those of tempests, less savage than his persecutors, that drift him to a returnless distance from his family and his home."

And such truly were Curran's words, descriptive of the social state of Ireland in this year of 1797; not – we request it to be observed – not the year of the rebellion in Ireland, and of the surpassing vengeance which it entailed upon the devoted population; but the year before that rebellion, into which visitations such as those spoken of by the orator chiefly tended to precipitate the people.

"That is all very well in its way," quietly observed the gentleman; "and all very beautiful language, I willingly admit; but surely the people of this fine country could not be subjected to such severities, if they had not given cause to provoke them."

His words now called forth a great flow of explanation and expostulation from the young man, and, even in his own way, from his father, to which, redundant as it was, their new friend listened with attention. He proposed questions, too, as if he would inform himself, according to their knowledge of facts, of the full subject in discussion; though, indeed, he really lacked no acquaintance with it, and put his queries solely to ascertain the extent and correctness of theirs, together with their incidental opinions and feelings. The statements they made are, however, interesting to our present reader, and we shall, therefore, condense them – again, as in the recent case of the quotation from Curran, not preserving the language of our immediate authorities.

But the rebellion about to break out, they said, no more originated with the people of Ireland, than did the American rebellion originate with the red men of the western continent. Its heads were descendants of English and Scotch colonists – Church-of-England Protestants, and Presbyterians – who, as their American prototypes had done, quarrelled with the mother country, because they wanted to rule independently over the land of their adoption. England overawed them with her disciplined troops, and then they seduced into their ranks the native population, who – to recur again to the model-contest across the Atlantic – bore, to the two parties really at issue, about the same political affinities as did the tomahawk allies of the American war to the true combatants in that struggle; so insignificant, in the eyes of their masters at every side, were then the "Catholic millions" of Ireland. Circumstances had, however, indifferently well prepared the Irish mass-goer for enlisting against the established authorities. For some time previously, a majority of the High Church colonists of Ulster had come to a resolution to banish out of their neighbourhood all aboriginal Papists; and, being more locally numerous than the objects of their aversion, and calling in to their aid fire and sword, and all legitimate means of extermination, they were very successful in their attempts to do so; for these were the fine old "hell-or-Connaught" times. The Protestant bands voluntarily organized on the occasion, dubbed themselves Peep-o'-day Boys; and the banished Papists, spreading among their own sect, wherever they wandered through Ireland, terror and hatred of their persecutors, counter-bands of Catholics became formed, in many parts of the country, under the name of *Defenders.*

Government had never openly countenanced or applauded the gratuitous loyalty of the Peep-o'-day Boys; the Defenders, however, did not think that it repressed or punished them as vigorously as it could and ought to have done; and those sitting in high places, consequently, began to share some of the feelings with which the illiterate Irish Catholic regarded his enemy; and, just at this nick of time, in stepped, amongst the fermenting Defenders, William Orr,

66

Arthur O'Connor, and their friends; and, as the Peep-o'-day Boys were Government supporters as well as Papist-haters, the Catholic people, hoping for ample and exemplary vengeance upon them during the struggle, soon became converted into United Irishmen – rebels, in fact, against English dominion in Ireland.

"An' that's the way *we* – the poor people o' the counthry, I mane – were made united men," continued the young miller; "though now it's we alone that bears the brunt on every side; ay, an' that are likely to be the only army General Abercromby 'ill meet in the field."

"Yes," assented his father; "yes, the misfortunate *spalpeens* – whoever dances, it's they must pay the piper."

"But who is this coming up to us, now?" questioned the son, stepping back, the infant still in his arms, and looking really alarmed. Two young gentlemen, in military undress, approached our party, along the bank of the river, from the direction of the town; and, owing to the increased twilight, they had come near before they were observed – their pace was hasty, and their manner anxious. The old miller more than shared his son's nervousness.

"Still fear nothing, Martin; these gentlemen are friends of mine, and only here to seek me. Farewell! I am authorized by your old fellow sportsmen on the river side, to take your hand." He did so, with an air of cordial though condescending urbanity; while Martin, his eyes reverting to the new comers, received, in an embarrassed and bewildered manner, the unexpected salutation. "And, farther, Martin, I have to inform you that the young Master Ensign Abercromby you spoke of awhile ago will be in your town to-morrow, and if you inquire for him at his quarters, pleased to see you, perhaps. Now, good night." He turned away, joined his young associates, and soon disappeared with them along the path by which they had approached, all conversing earnestly.

"Who are they at all?" resumed little Martin, his troubled eyes straining after them. "An look up there, father! – what's that?"

About half-way between the speaker and the town, a reddish spot appeared in the darkening sky.

"That's the sign of another house a-fire," answered the father, in a solemn, doleful tone; though we can't see the flames by reason of the high grounds between us and it."

"By the lot o'man!" half screamed the son, smiting his thigh with his disengaged hand, "it's the house of little Micky Glennan, our baronial secretary; and he had all the baronial papers under his roof; an' if they are found, we're lost men; or if HE is found, all the same; for the little tailoring *thrawneen* of a crature will never bear three lashes o' the cat-o'-nine-tails on his back without telling on the whole of us."

"What words are them you're saying, Martin?" asked his father, fixing his eyes upon him in misgiving and terror.

Before little Martin could make an answer, a feeble and tremulous voice cautiously pronounced his name. Both startled and looked round. The call repeated; and they could now perceive that it arose from under the bank near to the verge of which they were standing. They peered over the bank and imperfectly discerned beneath them, standing breast-high in the current of the waters, a little slight-built man, who with difficulty supported himself in his not unperilous position, by grasping at the roots of the ash-tree before mentioned as growing in this spot.

"I was right, I was right!" exclaimed young Martin; "it's Micky himself run out of the fire into the wathers, an' staling down through it all the way to us here under the bank, to give us a warning! Trot home to Mamman, Matty *avourneen,*" (he set down the child,) "an' tell her not to mind biling the pyatees for my supper to-night. Give us a hould o' you, Micky." He threw himself on his breast at the edge of the steep bank, stretched one arm downwards, seized the little scout by the shoulder, and landed him on his feet under the ash-tree. The poor tailor secretary stood dripping and shivering in the very undress in which he had jumped off his shopboard – namely, stripped to his waistcoat, and shoeless and hatless – upon the first alarm of the approach of the military to his house.

"Hurry, Martin, hurry!" he now cried, taking from between his clenched teeth a bundle of papers tied round with a strip of listing. "You know what these are, an' I just had time to save 'em for your hands – hurry into the mill and burn 'em – burn 'em well, well! or the whole world is desthroyed! you among all the rest! you and yours – hurry, hurry! No terrier could bring them better to you between his teeth, out of the fire first, an' out o' the wathers afther – hurry, man! – but, no – stop – there's no time for you to do it now, give them to your father there – let him make away with 'em – the sogers will be here on yourself in the turning of a hand! I see their bagnets bristlin' over the fence on the high-road above, dark as it's growin', an' they'll be down on the poor mill like a hawk on the wing! Yes, Martin, they have your name, as well as they had mine, an' the ould mill 'ill burn to-night, as sure as Mick Glennan's roof is burnin' beyant ther! Hurry, ould Martin, hurry, I bid you! – my duty is done here, an' I can't stop a moment longer. No, nor your bould son oughtn't to stop, if he cares for the breath he's brathin'! To the wather, again, wid me, for the bare life, an' for the lives of a thousand men along wid it. Follow me, little Martin, an' I'll shew you the way to a good hidin-hole. Follow me. It's across the river to the ould wood I'm goin' – an', oh, the Lord purtect me, for my life is worth a mint o' money."

The utterly terrified and yet self-important little man, delivered this speech in gasping and catches of breath, and almost in a whisper, while not only his features, but his hands, legs, and feet worked in spasmy gesticulations; and he had scarce ended it, when he dropped by his hands from the bank into the water, in the very place where, assisted by little Martin, he had made his appearance. His auditors, stunned by the nature of his communications and exhortations, had not been able to address to him a single word. Little Martin now first recovered presence of mind. He glanced up to the high road and saw indeed the glistening of the bayonets; he glanced at the death-fraught parcel in his hand, and felt that, as the tailor had said, fire ought that instant to consume it to ashes; he glanced at his father and perceived that he was so shaken by fright and consternation, it was impossible he could effect this object; then he ran headlong to the mill-house; gained it and disappeared into it by a succession of bounds, such as a race-horse might take, when pushed hard near the winning-post; reappeared and reproached his father, at the same speed; found the old man sitting helplessly, and with a pitiable expression of face, upon the curled roots of the ash-tree; flung himself on his knees at his feet, and addressed him.

"Tis all too thrue father, dear – I am the ruin o' you, in your ould days! The mill will burn to-night, as little Micky said, an' I must run like a hare to save my life itself from the hands that 'ill put the red fire to it! Father, can you forgive me? But the ould man has no speech for me, an' I can't stop till it comes back to him" – He eyed the high ground over the mill, and saw the soldiers jumping upon it from the road. "Father, listen to one word; they can't touch *you*, you know, for you're free o' the matther. When you see Anty, tell her to come look for me to-night in the ould wood. You heard what Micky said – didn't you, father?"

"Yes, avich, yes, yes," answered the old miller, incoherently.

"Tell Anty; then, as I bid you – and you'll come wid her – won't you, father? But don't tell her till all is over, an' the sogers gone – her grief might misguide her tongue. An' now, father dear, the good night, an' God look down on you, and pity you – an' forgive *me*!" He jumped up, took his father's hands, kissed his cheeks, gave one short look over his shoulders up the hill side, and the next moment plunged head foremost from the bank into the river.

The people in Ireland sometimes give strange names to places, names which purport or pretend to describe their characteristic features, but which, in reality, do no such thing; and indeed, had we time to pause for the purpose, we might perhaps show that such is the case in other countries also. In the present instance, at all events, the place of refuge spoken of by the little rebel secretary, as the "ould wood," was as unlike a wood as possibly could be. It was a bog, in fact; but perhaps, in the very olden times, trees had covered its surface, conferring a name which, even after its total decay or eradication, became hereditary in the neighbourhood.

It was an extensive bog, too, over spreading many acres; very little of it solid; and such spots of it as were so, connected with each other by strips of miry soil, or else almost quite separated by deep holes filled with water, across which it was necessary to bound with a sure foot and an agile limb. To those acquainted with its recesses, however, and well inured to jumping, leaping, and splashing, it could be explored partially at least; and from this description, we may infer that it afforded to our present fugitives a secure temporary retreat from pursuers not as well acquainted as they were with its statistics.

It lay about four miles from the town in the neighbourhood of which Martin Doyle's mill stood, or used to stand, and was distant perhaps fifteen miles from another town, a sea-coast one, whence small ships occasionally sailed to distant parts of the world. Some hours after his last disappearance from us, we discover young Martin Doyle, and his little shivering friend, Micky Glennan, accompanied by another man, who bore a pedlar's pack, crouching in the shade of a huge turf clump, upon a nearly isolated patch of almost quagmire in its centre. They had been conversing, but they are now silent, straining their eyes over the waste around them, as if in expectation of the approach of some person whom they anxiously wished to see. It was midnight, and, although an autumn midnight, cloudy, and moonless, and starless over-head; and altogether nothing could be more cheerless and dreary than their position. There was no running motion in the black bog-water to give it sound and life; there was no breeze abroad to stir the tufts of rushes or of flaggers – the only vegetation of the bog – which grew at its edges, or up through its stagnant wave; upon the shelve of the low line of falling ground which embasined the desolate place, no human habitation was in view; in fact, no object of interest met the eye upon the land or in the heavens; and the only sounds which now and then broke the painful silence, were the mouse-like squeak of the bat, or the angry hoot of the horned owl – each animal unseen – as it flitted or passed by them, or a sudden splash, through its dreams, of a sleeping waterfowl, near at hand.

And here little Martin and his two companions lay still, under the clouds of the night, wearily watching, as we have said, the coming of an expected visitor. But the grey morning began to break, and no one approached them; and, half-dressed and wet out of the river, as two of the three men continued to be, and unsupplied with refreshment of any kind, chilliness and hunger aggravated the misery of their feelings as outlaws, as houseless beggars, and as victims doomed to the death. Morning almost fully shone out, indeed, before Anty Doyle, with her little boy on her back, gained her husband's side.

They did not exchange a word at meeting, but embraced many times, the child encircled by their interwined arms – poor Anty only too eloquent in her incessant sobs and tears.

"Well, *ma colleen* – sure there's no use in asking – the ould mill-house hasn't a roof on it by this time?"

She could but cry on.

"Shure, I knew it, *alanna*; and what's the use of frettin' over it now? We're all safe, and all here together, anyhow; all but the ould man. Where is *he*, Anty? Why didn't he come the road with you?"

Still the poor woman was able to give only a weeping answer.

"He just staid behind to see what comfort or help he could pick up for us, an' he'll be with us in no time? – isn't that id, Anty? Musha, to be sure it is; and so, as I was saying, we'll be altogether, after the whole that is come an' gone; an' you and I are young and hearty yet, Anty; an' the world is wide, *achona*; an' – whisper in your ear – there's luck in store for us yet; ay, and nigh hand to us. Here's a friend o' Micky Glennan's," (pointing to the third man in company,) "an' he has room enough bespoke for us all aboard a good ship, only a few miles off; an', if the ould man id only come among us at oncet, we would be running off towards the sey this moment – couldn't we, Matty, *ma bouchal*?"

He snatched the child from her arms, and began to dandle and toss it about, singing and laughing, and even dancing to it, in an outbreak of false vivacity. "But *when* will he come, Anty? – did he tell you?"

"Martin, Martin," sobbed his wife, sinking down in a sitting position, and covering her face with her hands, "the ould man won't come to us."

"What's that you say, Anty? *won't* come to us? Is he so vexed with me entirely?"

"Martin, I mean to tell you that he can't come to us."

"Can't – what's to hinder him? They darn't harm a hair of his head; they darn't lay a hand on him. He has done nothing to deserve it from 'em. Where is he? Where is he, Anty? Where's my father?"

"He's in the sthrong gaol o' the town beyon, Martin."

"What's that you tell me, woman?" He stepped back slowly, put the child down as if a master-feeling had suddenly chased out of his heart all fondness for it, and then, looking deadly pale, continued in a slow, low voice – "The gaol! – how could that happen? What did they put him in the gaol for? I tell you again, he's as innocent of thrason against them as the child unborn."

"And I'll tell *you* how it came to pass, Martin. While the mill an' the house was burnin', an every chair and table we had were thurn into the flames to help them, they found the ould man and me whispering together. He was after telling me where to go and look for you then; an' they axed him about the road you took, an' he shook, and thrembled, and denied his knowledge of you, with such a weak, poor manner on him, that they easy guessed he knew well

70

everything about you; an' so they axed him agin, threatenin' him; but he denied them still, growin' stouter and heartier this time; an', at last, they dhragged him off between 'em to the gaol; an' your ould father's bare back, Martin, is to be flogged at their thriangle, afore breakfast time this blessed mornin' – ay, Martin, an' flogged, flogged, flogged, till he gives 'em the word where to find you."

The strong young man looked utterly overwhelmed; he changed colour again and again; his forehead grew moist, and he smote his breast solemnly, as, with upturned eyes, and moaning forth the words like a sick woman, he said – "O my God! my God! – Oh, the Lord forgive me! the Lord forgive me!"

His wife and he had spoken apart from his companions; now he turned slowly away even from her, walked round the pile of turf to a side of it where he could remain unseen, leaned an arm against it, and drooped his head; wept and sobbed, but not loudly; wrung his hands; and, as his thoughts and feelings rose fully upon him, even shivered; then he knelt, prayed, took his final resolution, and wiping the tears from his cheeks, returned to his wife, sat down by her side, drew her to his bosom, kissed her, and spoke again.

"It's now nigh hand to three years since we were married, Anty?" She assented.

"An' few poor couples, I believe, far and wide, has lived happier together, during that time, *ma-colleen*." – Her confirmation of this fact was given fondly and eagerly.

"This much I'll say of you, Anty: God never gave a betther wife to man, than you have made to me – an' I'm ready to say the same words wid my dyin' breath; an' did *I* make a bad husband to *you?*"

"What's the use in askin' me that question, Martin *a-graw*? Could I love you as I do, an' you know as I do, if you ever gave me rason to think such a thing?"

"But aint I givin' you rason for it now, Anty?"

"How, Martin, *ma-bouchalleen?*

"Aint I the cause o' your sittin' here this mornin', without house or home, Anty, an' without a hope for the to-morrow in this world? An' when I'm gone from your side – an' when you are left quite alone – you an' little Matty" –

"Me an' little Matty!" she interrupted; "left alone! how? an' where ud you be goin' from either of us? – What do you mane, Martin Doyle? Arn't we goin' to the ship together – we three – an' this moment, if you like?"

"And lave my father's bare back to be cut into the bone, Anty, as you tould me?"

"And how can you help him, Martin?"

"And on my account – to save *me* – me his son – his undutiful son; is it my own *corra-ma-chree*, Anty Doran, that give such an advice?"

"Why, what other advice can she give you, Martin? Go to the ship, or stay away from the ship, how can you, I ask again, screen the poor old man from their hands! 'Tis a terrible an' a sore thing to think of, an' many's the salt tear it has taken out o' my eyes, comin' the road to see you here; but, over an' over I say – what can you do to hindher it?"

"Listen to me, Anty. My father is to be flogged – ould and sickly as he is – an' the best father to me, ever since I could climb his knee, and larn the Lord's Prayer from him, that ever a son had – my father, I say, is to be flogged this morning and flogged until he dies undher their lash, maybe – because he won't tell them where to lay hands on me. Isn't that true, *allanna?*"

"Well! an if it is?"

"An' I have the knowledge of all this – isn't that thrue, too?"

"Well, Martin, well."

"An' here I am, wid that knowledge on me, an' time enough to make use of it – no more nor half an hour's good run from the barrack-yard, where they'll tie him up – and do you think now, Anty, I ought to let them tie him up, when stanin' sthraight afore 'em, an' just sayin' – 'Here I am!' would save him?"

"Give *yourself* up, Martin!" she screamed – "give yourself up from your wife and child! O my God! – Sure, well you know it isn't the thriangle alone is ready for you, but the gallows-three – the black gallows, Martin!"

"Well, an' maybe I do know it, as you say, Anty."

"An' you'd go and daare it!"

"I would, Anty; I will, Anty; I must."

"Never!" she again screamed – "never while the world is a world!" – (she clasped him tightly) – "never, Martin, unless you cut the arms out o' my body, never will I untwist them from around you, to let you from me on such an errand! Oh, our boy, Martin, our little boy! look at him!" – Forgetting, in the breath that uttered it, her threat not to release Martin, she now snatched up Matty, first springing to her feet, and held him close to his father – "Look at him, Martin, *ma vourneen*! look at his blue eyes – your own blue eyes – an' his roses of cheeks – an' his curly yellow hair – och! the good God never gave the sun to shine upon a more lovely babby! There – yes – take him and kiss him – well I knew you would!" – Martin, also standing up, caught indeed the little fellow in his arms – "An' talk of lavin' him, indeed! lavin' him on the wide world without a father! – hush! what nonsense!" and she laughed hysterically through her tears.

"Here – take him back from me, Anty," (he held out the child to her with one hand, covering his eyes with the other,) "and take him quick – I can never do what I have to do, if I as much as look at him. And don't be cast down, Anty; there is a good God to watch over him and you, when I am gone; and the poor ould man that I will save for ye, he will be a father to ye both, and make up for my loss; and, in a few years, little Matty himself" –

"Bad man, bad husband, and bad father, and bad Christian, too! you can never mane what you say – you can never mane to" –

"Husth, Anty, husth – bad Christian I am not, I hope – in this matther at laste. He is my father, Anty – the earthly giver of my life – and am I to be his murtherer? Against his advice, and against his commands, I have made my own lot – and is he to screetch to death, still sthrivin' to save me from that lot, because I am coward enough to skulk and to be afeard of it? Is that what you want the world to tell our little boy, when he grows ould enough to undherstand it? Is – but, huth! what *rammansh* I'm talkin' – spendin' the precious time here, givin' rasons for going to do what no living man, that has man's blood in his heart, could think of argufying for one instant? and so, Anty – Anty *mavourneen*!" – He extended his arms.

"Martin, Martin!" (she flung herself on her knees at his feet, speaking rapidly and hoarsely,) "listen to one word from me. A rich, a blessed thought comes into my head – a blessed thought to save you both – the ould man and yourself. – Listen to me well, I say – if go you must; do *this*, when you are face to face with them; they know well you have secrets that they would give you your life for, if you only tould 'em out plump. – Well, Martin, promise them" –

"Turn informer, Anty? – he drew back from her, his brows knitted – "save my own life, by swearin' away the lives of a hundhred other men in a whisper?

– dhry up *your* tears, by earnin' the curses of a hundhred poor women like yourself? No, Anty; our son shall never grow up to hear said of him a worse saying than this – "There goes the child of the man who could have made many widows, but made only one." And while the young miller spoke these words, there was an air of true, lofty dignity about him. "And come now, Anty, the last kiss for you, and for little Matty" – he raised her, and again took her in his arms.

"Oh, I'm lost! I'm lost! I'm lost!" shrieked the poor wife and mother.

"An' you called me bad father and bad husband, a while ago, Anty? Oh! the merciful Lord that looks down in pity upon me, this moment, knows that I am not; he knows that there never breathed a Christian crature than loved wife and child in the very veins of his heart, with it betther that I do! – ay, an' you know it yourself, *a-lanna,* and you just said them words without thinkin' – certain sure I am that you did. Here, then, *a-lanna* – here is the last kiss entirely for yez both – an' may God look down on ye both!" – he knelt – "and be a husband and a father to the widow and the orphan!"

"No; Martin Doyle! No, no! stir from us you shan't!" She clung to his limbs as he arose. "Matty, child, stay here by me and kneel too. Let him deny our prayers together, and let him kick us away together, while we are praying up to him, if he can! O Martin, *ma-bouchal* , life is sweet to man! – and the ship is on the sey for us, Martin, an' waitin' for us."

"Yes, yes, Anty, and the thriangle is put up for my father, if the lash is not already on his back! Hushth! I think I hear the sound of it, an' see the marks of it on his flesh! an' the ould blood that gave me life sthraming like wather! and his screeches, they are wringing in my skull. Let me go – let me go – let me go – or – Ah, poor crature! she can't hold me. Now, and now is the time to quit her. Here, Micky Glennan; come here with your crony." The men drew near to him. "Here, take Anty from my hand – kindly, kindly – the faint is on her, poor soul! Lay her down where she can come to herself, quiet; and, when she opens her eyes, tell her I kissed her again, afore I left her for ever; and our *gorsoon* too, our *gorsoon* too!" With streaming eyes and broken voice, he embraced, indeed, his insensible wife and his unconscious infant many times; then, before his friends could obtain a word of explanation from him, bounded like a chased stag across the bog.

Little Martin had erred in thinking that the place of his father's punishment was to be the yard of the barracks of the town, towards which he raced. In about the middle of the main street, and where it was spacious, stood the jail surmounted by the court-house, the united buildings falling back some distance from the line of ordinary houses at either side, and allowing an open space for them. On one side of this space, upon the morning we are speaking of, stood a triangle, on the other, a gallows. A line of soldiers were drawn up before both, and within their line appeared some officers grouped with loyal citizens of distinction; and without it, in the street, a crowd of the common people, of whom the countenances of some evinced compassion for what was going on at the triangle or at the gallows; while those of others grew pale in terror on their own account, perhaps a few among them looked on with scowls of indignation, or of longing vengeance. For, as we pause before this remarkable spot, neither the triangle nor the gallows is idle; nor, indeed, have they been so during the whole morning; for, above, in the court-house, sits an almost permanent court-martial, which can quite conveniently send off to the noose or the lash, as the case may require, without much loss of time, a convicted "Defender."

73

Two peasants descend together, well guarded from the court-house, the flight of steps which lead most immediately to the more important piece of mechanism erected for the fulfilment of the edicts of martial law; they had come in from the country tied on a common cart about half an hour before. They stand on two ladders under the gallows. In a twinkling, the steady swinging ropes are adjusted round their necks, and hand in hand, they direct their eyes amid the low wailings of the crowd, whose looks are fixed in the same direction, towards an open window in a house of the street immediately opposite the jail. At that open window appears a man stricken in years, wearing a portion of an ecclesiastical dress; his features seemed troubled, his eyes are red, his lips move in a murmured prayer, he extends his arms toward the doomed men – at a distance of perhaps forty yards; the rebels' eyes catch his, and their lips also move rapidly, and the next instant they are turned off the ladders. This circumstance asks a word of explanation. It was not, during this season of excitement, the etiquette always to allow rebels to be attended, in their last moments, by a clergyman of their own persuasion; an old priest endeavoured, as well as he could, to remedy the deficiency; he craved, and obtained permission of a friend to stand at a window in his house, conveniently facing the jail, as the sufferers were led forth to be hanged; they had previously got a whisper of his intention; when he extended his arms, they knew they were to join him in prayer, and they did so; and thus martial law became half-cheated of a portion of the full measure of its awarded punishment.

The bodies of the two peasants had not yet done struggling, when another man was guarded down from the court-house; but, as he was only on his way to the triangle the gallows did not require to be cleared for his accommodation. We have lately spoken of a little tailor, upon whose endurance of the lash, with a good many lives at stake, young Martin Doyle placed a very slender reliance; and this was another little tailor, and now in precisely the same position that Micky Glennan must have held, had his Majesty's troops succeeded in catching him the previous evening. But very different were the minds and hearts of the two little men. The individual before us was known to be possessed of information which, if fully imparted, would lay bare the whole conspiracy of Defenderism in the district; and, in order to argue him into confession, he had received five hundred lashes a few days before, but without effect. Upon this morning, having been again confronted with his judges, he was still contumacious; and he is now marched down from them to be tied up again; and he is tied up again; and, with scarce a loud cry, he undergoes five hundred lashes more, only praying for a drop of water, which is denied him. We will give a sentence more to this obstinate little fellow. Strange to say, he did not die under the lash; and, what is quite as strange, having been found proof against the triangle, he was not turned over to the gallows; for we saw him alive and well, twenty years at least after the year 1797; nay, and, with a great concourse of other people, of all political parties, we attended at his funeral; and his name was and is invested with heroism among the humble classes of his native place. We subjoin it for the curious in those matters – Dooly. Had he been a citizen of an older town, old Rome, and had he thus borne to be tortured in one of the streets of old Carthage, what would classic history now say of him!

The people knew that little Dooly had been flogged a few days before – indeed, had they been ignorant of the fact, his unhealed back might now have proclaimed it – and they therefore looked on at his present punishment with feelings of great commiseration; groans and lamentations – which called forth frowning glances of reprehension from the loyal gentlemen, civil and military, standing near the triangle – often escaping them. Now and then the flogger would be commanded to desist for a moment in order that some authorized person might reiterate to Dooly the prudent recommendation to save his back by turning informer; and when the stubborn little Defender only gave his invariable answer of – "Let me die asy – let me die asy, in the name of God;" – and when, in consequence of his pertinacity, the big-drummer's lash again descended upon his puny carcass with redoubled vigour, the cries of the spectators outside the line of soldiers, became quite too loud for the ears of loyalty. One man amongst them, in particular, aroused the angry notice of his superiors. He was taller by a head than any of his neighbours in the crowd; he had arrived hastily amongst them, running at his utmost speed; he was greatly agitated, though he seemed to make efforts to stand quietly and observantly; he was without waistcoat, coat or hat, and dripping with wet and covered with mire; and this person it was who, as Dooly silently cringed under a good blow, dared to call out – "Huth! can't ye hang the poor crature, to put him out o' pain? Ay! sthring him up at once, if there's a man's heart among ye!" – upon which he was sternly commanded to stand back and hold his tongue, at the risk of being dragged from where he was, and thrust into the jail.

"Huth! huth!" laughed the offender, "ye would not let me stir out of where I am, for a hatful o' goold this mornin'; stir out of it to go backwards, I mane."

A new incident appealed to the sympathies of the lookers on. When Dooly had nearly received his day's punishment, a second candidate for the triangle was led down the court-house steps. His appearance called forth a burst of lament from the crowd; and – "God of glory!" cried the man who had before spoken, while his eyes stared, and his teeth set hard. The rebel now to be flogged was tall, old, white-haired, and stooping from feebleness. His bleared blue eyes wandered vaguely around – his white lips moved rapidly – his hands were clasped. His guards stationed him behind Dooly, at a point from which, for his edification and the King's expected advantage, he might fully observe what was in store for himself, under a certain proviso. The moment they allowed him to stand still, the old man fell on his knees, fixing his roving eyes, as it was hoped he would have done, on Dooly's back; then clasping his hands tighter, and glancing upwards for a moment, his lips moved more quickly than before.

Dooly was taken down from the triangle, and borne, fainting, between two soldiers, into the jail. A fresh big-drummer, wielding a fresh instrument of torture, approached the kneeling old man, slapped him on the shoulder, and cried, "Strip!" The official was a black, of unlovely aspect, and his own shining, sooty, muscular arms and body were bared for his proposed task.

"Yes, Doyle, strip!" repeated another official, a gentleman of the civil corps; "or else change your mind, and give the information demanded of you."

"Yis, avich, yis – yis, your honour, yis!" answered old Martin Doyle, rising with difficulty. "Sthrip I will by all manes; only I'd ask again what I asked above in the court-house – couldn't I see aforehand, young Masther Insign Abercromby, for the love of God?"

The gentleman who had addressed him exchanged smiles with the friends around him, and all shrugged their shoulders; the big black imitated them, and the former spokesman resumed.

"You positively refuse, then, to declare your knowledge of where Martin Doyle, the younger, may at present be found?"

"Avoch," was the old man's reply.

"In that case, go on," said a sergeant of yeomanry who had accompanied him down to the court-house, nodding to the black.

"Come, old chap," commanded that important individual, tearing open the buttons of the old miller's white coat.

"Here, then, in the name o' God!" said old Martin, beginning to undress.

"Stand back, there!" roared a sentinel, who confronted the crowd outside the line of the soldiers – "Stand back, or I will run my bayonet through you!"

"Huth, man alive!" cried little Martin in reply, his voice good-naturedly toned, though, as will be seen, his actions proved none of the gentlest. "Huth, man alive! stand back yourself. I don't mane to hurt you, but I'm wantin' inside, there." He kicked up the musket; wrestled it with little effort from the sentinel's grasp; twirled him aside among the people; pitched it forward into the space before the jail, where it rang sharply on the pavement; pushed through the soldiers before him, with perfectly erect figure, and quiet, though prodigious strides; gained his father's side; put his arms round him; extended widely his gigantic limbs; and said, in a mild but firm voice – "Nobody is to touch this ould man; nobody has a need to touch him; nobody has a right to touch him; – all ye want of him is to make him tell where his son is to be found, and I can tell ye without botherin *him;* he is to be found here – here where *I* stand. I am his son; I am the Martin Doyle that ye called the younger just now; so tie *me* up; lash *me* as long as it plases ye, and hang me up aftherwards; but this ould man is to go his ways in pace."

Every one looked on in astonishment and silence – that is, everyone inside the soldiers; but the people in the street allowed to escape them great cries of pity and admiration; and so engaged were the feelings of all, that a burst of the music of a band, a few streets off, and the arrival, outside the military line, of a superior officer on horseback, attended by other mounted officers, remained for a short time unheeded.

"Is id you, Martin, avich?" cried old Doyle, hoarsely gazing wildly into his son's face. "Och, an' what ill luck sent you here? Go home again, little Martin," he continued, whispering incoherently. "Go home again to your wife an' child, in the ould mill. Go home, or they'll lay hands on you here, an' hang you. Go, an' never fear me. I won't tell; an' don't be throubled about what they can do to an ould man like me. I'm no difendher, an' so my life they can't take; an', as for anything else, why it's asy to bear id, avich. Sure a father ought to bear something for this own son – ay, an' for that son's son again; so go home, I bid you, I lay my commands on you to go home; or even, if it 'ill be too hard for me to bear" –

"Put on your coat, father dear," interrupted little Martin, kissing the old man, while his own voice broke. "Ye will let me help him, gentlemen?" turning with a smile to the authorities around – "ay, ye will, I know. Men are men to each other, afther all. There, father now you're fit for the road, and God speed you on it, an' do what you can to comfort poor Anty, father. An, now, gentlemen, here's my hands and arms for ye – tie them, and tie me, too, either there or there," pointing alternately to the gallows and to the triangle – "either there or there, which ever ye choose, as I said afore. I am ready for the one or the other."

"You must go up to the court-house first," said the person who had previously spoken; "but, stop a moment, men," as soldiers approached him, "here's the general after returning from inspection. Right about face! present arms!" he continued to the soldiers who enclosed the space before the jail, and they, obeying his orders, presented arms to the superior officer before alluded to, who still kept his horse stationary in the middle of the crowd in the street, earnestly watching from his saddle the scene between Martin Doyle and his father, while the troops which he had been inspecting in the vicinity of the town, came nearer to the court-house, their band playing loudly and gaily. As all eyes fixed on General Abercromby, many voices whispering his name, little Martin recognised the features of the stranger who had conversed with him and his father, the evening before, upon the river's side. The old miller, half-aroused into a confused perception of the same kind, and acting wildly upon it, cast himself on his knees where he stood, clasped his hands, and hoarsely shrieked –

"Mercy upon him, your Honour! Mercy upon ould Martin Doyle's only son, Masther Ensign Abercromby, my darlin'! "

The white haired general hastily turned his moist eyes from the pair, beckoned to an officer near the triangle, who hastened to attend him, and after some private conversation with this individual, rode away. Father and son looked as hopeless as ever, when a guard separated them, and led the latter into the jail. He was never led up to the court-house, however. In a few minutes afterwards, a servant in a rich livery came through the crowd to the old man, and after whispering him to an effect that brought light-of-joy tears into his old eyes, conducted him away from the triangle.

"I have often been obliged to curb my private feelings, Martin," said Abercromby to him, when, almost immediately upon this, he and his old fellow cross-fisher spoke together in a private room at the General's quarters, "but, perhaps, never with so much pain to myself as a while ago when I could not shake hands with you at once, down there at the jail; now, however, be of good cheer. I cannot, indeed, in these disturbed times, get Little Martin back again for you all at once; but they shall not hang him outright; and something he does deserve to suffer."

In less than two years after this day, there was a new mill built on the river's side; and, on a fine evening, old Martin might be seen fishing, as earnestly as ever, under the old ash tree; while little Matty prattled to him; Little Martin sang merrily with the hopper, and Anty was getting supper ready for the whole family.

The Rebel Chief: A Scene in the Wicklow Mountains, 1803 (1840)

"Well, sir; are you still disposed to proceed on the secret service which you volunteered?"

(This question was put by the late Colonel A – 'adjutant-general in Ireland at the period above stated, to a lieutenant of the – regiment, then on Dublin duty, who attended for the great man's orders.)

"I am ready, sir, at any moment, to proceed on my hazardous mission," respectfully answered the lieutenant, "but, considering the risks of such a service, I trust it may not be deemed unreasonable in me to request some pledge or guarantee from government, for the fulfilment of the terms on which I venture to undertake it – namely, promotion, and the promised reward, for the death or apprehension of the Rebel Chief; or, in the event of loss of life, a competent provision for my family."

The cold and cautious A – attempted to parry off any direct pledge on the part of government, not from any sinister views, but solely from official jealousy, which fired at the base idea of an inferior officer, presuming to dictate terms. He suggested to the subaltern, "whether he did not risk the favour of Government by doubting the strict performance of any promise made by it?"

"With the utmost deference, colonel," replied the subaltern, "to you and the government, I beg to refer to the case of the officer who lost his life on a similar service some months back, on the failure of his attempt, but with-out the slightest reproach on his courage or discretion; and whose widow is now dependent on the precarious charity of the benevolent – all parties in the state shifting the blame from themselves. The treasury required the vice-regal order to pay the compensation promised:– the lord-lieutenant, humanely disposed to yield, referred the claim for the recommendation of the commander of the forces; but that distinguished officer (who has assumed the command since the transaction occurred, and knows not the critical circumstances under which the deceased officer undertook this critical service) sets his face against it altogether, as offering a precedent for officers stipulating for personal reward for services which it is only their duty to perform. Thus, for a point of etiquette between public departments, the compensation to this hour remains in arrears. With this picture before me, sir, I trust you will deem me excusable in requiring some specific pledge, if merely an official letter, which would leave my mind at ease with respect to my family, whatever fate awaited me."

A frown on the brow of the man of office, and a cold bow of dismissal, with orders to await further instructions, sent the poor subaltern away in no very enviable mood.

The capture or death of Holt, the Rebel Chief of the Wicklow Mountains, had long been an object of deep anxiety with the Irish government. This extraordinary man, of whom little was previously known, save that he had been a farmer in comfortable circumstances, took the field in 1798, as chief of a formidable body of rebels; over whom he held a separate and uncontrolled command. Participating in the short-lived triumphs which the early successes of the insurgent army afforded, he subsequently shared in its defeat; but, being a man of uncommon vigour of body, great mental resources, and a master of that kind of vulgar oratory and persuasive address which is so effectual with the Irish, he succeeded in attaching to his green standard, under all his reverses, a tolerably large force of those desperate outlaws, the scattered remnants of the late formidable rebel army. With these he withdrew, at the close of the above year, to the fastnesses of the Wicklow Mountains, the wild scene of his nativity; with every glen and valley of which he had been familiarized from infancy. Within the mazes of this untravelled region, Holt found means to elude all the efforts of military skill and enterprise, to seize him by force or ensnare him by stratagem. The utmost ingenuity was exercised to mislead and harass the king's troops in this mountain warfare. The rapidity of the rebel's movements, and his apparent ubiquity, baffled all the plans of the professional soldier: military science was put to shame by the superior tactics of the mountain chieftain. In this manner he held all the powers of Government at defiance for upwards of four years.

On the breaking out of the ill-concerted and feeble insurrection of 1803, Holt once more descended from the mountains, in all his former terrors, to join a large body of rebels from the adjacent counties of Kildare, Wexford, and Meath, which, to the number of ten or twelve thousand, were to rendezvous in the vicinity of Dublin, and be ready to pour in their force in aid of the metropolitan outbreak, on a given signal. Holt had actually advanced, on the evening of the 23rd July, so near the scene of action as Rathfornham, (a village only a league from Dublin,) when his progress was suspended by the intelligence of the defeat and dispassion of the disorganized mass which attacked Dublin; and which, although contemptible in numbers and array, and without any known or ostensible leaders, took the government so much by surprise, that their precipitancy alone averted the most lamentable mischief.

Had such a man as Holt been at their head, there can be little doubt that the Lord Lieutenant and the officers of the State would have become the prize of this desperate attack; but in vain the rebels looked for a leader. They stood a volley from the infantry, and a charge from the cavalry, with desperate resolution; but, unled and unsupported, they fled in all directions through the numerous streets and alleys; and under cover of the falling twilight, escaped with comparatively small loss. The fate of this body decided Holt's movements. He saw the chance was lost by the rashness of this premature attack – and withdrawing his own followers from their allies of the hour, he made an instant retrograde movement, anticipating that every effort would be made to cut off his retreat to the mountains. His march was unceasingly pursued while the darkness of night afforded him an escape from observation; and the morning's light saw him and his band of followers safe within their old positions, unbroken in numbers, and unsubdued in spirit.

Holt, once more secure within his chain of posts, unknown and inaccessible to all except the experienced mountaineer, defied all the powers of the executive. Various expeditions were undertaken to bring him to action; but not one met with even partial success. His superior knowledge of the scene of warfare enabled him to anticipate and defeat every movement of the troops. His scouts were numerous and faithful; nothing in the garb of soldier or stranger could enter the mountain district without Holt being immediately apprized of the circumstance. Itinerant beggars, sham cripples, even children, were on the look-out to guard his haunts, and make some signal on the approach of danger. His depredations were confined to midnight attacks on the small parties of troops scattered along the extensive line of military roads which had for some years been in progress through the mountains. In the course of one night, his parties had been known to sweep away all vestiges of the labour of weeks – plunder the provision magazines – demolish the guard-houses – disperse and drive in the piquets, pursuing them, pike in hand, to the very gates of their stockaded barracks – then disappear, as if by magic, before the morning's dawn, leaving neither trace nor clew to their mountain retreat; while, on the very next night, a similar and equally rigorous attack would be made on a post thirty miles distant. "HOLT," the Rebel Chief, was at once a word of terror and reproach. Five hundred guineas of reward were offered by the government for his apprehension; yet, amongst the shoeless, ragged, half-starved outlaws he commanded, not one could be found to betray his chief!

The Officer whom we have introduced to the reader, as a volunteer for this dangerous enterprise, was a young Scotchman, of the humblest fortunes. He had served in Holland and in Egypt with much credit; and was esteemed by his corps as a man of distinguished courage, fortitude, and perservance. With a young wife and two children to support on his humble pay, his enjoyments, it may be supposed, were but few. Life he held at nought, except for the sake of his family, to whom he was fondly attached, and for whose benefit he volunteered this present hazard. The excellence of his character in his regiment gained for him favourable consideration at head-quarters; and the pledge he so earnestly requested having been unreservedly given, he prepared for his departure with his characteristic zeal and alacrity.

Whatever plans he might originally have contemplated to effect his purpose, they were forced to yield to one arranged by a conclave of Official dignitaries, before whom he appeared to receive his instructions. He was directed to select a non-commissioned Officer, and twenty of the most active, intelligent, and trustworthy men from his own regiment, to accompany him as the expeditionary force. The soldiers were to be disguised in the uniform of the drivers of the commissariat waggon train, himself wearing that of a sergeant-conductor of that corps. Thus equipped, the whole were to be incorporated, and march with a detachment of the commissariat train conveying the monthly supply of provisions and stores to the several depots established in the new line of road in the mountains, (in the progress of which the Officer was to collect all the information he could obtain of the Rebel Chief and his parties.) This duty performed, the whole party were directed to take the short route across the mountain, on their return towards Dublin; on which track it was supposed they might fall in with some of the parties of the Rebel Chief, and, by possibility, himself. – This *ruse* was suggested, it was said, by the then commissary-generals as a bait for the rebels – several small bodies of whom had, on former occasions, intercepted detachments of the waggon train on this route; and to whom they offered no molestation, (that corps being an unarmed body,) except a rigid examination for concealed arms or ammunition. Several of the drivers attached to the present expedition alleged that, on some of these former occasions they had seen the *General;* but subsequent events proved that his precautions to conceal or disguise himself were so effectual, that, of the various descriptions published of his personal appearance, and equipment, not one was found to be correct.

Plunder, beyond the means of subsistence for his daily diminishing force, no longer appeared to be the object of the Rebel Chief, whose hopes of a successful rising had all been abandoned when he learned of the capture and execution of that ill-fated youth Robert Emmett; and as a last resource he contemplated an escape to America; previously to which, he sought to reduce his followers, and eventually disband them as opportunities offered for their return to their distant homes with safety. They had stuck by him though all the vicissitudes of his fortune, and he determined to share their perils until he alone was left to encounter the last danger. This state of the Rebel Chief's affairs was in part known to the government, and it was imagined he might be captured by a *coup de main* in some unguarded moments of fancied security: such was the object of the present expedition.

The convoy marched from Dublin, about forty strong, including the military whose arms were concealed on the carriages. After a march of four days, during which the whole line of posts were supplied, the party proceeded on their return with the empty cars, taking (as previously arranged) the old mountain track – a road so little used, since the year 1798, as to be scarcely distinguishable from the naked face of the barren mountain. On leaving behind them the last military post, the party halted at noon to water and feed the cattle, forming a bivouac beside a mountain stream. The lieutenant took that opportunity of distributing the arms and ammunition, and giving his final instructions. Each soldier was directed to seat himself beside a musket on a car, to be ready for instant action, but on no account to make any display of the arms until the moment for using them arrived.

An idiot boy, (who either was, or assumed to be dumb) in a state of destitution, had attached him to the party the first day it entered the mountains; and who, for the reward of a biscuit, and fragments of the men's rations, had rendered service by fetching water, and cutting heather, for cooking, on the three preceding days' marches. Of this wretched object no suspicions whatever were entertained; but his sudden disappearance, during this short halt – no one could tell how or where – raised a momentary alarm; and although it was accounted for, by some, as the boy's terror at the sight of fire-arms, the lieutenant could not divest himself of the suspicion of treachery, and therefore drew together his party in as compact a body as the long line of cars admitted, enjoined the strictest silence, and concealment of the arms. The party proceeded unmolested, and apparently unobserved, for two or three hours, gradually surmounting a long range of hills, which they had been ascending since morning; when on rounding a projecting knoll which lay in their route, the ears of the lieutenant, who had ridden a few yards in front, were saluted with the whizz of a ball, which passed within a few inches of his head. The order – "*Halt! stand by your arms!*" brought in an instant twenty fine light-infantry men into rank, and ready for action. As yet, however, no enemy appeared – The party then cautiously advanced, until, having left the knoll a couple of hundred yards in the rear, the lieutenant halted and prepared for action. Feeling satisfied that they were in the presence of an unseen foe, he made a keen reconnaissance of the position, and more particularly of that part over which the thin blue smoke of the lately discharged fire-arms still lightly floated. Orders were given to the sergeant of the drivers' corps to form his cars in a hollow square, into which the party might retire and sustain the battle, in the event of an attack from superior numbers. This precaution taken, the officer dismounted, and armed with his double-barrelled gun, proceeded to take a nearer view of the localities of his ground. In front, and about a mile distant, was the towering summit of the Ram's Head; beneath the craggy base of which stupendous cliff, lay their scarcely discernible route: on the right, an open and partly broken range of sterile mountains for many miles, extended towards Blessington: between which and their present position, and not above three miles distant, a small military party was stationed during the day. The left presented the rough and tangled side of the mountain, sweeping with a continuous descent as far as they could reach into the deep and lonely valley. The chief object in their rear was the knoll they had so lately passed, between which and the party nothing could approach unobserved. There was not a tree or shrub of sufficient size to form an ambuscade for any number of men within the whole range of his vision; but the lieutenant's ready eye saw that the low brakes of furze and tufts of fern, as well as the detached pieces of rock, which lay scattered about, afforded a secure shelter for a single lurking foe. The afternoon was overcast and sultry; that awful stillness, which is only to be found on the mountain or in the desert, reigned around, unbroken by a single sound from the lips of the well disciplined soldiers. Silence and the most intense anxiety prevailed for a quarter of an hour, without a move, without a whisper, when the lieutenant fancied he perceived a slight motion in a brake of furze about fifty yards on his left. He stealthily approached the spot, with a keen and fixed gaze, when his suspicions were confirmed by seeing a human face cautiously rise from the furze, and, after casting a wary look upon him, again bury itself in the brake. He had just time to send a bullet in that direction, when he beheld the idiot boy rolling and scrambling down the slanting mountain side, as he conceived, wounded; he soon, however, sprang to his feet bounding off like a deer, and, before the lieutenant could discharge his other barrel, his figure disappeared, as if the earth had opened to receive him. With greater caution the officer rushed forward to secure the traitor, shouting to the sergeant to send a file of men to his aid; but just at that moment a body of rebels, to the number of fifty or upwards, sprung up from every brake and tuft, like tigers from their lair, roused by the lieutenant's fire, and commenced their attack on the party with a fury, sufficient to appall more gallant hearts. Their assault was met by a steady volley, which checked their advance, and sent some of the assailants, writhing in agony, down the mountain's side. Nor was the rebels' volley ineffectual. Three soldiers fell wounded by the first discharge; after which several attempts were made to storm the position into which the soldiers had taken shelter, but each attack was met with vigour. But it was not in human nature to hold out much longer; the insurgents were gaining ground each moment; every effort which skill and courage suggested was made, but the odds were overwhelming. At this awful moment, the distant cheer of friendly voices (so different from the rebels' wild "Hurra!") broke on their ears, and revived their sinking but unsubdued hearts. In another minute, on came a party of fresh troops, headed by an officer, at a running pace, whose appearance soon turned the tide of babble. A few bullets were sent after the fugitives, but with what effect could not be known.

The former position regained, the drivers, the horses, and carriages, were found uninjured. The rebels had disappeared at the same time with the troops, and no fresh party had approached. Having, in their united parties, thirty effective men, the officer directed his attention to a search for the missing lieutenant – a task which the sergeant, with half-a-dozen of his own men, anxiously undertook; but, after an hour's absence, they returned unsuccessful; and, to add to their fears for their officer's safety, the two drivers, who had been sent in pursuit of him during the action, returned about dusk, exhausted with fatigue, and in utter despair at what all now considered the certain loss of the gallant lieutenant. They had traversed miles in various directions without seeing a human being, or any trace of footsteps save in the immediate vicinity of the position; and also the impress of the bodies of the rebels in the clumps of furze and fern. It was evident that they had withdrawn from that side of the mountain for the present. The wounded soldiers were dispatched, on a car, to the nearest military post, for surgical aid, and with a demand for a reinforcement. The united party made their arrangements to bivouac for the night in their present position, placing sentinels at all points, and lighting a fire to attract the attention of the absent lieutenant, should he still linger in their vicinity.

We must now return to the luckless adventurer whom we left in full chase of the idiot boy, and whose sudden disappearance so astonished his pursuer. In the ardour of his pursuit, and with eyes intently fixed on the spot where the boy had so unaccountably vanished, the lieutenant fell headlong into a narrow but deep ravine, or mountain gully, with a grassy bottom, the edges of which were so thickly fringed with a border of luxuriant fern, as to be almost entirely concealed. In a few moments he saw himself surrounded by a small party of the insurgents, and being hemmed in by at least a dozen of pikes, was compelled to surrender. He was then seized, disarmed, and hurried, or rather dragged away, he knew not whither, by four of the party; and, after a harassing march, or rather run of two or three miles, within the mazes of the trackless mountain, the prisoner and his escort descended into a wild and savage glen, which presented no other token of human habitation save a faint stream of dusky smoke, which stole along the heather, scarcely rising above its surface, as it issued from a low heath-covered hovel, towards which the lieutenant was conducted by his guard. After challenging those within, in the Irish language, and receiving their answer, one of the escort proceeded to blindfold his prisoner, by tying his handkerchief over his eyes. The first and most natural suspicion in the poor lieutenant's mind was that his last moments in this mortal life had arrived; and he prepared to meet his fate in uncomplaining silence; but after the lapse of a few minutes, the bandage was removed; the party who had been within the hovel on his arrival, having, as he presumed, retired during his temporary darkness. He was led inside. The floor of this wretched hut was some feet below the level of the surrounding turf, and had evidently been hollowed out to form a cavern of retreat. Here he was deprived of his watch, money, pocket-book and his instructions from head-quarters: and it was intimated to him, that no further removal was intended until they received the *General's* orders. The poor prisoner, with a heart overwhelmed by grief and disappointment, gave way to the most poignant feelings of self-reproach, at his indiscretion in allowing himself to be betrayed to such a distance from his party. The thoughts of his own death, which he looked upon as the inevitable consequence of his capture, did not affect him with one-half the bitterness of sorrow which his reflections on his failure and disgrace brought to his agonized mind. The evening already lowered; the dark clouds rolled down the mountain's side in gloomy masses; the sun for a moment appeared, and, shedding the blood-red tinge of its departing rays on the peak of the lofty Sugar Loaf, sunk beneath the dark and distant hills. An awful gloom hung over the dreary scene! The lieutenant, overpowered by chagrin, and worn out by fatigue, sunk on his rude couch of fern and heather, to seek a brief repose, when his second hour's unsettled slumbers were disturbed by the tramp of many feet outside the hovel, and the piteous groans of some persons, whom he concluded to be the wounded of that day's action. One of the two men who had been left to guard him, repaired to the opening of the hut, and, after holding some converse with a party outside, whose tone (although in a language not understood by the lieutenant) seemed to imply command, the guard returned to the side of the rough bed of the captive, intimating, that the shelter of the hovel was required for some of their wounded comrades. Misery levels all distinctions! The poor lieutenant was preparing to resign his humble berth; but this the guard refused, and even, in respectful terms, expressed his concern at the inconvenience the officer would be exposed to in that miserable place. Four unhappy wretches, with gun-shot wounds, were borne in, and a rude litter of heather spread for their repose. But a night of horror ensued. Distant thunders rolled along the desolate range of mountains which surrounded their dismal glen, through which the moaning wind swept, in sad accordance with the piercing moans of the unfortunate unattended sufferers within this narrow prison. As the night advanced, the elements seemed to be engaged in horrid conflict; the awful peals of thunder following each other in rapid succession, united in wild reverberation, while the vivid lightning seemed to bestow permanent illumination on this contracted scene of human suffering and terror!

The night was one of unmitigated horror within the wretched hovel, and with the detachment on the distant mountain almost equally so. After a night of care and anxious watchfulness, their morning broke without tale or tidings of the respected and now lamented officer. The Dublin party proceeded on their march to head-quarters, with the painful conviction on their minds that their gallant lieutenant had fallen a victim to the savage vengeance of the rebel Holt.

When the first beams of the morning's light broke through the crevices of the hovel's roof, the lieutenant implored his guard to allow him to enjoy the invigorating air of the early morn, if only for a few minutes. His jaded senses required that relief; he had awoke from feverish dreams only to the keener reality of his error and misfortune. Great was his surprise and gratitude at finding his request complied with; and his guard was in the act of assisting him to rise, when some voice of authority suspended the movement, until the bandage was placed over his eyes: this done, he was led forth. Some person appeared to enter as he departed; and he fancied he heard a prayer, in the Latin tongue, uttered in a low tone of voice. By the time he had reached, according to his calculation, a dozen yards from the hovel's entrance, he was halted, as if for the inspection of some, to him invisible, spectator; after which an order was given, in a tone of authority, (but in the Irish language) which, after a few moments' preparation, set the captive and his guard once more on the march. More than half-an-hour elapsed, during which period they were constantly ascending, ere the bandage was removed from the eyes of the lieutenant, when he was invited to repose by the guard, which had been increased to *four*. He cast his eyes around, but sought in vain the scene of last night's horrors: all about him breathed peace and tranquillity. They had reached a verdant and sheltered spot, where the blooming heather, refreshed by the late rain, scented the air with its grateful perfume. The morning breeze, playing over his burning cheek, revived, with almost magical effect, his physical powers; while the painful certainty of his hopeless captivity, and probable execution, before that glorious sun which now rose in splendour over the glistening mountain-top should again set in darkness, weighed heavily on his heart. After a silent march of two or three hours, they gradually wound their footsteps down the mountain side, and at length reached a secluded valley, through which a narrow rivulet flowed. On the bank of this stream stood a solitary cabin, of rude formation, two sides being afforded by nature, in the projecting points of a moss-covered rock; the others by walls of mud and straw; the roof securely thatched with the rough produce of the soil. There was an air of security in this romantic spot, (which appeared to be shut out from human observation,) that rendered it a most fitting place of retreat. A few domesticated goats browsed about, undisturbed, in this peaceful little valley; all beyond and around which was wildness and desolation. As the party approached the cabin, three half-clad but robust children ran forth, as if to greet with their embraces some anxiously-expected visitors. The sight of these little ones kindled all the father's feelings in the heart of the poor captive; and when, on nearer approach, they accepted his proffered hands, he took the little savages one by one to his arms, while tears of fond recollection poured down his manly cheeks. The mother of these children, who appeared for a moment at the door of the cabin to answer the inquiry of one of the guard, beheld this affecting sight with all a mother's tenderness, and, retiring within the cabin, she returned in another minute with a large basin of milk and a piece of girdle-bread, which was respectfully presented to the lieutenant by one of the guards. Seated on the rivulet's bank, a short distance from the lowly dwelling, and surrounded by the children, he enjoyed in thankfulness his humble, and, as he imagined, his last repast. During this period of repose and refreshment, he perceived, as he thought, a degree of restless anxiety in the countenance of his guards, who had evidently expected to see some superior in that lonely valley. One of the two men who had kindly relieved his wants the night before ascended the mountain's brow, at the desire of the woman; but returned to express, as the lieutenant supposed, (for the conversation was carried on in Irish,) his disappointment. A long consultation took place, the woman apparently urging delay, in which she was seconded by the guard who had passed the night at the hut, while the two strangers who had that morning joined seemed much disinclined for any. The lieutenant heard the word *general* mentioned, as, on each occasion, one or other of the party looked up the mountain track. After a racking suspense of nearly an hour's duration, the guard moved slowly from the cabin, encircling their prisoner, who moved his hands in grateful thanks to the woman, as he cast his last look on her and the children. Leaving the rivulet's side, the party proceeded through the valley, which darkened to the view as the impending rocks rose in awful and abrupt masses on either side, screening from sight the noonday sun. Suspicious looks, and low whispers passed between the guards. The impatience of those who had that morning joined, and the undisguised reluctance of the others, to execute some important order, of which he was, of course, the object, left no doubt on the lieutenant's mind as to his approaching fate. Not more than a quarter of an hour had elapsed since they left the cabin, the direct distance from which could not have exceeded a furlong, when, after a brief altercation between his guards, one of those of the preceding night approached to his side, and, with evident emotion, announced that "their march had ended!" a sentence which struck on the ear of the captive as the signal for immediate death. His heart for a moment sank under the shock; the colour forsook his manly countenance as the thoughts of all most dear to him rushed on his distracted memory; he cast his eyes towards the blue unclouded heavens, which shone like a narrow streak of light above the horrid chasm, and on his knees resigned himself to silent prayer! With his face buried in his hands, he remained undisturbed for several minutes, and almost unconscious of existence, when he felt himself gently enfolded in the arms of some kind benevolent being. On opening his eyes, he beheld, kneeling beside him, a venerable-looking man, in soiled and faded black clothes, who, with all the fervency of the priestly profession, entreated him to accept the consolations of religion in these his last moments of life!

The guards, on the approach of the priest, had withdrawn to some short distance; but as the doomed one cast his bewildered glance around, he perceived one of them armed with his own double-barrelled gun. Hitherto he had anticipated a horrid and ignominious death by the pike or the halter: it was, therefore, a relief to the gallant soldier's mind to think (as appearances indicated) that he would at least meet a soldier's death. Even that thought brought its consolation. Grateful for the attentions of the reverend father, he felt all the difficulty of declining, without offence, his spiritual aid; but the kind pastor, availing himself of the privilege of this sacred office, to extend the respite between life and death to the latest possible moment, listening to those communications on his worldly affairs which the afflicted lieutenant thought fit to confide to him. He was requested to write to his wife (whom her devoted husband already considered a forlorn widow) all the circumstance of his capture, his sufferings, and ultimate fate. Then, taking a kind farewell of the deeply-affected priest, he declared to his approaching executioners his readiness to meet his fate. With trembling hands and palpitating heart, the good pastor took on himself the last sad office of placing the bandage over the eyes of the victim; and, with a fervent benediction and invocation to divine mercy, was about to hurry from the horrid scene, when the shriek of a female voice – the cries of "Stop! stop!" – the sound of fast approaching footsteps, fixed him to the spot. Standing, with uplifted arms and exposed breast, in front of the kneeling lieutenant, he suspended the execution. In another minute, the bandage was torn from the captive's eyes by that generous woman, who had so lately and kindly relieved his necessities. She was followed by a stern but care-worn looking man, in plain attire, but armed at all points, whose angry chiding could not for a moment arrest her humane purpose. After him crept the children, with fearful step; and when they saw their mother raise the drooping lieutenant from his kneeling posture, they instantly ran towards him, and renewed their caresses.

'O spare his life, husband of my heart!" cried the woman. "O father of my children! have mercy upon him! On my bare knees I ask it."

The poor children, seeing their mother on her knees, in the attitude of supplication, happily unconscious of the awful cause, knelt beside her; and, catching the infection of her tears, put their little hands, and cried aloud, "O father! father!"

The husband advanced towards his captive with haughty stride and scornful brow, while his quivering lip and moistened eye betrayed his better feelings.

"Look," said he, while his varied passions almost choked his utterance, "look upon that poor woman, now pleading on her knees for the life of him who came, under a mean disguise, into the last wretched retreat your cruel government has left us – our wild and desolate mountains, to destroy the life of her husband, her only support or protection on earth, and throw these poor innocents, destitute and despised, on a hard, unfeeling world! Behold the REBEL CHIEF – the proscribed, the hated HOLT, whose blood you were sworn to shed, now before you! These," pointing to the papers of which the lieutenant had been despoiled the previous day, "inform me of all your plans; and this proclamation shows for *what* you sought my blood. Oh!" added the

86

rebel, in a subdued and melancholy tone, "one-half of this reward would have transported me and mine to a far distant land of liberty; but nothing but my blood will satisfy your rulers. You see, sir," said the chief scornfully, "that we can yet defend ourselves."

The lieutenant would not condescend to offer a word in vindication of his share in the expedition; and, scorning to supplicate for life with such an enemy, he folded his arms, and coolly said, "I am in your power, chief – take your revenge!"

The peculiarly broad Scotch accent in which these words were uttered seemed
to startle the chief, who hastily called one of the guards to his side, who received from his chief some angry rebuke, and a command to order the others to fall back. Turning to the lieutenant he again addressed him, saying:–

"No, sir, your life is now safe; but had you been an *Irishman*, as your name implies, by Him who died for us on the cross, you should have been shot like a dog, and your bones left to bleach on the wildest crag of our naked mountain! As it is, your life is no longer in danger; thank that broken-hearted woman for the delay that saved it! She saw you caress her children; she felt that you were a father; and, for the sake of *that* father, who, God knows how soon, may stand in need of all their prayers, she pleaded for your life, and it is now granted."

The rebel chief then raised his still kneeling wife, and pressing her fondly to his heart; then, turning once more to the captive, said:

"You must be content to remain our prisoner, and share our mountain misery for a few days. The same men who have been your guards shall remain with you, as well to prevent escape as to protect you against the vengeance of others. The blood of five poor souls lies on your head, and those who sent you; but fear nothing from me."

Then, taking up a child in each arm, whom he alternately kissed, he strode away toward the solitary cabin, closely followed by his wife. The good priest, with tears of joy in his eyes, took an arm of the lieutenant in kind support, who on the other bore the youngest child of this ill-fated pair, whose little arm was entwined round his neck. In this order, followed by the guard, the whole party reached the miserable cabin, into an inner apartment of which the lieutenant was led; the interior, consisting of three comfortless chambers, presented a melancholy picture of that state of danger and privation to which this once respectable family had been reduced. Here, left to his reflections, the poor captive found leisure to contemplate his strange and anomalous situation. But, half-an-hour before, the doomed and detested enemy – now the pardoned and protected *guest* of the rebel chief! While pondering on the strange events of the last twenty-four hours, and still half-doubtful of his ultimate fate, one of the men left to guard him broke in on his reveries, to intimate that the priest was about to take his departure, and had obtained the chief's leave to receive the lieutenant's commands. The worthy man entered; and, having expressed his joy at the termination of the captive's late heavy trial, renewed his promise to write to the wife of the officer. But how to announce the glad tidings of his safety?

"My mission," said the priest, "into these wild scenes is now accomplished. I am permitted to communicate to your family your personal safety – more I know not. Led into these dreary regions in the darkness of the blind, even so must I return on quitting this valley. Miles must be traversed ere I gain my well-known road, and then the light of heaven will be restored to me. Though death and danger stand in our path, the ministers of our religion dare not deny the Christian's right whenever 'tis demanded, even to the guilty outlaw. Farewell, stranger! Your bidding shall be faithfully performed; and, oh, may the mercy of the rebel teach *your* heart the lesson of pity and forgiveness! Heaven prosper you!"

In a few minutes the noise of a horse's footsteps called the attention of the lieutenant, who, peeping from the single pane which formed the window of his prison, beheld the good pastor depart with bandaged eyes, taking the route up the mountain side by which he had himself that morning descended. The horse was led by one of the ragged crew, while another walked beside it, each armed with a pike and pistol. Exhausted by fatigue and anxiety, the prisoner sought that repose which his late sufferings demanded. – And here we must leave him – secure at least of life – to take a view of what was passing in the capital.

On the evening of that eventful day, the defeated party reached Dublin. The sergeant who took the command on the supposed massacre of his officer, was next day examined before a privy council, to whom he gave a circumstantial account of all their brief but calamitous expedition. Rendered furious by fresh defeat and disappointed vengeance, that sanguinary party, to whose dominion the destinies of unhappy Ireland had been too long committed, were loud in their demand for fresh sacrifices. All moderate measures, all intimations to concession and surrender were denounced, and vengeance was their cry! Alas! against whom? A poor unfortunate outcast, who scorned their power; but yet one whom a word of kind promise would have brought a voluntary captive within the castle gates. Blood had already been profusely shed – accursed martial law, with all its horrors, had contaminated and despoiled the land. Executions, attended with all the brutalising and disgusting butcheries consequent to a conviction for high treason – the *hangings, beheading,* and *embowelling,* (*literally* performed,) had stained and polluted every leading street of the metropolis. Yet there was ONE party unsated, whose cry was still "more blood?" A fresh expedition to the mountains, consisting of one thousand like troops, was recommended; a renewed proclamation issued, increasing the reward for Holt's body, dead or alive, to ONE THOUSAND GUINEAS!!! and a free pardon to his betrayer or assassin. These had scarcely been posted on the walls of the city, when intelligence reached the family of the lieutenant of his perfect safety, with the addition that he owed his life to the clemency of the generous Holt! The letter, written by the priest to the lieutenant's wife, appeared in all the papers; many of the proclamations were, in the course of that night, torn down or defaced, and songs and placards in praise of the brave Holt substituted. All this was wormwood to that odious party whose names will descend to posterity with merited exception.

The untalented, but merciful and humane Earl Hardwicke was the viceroy of that day; who, following the counsels of the British cabinet, had hitherto resigned himself to the guidance of the dominant party, but now called to his confidence and aid the few enlightened patriots who boldly withstood their country's degradation, and proudly maintained their independent station, untainted by bigotry, unsubdued by corruption, and unawed by those terrors which sent to exile or the grave so many of the friends of freedom and law. Under their advice, the plan of a general amnesty was drawn up, in order to be submitted to the British government, and one which would embrace the greater number of the deluded rebel party that yet remained in arms. This measure was, of course, warmly opposed by those whose trade was discord, who lived on the distractions of their common country; but was hailed by the more humane and politic as a coming blessing to the long-distracted nation. In the course of a week the lieutenant himself arrived at the head-quarters of his regiment, having been unconditionally released. He reported that, within the last few days of his captivity, an important change in his treatment had taken place; his gun had been restored to him together with his watch and other property; he had been allowed the range of the mountains, with only one man as his escort, and him, he considered more as a protector than a guard. The chieftain's band had been dissolved, and had retired by numbers each night to their different destinations: but few remained of the once powerful Holt's rebel party; and those apparently his own relations or dependants.

The chief himself disappeared for a few days; but, on his return to his lonely cabin, he hastily removed his family, and, within a few minutes from their departure, the humble fabric was consigned to the flames! Holt, seizing the arm of the lieutenant, and pointing to the blaze, exclaimed – "Behold, sir, the last poor shelter of the Rebel Chief is now destroyed! You are free! Your guard shall guide you within a short distance of a military post. We have now nothing to conceal; and you will travel with open eyes. – Farewell!"

The lieutenant expressed his sense of this generous conduct; and, taking the chieftain's hand, bestowed a grateful pressure, as he bade him farewell, wishing him happier days.

"One week more, sir," replied Holt, "and I shall be happier or in my grave!" Then, pressing the officer's hand, he hastily withdrew.

A few days subsequent to the lieutenant's return, an unusual bustle and whispering in the castle and its purlieus, indicated that some important event had occurred. The preparations for the march of the battalion of light infantry for the Wicklow Mountains, were all at once suspended: and, to add to the surprise of speculators, a regiment of Highlanders, which long occupied the position on the new line of road in that district, for defence of the works, was called in. The usual conjectures – a French fleet off Bantry Bay, or Loughswilly, or Galway, formed the gossip of the passing hour; but, in another day, the mystery was cleared up, by the public announcement, that the rebel general, Holt, was a prisoner in Dublin Castle!

The lovers of military law, and of the atrocities which that law sanctioned, were rejoicing in the prospect of another victim, when their hopes and expectations were suddenly checked, by a piece of intelligence, which set the "loyal" in a frenzy; no less than that Holt had made his peace with government, and was to be allowed to depart, himself and family, to the colonies, under his Majesty's pardon, and at the expense of the crown!

It was not until the lapse of some weeks that all the circumstances of the surrender of this extraordinary character became known; and, as they were of a romantic, and rather heroic description, the name of Holt obtained a degree of honourable celebrity for the while, which his former fortunes could not have promised; while they threw a veil of pity over his past errors.

On the dispersion of his followers, he collected from the various places of concealment in which they had for years been secreted, whatever remained of his once respectable property; and having released the officer, and restored those articles of which he had been deprived, he removed his family to some place of safety; then, assuming the plain dress of the ordinary farmers of that county, found means of eluding all the military posts and patrols during a rapid night march, and arrived in the suburbs of Dublin, unobserved and unknown.

Here, it would appear, he must have remained a day or two in secret, collecting such information as the newspapers afforded, or as his private friends in the city could convey. He learned of the safe arrival of the lieutenant, and saw the fresh proclamation for his apprehension or death, in which his person was (fortunately for him,) most inaccurately described; a copy of which he found no difficulty in obtaining. With that in his pocket, and a paper, written by a friend, in the name of Fitzpatrick, addressed to Mr. H – , a magistrate of the County of Wicklow, (and a gentleman holding a confidential office under the crown,) in which offers were made to give some important intelligence respecting the rebel Holt, he boldly rode off for that gentleman's residence, situated about fifteen miles from Dublin. This was a daring proceeding of Holt, in his native county too; but he had set his life upon the hazard.

Arriving at an early hour in the forenoon, he found, paraded in front of the mansion, the corps of yeomanry which the magistrate commanded, many of whom had been within the length of the rebel's pike in the hour of action; but before whose gaze the late formidable chief now quietly passed unheeded, to present his credentials to the servant in waiting.

In a few minutes he was summoned to the study of Mr. H – , whom he found at his table, amidst a mass of papers, the most prominent of which was the new proclamation. The chimney-rack was filled with arms of all description; and the captain's holster pistol, which he had just finished loading, lay beside him on the table. He eyed Holt with a scrutinizing glance as he entered, but could perceive nothing in his calm and quiet appearance to excite fear or suspicion; however, to show that he was not to be taken by surprise, he took up one of his pistols, as if examining the priming, remarking that, "in these times, it behoved every one to be on his guard; and now Mr. Fitzpartick, be seated." Holt drew his chair close to the magistrate's table, whose hand still rested on his pistol, and who thus continued – "You tell me in this letter that the person of Holt is known to you."

"Perfectly, sir, as well as my own brother's. I have known him from childhood," answered the rebel.

"Look, then, at this description," said the magistrate, offering the proclamation to Holt.

"I have one, sir," (unfolding that which he had brought from town,) "and certainly see some slight difference; but to me all descriptions are unnecessary; and, furthermore, sir, I can now give you a solemn assurance that I have the means of placing the rebel in *your* hands!"

"Then the reward shall, in that case, be yours; but why not have given information at the castle? when a sufficient force might have been sent with you to insure his capture."

"Force captain! ah, no! Holt can never be taken by force! You shall shortly know my reasons for making *you* the instrument of his capture; but for myself, it is not the temptation of the high reward that leads me to surrender him; for, O God! 'tis hard to give up a fellow-creature to an ignominious death, for the sake of paltry gold! to sacrifice a broken-hearted, and, perhaps, a penitent man and his innocent family, for the lucre of money; not a guinea of which could ever bring luck or grace on the betrayer. No, sir, there are higher and better motives for my appearance here – the peace and tranquillity of the country I love."

"Whatever are your motives, Mr. Fitzpatrick, I trust you do not mean to deceive or baffle us; if you do, sir, we have our remedy, you know. You should recollect that this rebel has been for years the terror of our country, the enemy of his King and his government."

"No, sir," suddenly exclaimed Holt, with an energy that rather startled the magistrate; "of the *government* – not of the *King*. It is my belief, that were the Lord Lieutenant to offer the poor man his life and liberty, he would withdraw for ever from the scene of his past crimes, and from the country in which he has now neither house nor home, friend nor protector."

"That may be your opinion, sir, but no terms will ever be made with the rebel until he is in the power of government; for what security could he offer for his compliance, even supposing that the Lord Lieutenant humanely consented to accept of his submission on these terms?"

"*His honour*, sir!" replied the rebel, with an emphasis which in an instant raised a feeling of suspicion in the magistrate's mind that he was conversing, if not with Holt himself, with some one of his band in the immediate confidence of the chief. He grasped his pistol, while he alternately glanced at the description given in proclamation and the form and features of his visitor; then fixing his full dark eye on the yet unmoved and firm countenance of the stranger, authoritatively demanded –

"And pray, sir, who are *you* that thus so confidently vouch for the honour of the rebel chief!"

"*Himself* ! – the unfortunate HOLT!"

The magistrate attempted to raise the pistol, on which his hand had for some time rested; but ere he could accomplish the movement, one was close to his head, in the firm grasp of the rebel's hand, who, in a tone of humility and supplication, cried –

"Easy, easy Captain! Your hand, sir, must not be soiled by my poor blood or, if it must be so, *we die together!* Hear me, sir. I promised to explain why I made *you* the instrument of the rebel's capture. You have been a blessing to our poor country under all its misfortunes, and often arrested the hand of the murderer from the throat of his unresisting victim. Unable to check the atrocities you hourly witnessed without compromising your own character for *loyalty* (that hackneyed cant-word of the tyrants of our island,) you have seen our poor houses in flames – our herds destroyed or plundered, our crops trampled upon – and ourselves hunted like wild beasts, by a brutal soldiery, or the still *more* savage native yeomanry, let loose upon us to drive us to that rebellion which the government itself provoked. You have seen all this; but *you*, sir, never wantonly oppressed us. Not a stick of your plantations, not a hair of your cattle, nor a sheaf of your crops, have ever been injured or plundered by me or mine. Whilst others were the firebrands to keep alive the flame of rebellion, you, sir, were always the peace-maker to mediate between the weak misguided rebel and the all-powerful government. To *you*, sir, I surrender myself! – do all you can to protect my poor wife and children, then dispose of me as you please."

Then, drawing from beneath his coat another pistol, he placed the muzzles of both towards his *own* breast, while he thrust them forward to the hands of the magistrate, saying, "*Now, sir, the Rebel Holt is your defenceless prisoner.*"

A thousand conflicting feelings agitated the breast of the magistrate, a man whose humanity was equal to his courage, (and both were unquestionable.) All that rancorous feeling which a few moments before he entertained towards the daring rebel gradually yielded to sentiments of pity for his misfortunes, and admiration at his magnanimity. Ardently did he long to save him; but there was

91

a bigoted council, and justly exasperated government, to be won over to the side of mercy. His chief hopes rested on the well-known humanity of the Lord Lieutenant. To see his Excellency – to make the *first* impression – was that great object of the magistrate's solicitude. A pledge once given by the humane Hardwicke would insure the safety of the rebel's life. His resolve was instantaneous. Ringing a bell, he ordered four horses for Dublin, without a moment's delay; and intimated to Holt the necessity for his being confined to the house till his return; assuring him that his name should not be divulged, and that no restraint, beyond confinement to the house, would be imposed on him. The officer next in command of the troops was called in, and informed that the *stranger* had made some important disclosures, and had still further communications to make to government, and must not be lost sight of for one instant; but no questions were to be asked or answered, except as to his personal wants, which the servants were ordered to attend to. With a mind oppressed by anxiety, but still not wholly divested of hope, the worthy magistrate set out for Dublin Castle; and in the course of a long and secret audience with the Lord Lieutenant and Chief Secretary, he rendered a full, and, of course, the most favourable account of his most extraordinary interview that morning with the Rebel Chief, concluding with the announcement of his unconditional submission to his Excellency's clemency. Pity, mercy, and sound policy prevailed over all narrow or vengeful feelings. The pledge *was* given; and Mr. H — that evening returned to his mansion, the joyful messenger of pardon and of peace.

Next morning, without any parade, or even an escort of troops, the magistrate conveyed Holt in his carriage to Dublin Castle, where, for safety, he was lodged in the apartments appropriate for State prisoners.

Every information which the grateful Holt could afford was given with fidelity, and with no ordinary show of talent, shrewdness, and good sense, during his several examinations before the Privy Council. He acted as guide to the band of general and engineer officers who proceeded to the Wicklow Mountains to examine the various positions in which the rebel chief for so many years had sustained himself. Passes through apparently unfathomable gulphs, (the mere existence of which rested but on traditional accounts) – by means of which communications were held with distant posts with a rapidity which baffled all professional calculation – were explored under his guidance. New lines of road, branching off from the great military way then in progress, were suggested and marked out by the intelligent Holt, as opening a ready access to the very heart of the mountain recesses. Those, and every other service he could render, were his peace offering and atonement for past offences, and an humble testimony of gratitude for royal clemency.

In another month the fallen chieftain, from the deck of the vessel which conveyed this wretched family to a far distant shore, cast a long and lingering look on the blue hills of romantic Wicklow, the scene of his triumph and of his sorrows; and, pressing to his bosom the faithful partner of his past perils and future fortunes, he bestowed a tear and a blessing on the country of his heart.

The Desmonds: A Tale of Landlordism in Ireland(1845)

"Mary, alanna, don't trouble yourself; 'twas a hard struggle, acushla; but 'tis over – and God forgive them that drove him to it," said an old crone, addressing her younger companion, as she leant over the dying embers of a turf fire strewed upon the hearth in one of those wretched huts so common in the south of Ireland.

The scene was a striking one. By the glimmering of a rushlight, stuck in a broken bottle, might be seen the two females, – the elder sitting on a low stool, with a short pipe in her mouth, and rocking her body to and fro, as she now and then gave utterance to a querulous lament; while the younger was kneeling at a settlebed, seemingly absorbed in prayer. And on that bed lay the corpse of a man who might perhaps have numbered some six-and-thirty summers, and who had once been eminently handsome; but his features were now horribly distorted – and a terrible mark around his neck showed that he had died a violent death. Yes, there, in that miserable hut, lay the remains of Gerald Desmond, the last of a time-honoured house, which had borne a distinguished part in Irish history.

Let us, however, recite the sad incidents of Gerald's history in due order. The revolutions of society and the confiscations which property had undergone, had gradually reduced the Desmonds to the class designated as "wealthy farmers;" and Gerald's father *rented* the land which his ancestors *owned*. However, he was, as the saying is, "a man well to do in the world;" and, the land never having been in *his* possession nor in that of his father, he was quite contented to have it at a moderate rate, so as that he could make his own out of it, which he did – and something to spare. At his death he bequeathed his interest in his farm to his elder son, Thomas; and to his younger son, Gerald, he left £700 in ready money. Gerald resided with his brother and mother at the farm; and for two or three years everything went on as smoothly as during the father's life time. But matters were soon destined to change; and the alarm of Thomas knew no bounds, when, on an application for a renewal of his father's lease, he met with a stern refusal. This blow was aggravated by the appearance one morning of a surveyor, who had been sent by the agent for the purpose of valuing the estate. Mr. Hill, the proprietor, was a wealthy commoner; but the circle to which he was introduced by a noble matrimonial alliance which he formed, and by the appearance and expenditure which it required, would have easily disposed of a greater revenue than that at his command. Year by year did he find his income narrowing; and year after year did he write to his agent to send him every penny he could screw from his unlucky tenants. The Desmonds's farm had long been looked on with a greedy eye both by landlord and agent:– it was let *too* cheap, – and many were the devices and plans proposed to foreclose the lease; but old Desmond was too prudent a man; – it would have taken a run of many bad seasons to put his affairs in disorder; – and then he was so punctual in paying his rent, that both master and man gave up the hope, during *his* lifetime at least of turning that portion of the estate to more value than it was worth.

Meanwhile the other tenants, who had the misfortune not to be in such independent circumstances as the Desmonds, were rack-rented to the last farthing. And now that old Desmond was dead, and that the lease had expired, an opportunity was afforded for the carrying out of the fatal system which unhappily prevails in Ireland. The farm was valued, and at the rent set upon it did Thomas receive it back, without even the security of a lease.

It was a hard bargain. With the funds at his disposal he could have easily obtained a better in the neighbourhood, – for many would have wished to have the Desmonds as tenants; – but the farm had been in his family so long, and was so associated with his earliest impressions, that he could not resolve to part with it.

But we have not as yet introduced our reader completely to Gerald – the quiet Gerald, who, from his amiable disposition, was naturally the pet of his mother.

He was now nineteen; and, as his only surviving parent would not part with him, nor allow him to follow any avocation, he was compelled to lead a life of dreamy indolence, wholly unacquainted with the desperate state of his brother's affairs. He spent most of his days in a wood, through which the sweet Blackwater rolled its silver tide; and there, stretched upon a bank, with book in hand, he was accustomed to sink in reveries until the approach of night drove him homewards.

He had lost himself one day in these musings, when his attention was aroused by the figure of a lovely girl near him. For a moment he did not know whether the being he beheld was not one of those happy spirits with which he had been peopling the Heavens. 'Twas Mary Neale – the daughter of rich Neale, the grazier – the pride of the village – the admiration of all the men, and the envy of the women; for she was handsome and withal an heiress. And there she stood before him in her loveliness – the very perfection of those charms which Gerald had dreamed as necessary to constitute his happiness. Her rich auburn tresses were slightly discomposed from the wind playing with them; and her face was flushed with excitement. One look was sufficient to explain the cause of her appearance:– she had been gathering wild flowers upon the bank of the river – and, in over-stretching, her light straw bonnet, which was unfastened on her head, had fallen in, and was now floating gently down the stream. She had followed its course, hoping that each succeeding wave would bear it within her reach. Gerald was not long in rescuing the prize from the covetous water; and he presented it to the delighted girl with so much modesty and taste that her fears were at once allayed. Offering to be her guide, he escorted her almost to her father's house, and felt grieved when she refused him permission to accompany her further, stating her intention of keeping the accident and rencontre a secret from her parents. He ought to have felt rejoiced; but, entirely unskilled in the female heart, he was not aware of the impression he had made upon an artless girl. Need we follow this portion of the tale further, or enter into the thoughts which agitated the breasts of our young friends? It will be sufficient to say that they met and loved; and that the wood had now more attractions than ever for Gerald. For there the youthful pair spent many a day! Hours of enjoyment glided over them, when the full heart, intoxicated with its own bliss, seeks happiness and finds it every where, – in the verdure of the trees – the murmur of the brook – or the warble of the feathered songsters.

It was after one of these delightful evenings spent in the society of his Mary, that Gerald stood in his chamber gazing at the distant wood, whose tops were silvered by the moon. His thoughts were not on the glorious scene which spread its witchery before him – they were with her who had on that day plighted to him her faith. What dreams of happiness did he not picture to himself: – they were as glowing as his young heart could portray them in the fullness of its joy.

"Close up that window, Gerald!" said a hollow voice beside him; "I am cold and sick." Gerald turned and beheld his brother, whose cheeks were ashy pale and whose eyes were wild.

It was the first time Gerald had observed the sad alteration which had taken place in his brother's countenance, – telling a long tale of care and woe – hopes blighted – affections thwarted – and the fearful struggles which he had made to keep up former rank and appearances without adequate means. After gazing a few moments at him in a kind of stupefaction, Gerald earnestly inquired the cause of his illness.

"I – I – cannot speak it!" said the wretched man, bursting into tears. "I have ruined you – myself – my mother – and all!" – and, laying his hand on his brother's arm, and tightening his pressure to torture, he added, in the deepest undertones of his voice, "*I am to be – and must be hanged!*"

It was some time before Gerald could soothe his brother and bring him to talk rationally upon his misfortunes, the story of which was as follows:– Having, in vain endeavoured to keep pace with the increased rent of his farm, sunk all the money left to him by his father, he had been tempted to forge a draft upon his mother's banker for a considerable sum, in the hopes that a good season would enable him to restore the amount with interest. The season, however, proved unfavourable; his cattle died; and misfortunes crowded upon him. The agent would give him no relief; and what was he to do? Should he resign his holding? *That* would have been to have gone out upon the road side and starved; for he had not then, as he had at his father's death, a capital to place him in another farm. He was at the mercy of the landlord, who was inexorable. Under these circumstances, he was again tempted to forge a draft for a more considerable sum: but he was again unlucky. In vain did he toil and struggle; Providence seemed to have forsaken him. A third time tempted, he a third time yielded, until he had drained every penny of his mother's property; – and, not resting there, the wretched man had forged the name of a wealthy farmer upon a bill, which was then lying at the bank. In a day or so exposure and infamy were certain.

To give up his patrimony, in order to save his brother, was the instant determination of Gerald. He felt that he would lose his darling Mary by acting thus; but the thought did not check the generous impulse of soul. Through the medium of Gerald, the honour of the family was saved. As for the wretched Thomas, unable to bear the recollection of his guilt, he shortly afterwards terminated his miseries in the grave of a suicide.

His aged and fond mother died of a broken heart when informed of his fearful end; – and thus were they both victims at the shrine of landlordism!

And now Gerald stood alone in the world; – not quite alone – for there was one pure and devoted being to whom his heart turned for support. She had loved him in his prosperity – she adored him in his poverty. He explained to her the desperate state of his affairs; houseless and homeless, he painted to her the risks she was about to run – her father's certain anger – the loss of wealth –

the bitter pangs of poverty; – but she, in the depths of her woman's heart, found a courage to meet all – to share all!

The church joined the hands of those who were already united by holier ties; and now, out of the wreck of his brother's property, there remained to Gerald about fifty pounds.

Within a few miles of his former abode, there was one of those large tracts of waste land so common in Ireland – the property of Mr. Lawson, a rich proprietor who resided the greater part of the year with his family on the continent. Having heard of Gerald's misfortunes, he granted to him a short lease of some hundred acres of those lands at a low rent. To work Gerald went with a grateful heart and a willing hand; and his toils were lightened by the presence of his Mary, who worked by his side. After a few years, their industry was well repaid: – the place, formerly a wild moor, became a snug farm. The success of Gerald stimulated many poor persons to take tracts of the same land and settle around him. Years rolled on: he was becoming rich and happy, and his cottage fire-side was well known by the poor for many a mile round; when a storm was gathering in the horizon to burst over him, charged with irreparable calamity.

Mr. Lawson, the landlord of Gerald's holding, had, like Mr. Hill, lived far too extravagantly for his means; and, to enable himself to purchase a box at the opera for his wife, had sold his estate to a Mr. Abel Crawford. This gentleman was bent upon making his newly acquired purchase a sort of paradise; and, amongst the improvements which his scientific mind had suggested, was the razing of the little hamlet that had been reared around Gerald's land, for the purpose of beautifying a park. To conceive the idea was to put it into execution. In vain did the poor tenants wait upon their cruel tyrant; in vain did they tell their tale of woe. He was deaf to all remonstrance – to compassion he was a stranger. Yet still they could not persuade themselves that they would be turned homeless on the world, and deprived of the very land which would have been bog but for them. Unfortunately none of them had made provision for the evil day. It were impossible they should; for in Ireland the peasant's wealth does not consist of gold and silver, but in the store of food that each is enabled to lay up for the year. But food would not procure them shelter: – they could not sell their lands; they had not interest therein:– they could not sell their crops; they were not ripe: – without money they could procure no home.

The fatal day at length arrived. Early in the morning – 'twas November – Mr. Abel Crawford attended with a strong body of the military and police; and the work of destruction commenced. A few hours sufficed to complete it, and ensure years of misery and destitution. Silently and moodily did Gerald and his unhappy brethren view the ruin of all that was dear to them. Sisters, and wives, and children wept; – but the men had no tears: they burned for vengeance. Two or three wild boys in the paroxysm of their grief threw stones at the police when departing:– these functionaries, considering doubtless their lives in danger, fired into the crowd, and one poor, unoffending, blind old man was shot. The peasants looked on in silence: what could they do?

When all was over, the homeless ones sought a refuge from the inclemency of the weather behind the banks of the ditches – for, as the evening closed, a heavy rain began to fall. As it grew darker, not a breath was heard: a low moan, escaping at intervals from some poor sufferer, only served to render the stillness more wild. It was a fearful night; and many a fervent prayer was silently offered that the morning would soon come. And when morning did at length arrive, it only brought renewed sorrow: nine persons had perished from the cold and wet; and Gerald Desmond's wife and children were amongst the number! Bitter was his grief, and dreadful were his denunciations against his destroyer; – his meek and enduring nature was changed – and he was now an infuriate, panting for vengeance!

A few evenings after the fatal events just related, – and as Mr. Crawford was returning home with his son and daughter, – the youthful pair, as they entered the park, set their horses to a gallop to try which would reach home the sooner. Their father remained behind. An hour elapsed; and he did not follow. But perhaps he had taken a turn in the park? Two – three – four hours – and still he came not. His family grew alarmed: search was made, and his horse was found tied to a tree. Surely he could not be far off? Presently his hat was picked up in a part of the meadow where evidently a deadly struggle had taken place. A few yards off, the corpse of Mr. Crawford was discovered in a ditch. The head was completely smashed as with a heavy instrument; and at a short distance a huge stake was found, clotted with gore!

Although Gerald's companions in misfortune had heard the threats which he had levelled against the landlord, not a lip breathed a murmur calculated to betray him. But the conscience of the wretched man was his accuser; and, after wandering for three whole days and as many nights about the fields, without tasting a morsel of food, he delivered himself up to justice. In due course his trial came on: he pleaded guilty – was sentenced – and executed!

The corpse was given up to two poor women, who, though total strangers to Gerald, were still deeply affected by his sad history; and they had claimed the body under pretence of relationship, but in reality to afford it a burial *outside* the precincts of a gaol!

The Meal-Mongers: Or, Food Riots in Ireland (1848)

About forty miles from Dublin, in a S.W. direction, skirting the "Great Bog of Allen," there are a number of neat and somewhat superior class of villages; like many of their unhappy kind in Ireland, they are the property of an absentee nobleman, Lord Digby, of Sherbourne Castle, in the county of Dorset. One of these villages, from whence he takes his title as "Baron of Geashill in the King's County," was given as a marriage portion about 1590, with Lettice, daughter of Gerald Lord Offaley, ancestor of the present Duke of Leinster.

The present sketch of "Food Riots" is taken from this food-sequestered village, and is not, alas! of unusual occurrence in some of the S.W. counties in Ireland, a strong opinion being entertained by the peasantry, that parties of "Ingrossers," or small farmers whom they denominate "Meal-mongers," had combined to bond up their oats and meal, in order that, by having an insufficient supply in market, they might enhance the value of their grain, and raise their prices at the expense of the poor. It was no great wonder, then, that the poor people looked upon these men as their worst of enemies; as men, in fact, to use their own expression, "who were taking their bit out of their mouths," and many were the schemes suggested by the "Geashill boys" to make the mongers believe that their meal-hoarding propensities were duly appreciated by them. In this village lived a family of three brothers, who followed the graceful occupation of meat butchers, and whose name, "Delany," rendered them of rather doubtful Milesian extraction; but who, nevertheless, were in the full confidence of their village companions, although placed rather above them by more favoured circumstances; still were they always on a level with them whenever there was anything to call out their natural propensities for what they would call a "bit of shindy." Mike, the eldest brother, who from his natural love for the "Fancy Art," was called the "Buffer," was a harum-scarum, cracked-brained sort of a fellow. If he heard of a wake, or a wedding, a dog fight, or a bull bait, a fair, or a frolic, within ten miles, smack went his whip, round went the wheels of his little buggy; or mayhap he would jump into the natural saddle of his short-tailed nag! with a crooked stick in his hand by way of a bridle! Away he went, bounding over the village stream as if in mockery of its gentle gliding, at such a frightful pace as none but a real cockney son of the pouch and steel could envy. Ned, the second eldest, was quite the antipodes of Mike; no one ever knew Ned to bestride a living horse; his whole delight was in strutting about the ring of a cock-pit, or trotting thereto upon Shank's mare; wherever there was a main of cocks to be fought there was Ned in the midst of them. Twenty miles would be but a pleasant morning's walk for him, if he had but the glorification of standing twenty minutes in a cock-pit! With Ned fair play was a jewel that he prized dearly, in support of which every particle of Ned's dress seemed disposed to second his efforts, each acting the part of a free agent; his shirt-neck and stockings alike scorning the tyrannical trammels of button or band! Even the knee-strings of his unmentionables seemed to pay due regard to his self-devotional exercises in the ring of the cock-pit; but he, too, dearly loved a bit of a row, and was never backward in coming forward, even after a retreat had been sounded by some of the stoutest of his own party. The youngest, James, or as he was commonly called, Shamus, or "Crutchy Delany," was, at one period of his career, the wildest of the three; but was cut short of a leg, and deprived of an eye, in one of those party feuds whose belligerents rejoice in the unmeaning cognomen of "Black Feet," or "White Feet;" whose successors were the far-famed "Terry Alts," and the still more recent brotherhood of "Molly Maguires," not to speak slightingly of the noble house of "Captain Rock," of whom it was said, that -

"Through Leinster, Ulster, Connaught, Munster
Rock was the boy to make the fun stir."

Nevertheless, Crutchy Delany was no mean authority to be consulted on important occasions, as in the sequel which we are about to relate will be seen. The conspiracy against the meal-mongers was planned under the spreading branches of an old oak tree that grew on the centre of the village green. After mass on a Sunday morning, which service was performed in an old barn which for some time back had been rented as a Catholic place of worship, for want of a better, Barny Cavanagh, the brogue maker, was the last man that left the shed, barrin' the priest, who waited for the congregation to depart to divest himself.

"Oh! boys, jewel," said Barny, "did ye'z hear the sarmon?" throwing himself down on the elevated green bank beneath the spreading branches of the old oak tree.

"What was it about?" inquired a dozen voices at once, who had just returned from a foot-balling, and had placed themselves in a conspicuous position for the twofold purpose of concluding their plans, and being seen by Father Scully on his return from mass. "What was it all about, Barry?" reiterated half a dozen voices, more impatient than before.

"Oh! by gor, Father Scully did cum out, shure enuf,"

"Not yet we hope," said two or three voices; "for we want him to see us," said another.

"Oh! the divil go from you," said Barny; "I mean he cum out about the 'meal-mongers.'"

"Philelew!" says Shamus Delany.

"Somebody tauld him," continued Barny, "that we intend to give the meal mongers a drubin', and he ses the very devil himself will have nothin' at all to do with uz, if we meddle with them, because, as he ses, the Liburathur says that we must let the meal pass; and besides, boys, I'm got good news for ye'z; the clark tould me as how the bog stuff is all to be taken out of the bog holes, and to be filled up with clay, to make railroads."

"Shure that'll give uz plenty of work for a twelmo'th an' a day," says Crutchy Delany, giving a shrewd doubtful nod of his head.

"What de ye zay, Crutchy?" says Barny.

"Why I zay those tales about fillin' up bog holes 'il never fill our bellies; and as for the advice of the Liburathur to let the meal pass, I only think, as if he had our empty stomachs he wouldn't take the advice himself (Bravo, Crutchy). I only wish, begor, that we had all the pennies ever we sent him and we wouldn't be as we are. ("That's true enuf," said several voices). However, if ye'z are all of my mind, we'll fill our childers' bellies, instead of the bog holes. As for myself, I'm a rale young Irelander, and ye'z may depend the gentry 'il give huz nothing until they're forced, or till they sees the half of huz cut off wid starvation; and maybe its then they'll begin to think of who's to till the land for

99

them, or pay them their rents. So if ye'z are of my mind, let us all meet at the widdy Rouse's on Thursday evenin', and then I'll warrant ye'z," said Crutchy, arising his crutch in such a manner as required no further explanation of his intention; "we'll fill our childers' bellies instid of the bog holes!"

Seeing the priest coming they moved slowly along, muttering to each other in an under tone, "Faith and begorra, we'll fill our childers' bellies instead of the bog holes!" and they kept their word.

Thursday evening is come, and the whole party are seated in Judy Rouse's cabin, smoking their short pipes round the expiring embers of a portion of the great bog. Crutchy Delany sits in the dark corner, amusing himself cleaning up what seems to be the remnant of a cow's horn.

"Hard times, Shamus," said Judy, as she turned about half a dozen of potatoes into a circular frame, which were as quickly rescued by as many little hands, and devoured as eagerly as though they were sugar plumbs, instead of what they were:–

"Sickly, soap like vegetable matter."

"Hard times, Shamus," said she; "but wirra strew avic! what is to become of huz. Sure God knows I didn't care a traneen what becomes of myself, but these poor babbys – shure its enuf to drive one mad to think of it. Oh! Shamus, jewel," said Judy, in seeming great agony, as she dipped her lumper in a mixture of salt and water, and instinctively held it to the youngest child's mouth, "What am I to do for another meal for my poor childer? God knows I've been out all day, and the hearts of everybody seem as hard as a stone; the poor hav'nt it for themselves, and the rich wont give huz anything. Sure, I don't know what use it is buildin' so many school houses about the barony, and the poor childer starving; shure, its food the poor creathurs want insted of larning, God knows. I wondthur how Mr. Richard Digby, or Mr. Benjamin Digby, or Mr. Kelm Digby, or the great lord himself, who hasn't put a foot in Geashill but once these forty years, can expect poor childer to get whole chapthurs of the Bible by heart, without a morsel of food in their little stomachs; shure, its enuf to sicken them for ever agin religion, to make them live on it in that sort of way; unless" – here poor Judy faltered, she wished to say something about conditions – but her feelings overpowered her; the last words were uttered with such phrensied gesticulation, that betokened the struggling emotions of the heart, desperately contending with difficulties – nor was Shamus unmindful of the poor widow's appeal to his sympathy, for he had already disappeared, and in a few moments returned to his seat in the corner, having left a small wooden bowl on the table. "Now Judy," said he, "there's a handful of rice, and a bit of oatmeal, you can make the childer a bit of stirabout for supper; keep your spirits up, I'll warrant you'll have more in the mornin', without prosilting the childer." At the sight of the meal, and the last cheering words of Shamus, poor Judy seemed suddenly metamorphosed into another being – the grateful tear rolled down her joyous cheek, as she hugged her little ones to her bosom, and exclaimed: "May the great God bless you, Shamus, this night; its the poor that can feel for the poor; that's more than the parson ever gave my poor childer since the first day ever he cum to Geashill, though many's the price of a good pig ever poor Larry paid him, God rest his soul in glory." The latch had risen just as Judy began the last sentence, and ere she had finished it, Mr. Fogarty, the village school-master was looking Judy full in the face.

"Well, but Mrs. Rouse," said he "you know the parson is a very good man, and its your fault, or defect, as Dr. Johnson says, if you are not a recipient of his *more* than Christian-like bounty, and remember, Mrs. Rouse, all you have to do is to send your children to school, myself and Mrs. Fogarty will bring them up in the way they should go: that is, in the reformed way of the church: that is, according to Dr. Johnson, a change from worse to better! they will be clothed from head to foot with good linsey woolsey covering; but its a strange feeling, or fatality, as Dr. Johnson says, that you poor people will not be advised by your betters, who must be allowed, or tolerated, as Dr. Johnson says, to know what is best for your souls as well as your bodies." This speech of Mr. Fogarty seemed, for a moment, to paralyse the volubility of poor Judy's tongue, delivered, as it was, with such an air of earnest commiseration, that entirely hid from her view the subtlety of the proselytising old serpent. "Dear knows," says she, "I would do anything in the world for the good of my poor childer."

"I should think so," rejoined Mr. Fogarty, chuckling with a degree of self-satisfaction at the impression he had made upon the phrensied mind of the poor woman; "I should think so," continued he, as he rolled his bone headed cane between his hand and his knee, after the manner of an apothecary making pills with a palate knife, "people, now-a-days, ought to consider their own interest, and not put their best friends against them, or in opposition to them, as Dr. Johnson says."

"But s'pose Mr. Fogarty," said Barny Cavanagh, the brogue maker, who more than once whispered to Crutchy Delany, that he didn't half like the goings on of the old gentleman latterly, "s'pose Judy was to give up the childer, would they be obliged to learn the Bible, and go to meeting or church instead of to chapel on Sunday? or s'pse Judy was to givin to the kitchen of the glebe house, would she have to attend prayers every evening, and worship God the parson's way, instead of her own?" The last question was a settler for Mr. Fogarty; he saw, to answer it would undo all he had done before and perhaps expose him to the ridicule of the villagers, who, through "ages of misrule and wrong," clung to the insulted religion of their fathers, still preferred the damp floor of the thatched barn, to the cushioned pew of the "law-made church,"

"For which they paid, but would not enter."

Mr. Fogarty, therefore, wisely contented himself by saying, that he thought the present was not a proper time nor place to answer such questions; but if Mrs. Rouse would call upon Mrs. Fogarty in the morning, everything should be arranged according to her desire; he would wish them all a very good night: "Late hours," continued he, "are signposts of ungodliness, or impiousness, as Dr. Johnson says, and leadeth man into vicious ways!" The latter portion of the sentence was delivered in a sort of a drawl, with his eyes raised towards heaven, and his cane towards his mouth, a veritable Obadiah!

The absence of the old man was desired by the whole party; they therefore had no great desire to prolong the conversation, lest it should trespass upon their time, which they thought was about to be employed in a much more profitable manner; there were twelve or thirteen of them, able and willing to work, but up to Thursday evening none of them had earned a sixpence, though

101

some of them had wives and small children looking up to them for the means of existence. After the departure of the old man, silence was broken by Crutchy Delany exclaiming:–

"Its time, boys – the meal-mongers war comin'."

"Och, musha, elana," said Judy, "the'l be here time enuf with their great car loads of meal, as big as clumps of turf."

"It would be betthur for Vexeter Hall," says Barny Cavanagh, "to buy the meal up, instid of bibles and testaments, than laving it to the mongers, that wont let us have a morsel of it, unless at a price that nobody can give them, for a bit of it."

"Faith, we'll pay them off for it to night, any how," said rollicking Ned, twisting a straw band round a punch bowl shaped covering for the head, locally called a *caubeen*.

"Why don't ye'r keep a look out there," said Paddy Dunahan.

"Lend me the horn," said Mike the Buffer.

"Blow hard," said Crutchy. In a few minutes, Mike ascended the old castle walls, a sort of inclined plane, leading, some fifty feet high, to an old ivy-clad tower, from whence he could see any object for at least two miles along the desolate highway of the great bog. From the elevated position of the old tower, he could also give timely notice, by means of the cow's horn, of the mongers approach, to the boys of Raheen, and Clonneygown, whose localities from the village, through swamps and through mire, made them rather uneasy, lest they should be time enough to be too late for the meditated attack on the money-loving, famine-seeking "meal-mongers," whom they looked upon as their grave-diggers from England's "merchant princes," whose wealth had enabled them to monopolise the markets, by buying in cheap and selling out dear, realising a profit, it is pretty certain at present, of as much as ten pounds on a single ton of meal ! It was usual for the meal-mongers to halt at the village for the night, on their return from the adjoining market town; one of these evenings was selected by the King's-county boys, "for thrashing the corn out of them."

It was a beautiful evening in the latter end of August; the day had been made up of sunshine and showers, which made the market close somewhat sooner than was the custom, and the rich radiance of the fading rainbow, as it blended in variegated hues with the golden rays of the setting sun, seemed to linger longer than usual upon the dark ruins of the old castle walls, the crumbling turrets of the once splendid mansion of the renowned Baron of Geashill ere it had been quite so fashionable to live in English castles, and hold Irish estates in trust for the benefit of their numerous progeny, and poor relations, who grow fat and insolent upon the good things which conquest had sent them, and who look upon the peasant's pig as a more essential adjunct in the cabin of the poor man, than is the partner of his sorrows or the child of his bosom.

Mike had not been long in his elevated position, till he descried the meal-mongers tracing their slow and steady course along the fenceless road, which twined itself like a great serpent across the barren heath. Pwhoo-hoo-hoo-hoo; went the cow's horn! Hector's trumpeter could not have given a better blast! re-echoing from hill to hill, like a truthful messenger, its new-born mission.

"O, be the powdhers of Moll Killy," said Crutchy Delany, "ther coming at last," and the whole party darted towards the door.

"O, for heaven sake, boys, jewel," said Judy, "what ever are ye'z up to, this night?"

They had disappeared! The whole village was in an uproar in an instant, for, till then, the matter had been kept a strict secret from the women and children; confusion was here; helter skelter was there; the interjection, "Oh!" with its accompanying relatives "What ever!" was uttered by a hundred voices together, while a little incident, connected with poor Judy, helped in no small degree to add to the general rising of the whole village; men, women, and children were seen running from all sides towards the old oak tree on the village green – the appointed place of rendezvous. Mike, in his descent from the old tower, had taken advantage of the general tumult to rescue poor Judy's donkey, which had been impounded for a trespass a few days before; he had succeeded by main strength in getting the donkey over the pound wall, and was carrying poor Neddy across the village green, when, lo! just as he came to the old tree, Neddy thought proper to express his thanks to his liberator in the most public manner, which called forth an encore from no less than one and twenty of his comrades, who came running and roaring from the adjoining skirts of the bog, with pricked ears and cocked tails, no doubt rejoicing at their lost brother that was found; the donkey storm of bellowing set the whole rookery in the beech trees of the old churchyard a-cawing; what with the women and the children, the donkies, and the crows, and hurras for the fight, a looker-on might be led to think that another Charles, or the Devil himself, was centred in the old oak tree on the village green; like a grand centrifugal magnet, it seemed to possess the power of repulsion as well as of attraction, for suddenly the whole body of noisy brawlers, above and below, diverged in uproarious tumult towards the road which led across the far famed Bog of Allen. The cavalry of donkies led the way; next followed the invincible "Buffer," on his short-tailed nag – his legs and arms in rapid motion, like the wings of a windmill – surrounded by a company of sharpshooters, with muskets from the wood of Shililagh, whose duty it was to urge the cavalry in a direct course, and not allow any fugitive "meal-mongers" to escape. Then came Ned and Crutchy Delany, the former carrying a tolerably sized sieve slung over his shoulder, anticipating a supply for his darling cocks; while the latter acted as fugle master with the cow's horn; the rear was brought up with what might not misapplicably be termed, a motley number of squatters and camp followers, while the carrion crows seemed to point out the field of battle by alighting in great numbers on the road, mid-way between the belligerents; daylight was retiring beneath the horizon, evening was wrapt in her mantle of grey, and night – sable night – was fast approaching, to throw his pall o'er the dread meeting of *Famine, Monopoly, and Revenge*.

The meal-mongers were not so strong in numbers as their assailants, but they had flesh, and sinew, and bone, and stout weapons, and they knew how to use them; they numbered thirteen; each carrying a loaded whip, of which the English reader may form some notion of the defensive and offensive properties by the following description:– Its length is a yard, one foot of which is square piece of tapered iron, bound to, and strapped all over with stout pieces of whalebone; a handle of lead is often cast over the piece of iron, and all bound tightly over by heavy weights with stout catgut. They met in deadly conflict on the narrow fenceless road, the whips made woeful havoc on the heads of the peasantry, and the poor donkies, by getting entangled with the carts and horses, suffered not a little; but they ought to have known better than to have got themselves into such a scrape – we cannot say much more in their favour, it was certainly not uncalled for by them – and we hope all other asses will take warning by them; they were half a mile from the village; a sort of a running fight was continued for about a quarter of a mile, the mongers endeavouring to gain the village by alternately whipping the horses, and beating back their assailants; the bridles were cut, and the horses becoming unmanageable, a desperate conflict ensued to gain the mastery; each man assailed his fellow with whip and cudgel, then came the desperate grasp; one young fellow was thrown right over a donkey into a woman's arms, and as she tied a handkerchief over his head, which was bleeding profusely, was heard to exclaim, as he seemed to shiver in the limbs with sheer weakness – "Och Nancy, avournee, macree: shure, its not the mungers thats beaten us, but the hungers." He rushed again into the midst of the fray, and made up with valour what he could not do with strength. The fortune of the night was now turning in their favour; they had succeeded in capsizing most of the meal-mongers into the bog holes – the last was on his legs in a death-grasp-like struggle with the invulnerable Mike: they were both powerful men. "I have you at last," said the monger, as he pinioned Mike up against a meal cart; when the latter made a desperate plunge, seizing the arms of his adversary in return, as he often would do with horns of a restive bullock – the next moment he had him on his hip – when, with the well-known jerk of the practised wrestler, Mike set his assailant first into the air and then into the

"Dark and dismal swamp,"

A tremendous cheer for "Geashill and the sky over it," suceeded, after which the cars proceeded in glorious triumph towards the village, the victors returning in nearly the same order as they had left, the donkeys bellowing, and the crows not seemingly quite pleased with the result; but as it is not all gold that glitters, so victory also sometimes has its dark side as well as its bright. The meal-mongers, after somewhat recovering their sousing in the bog, had taken a short cut to the village inn, and having regaled themselves with a drop of the creature, sallied forth like giants refreshed, to regain their lost ground while "the boys" contented themselves by consigning the meal carts, meal and all, to the tender mercies of the women and children, while they further employed themselves making a sort of ring fire round the old oak on the village green, in commemoration of their victory; while, to do the meal-mongers justice, they seemed noways disposed to fight the battle over again with a handful of ragged, hungry women and children.
One little urchin seemed, however, inclined to bring matters to another issue. He had ensconced himself in the centre of one of the meal cars, and having untied one of the sacks kept stowing away into his upper garret, which seemed as capacious as the pocket of Grimaldi. The full moon had suddenly cast off the trammels of a dark cloud, and in the intruder we beheld a sort of hunchback, with head of monstrous size, and forbidding aspect; his eyes seemed of unearthly glare; his forehead was sunk back; a slight elevation of the nose took place just above the nostrils; the under part of the face protruded much, while the flabby skin of his sunken cheeks hung widely over the tying of a tabby cat-skin cap, the attached paws of a poor puss, at either side, giving it the appearance of ears: they whipped at him in vain, his unsuspecting little hand would coil round the thong, and the whip would follow, till he had deprived some half dozen of their weapons; and when they would mount the cars to come in closer contact with him, his cheeks would swell up like bladders, and a sudden gust of meal dust would meet his chagrined assailants, who at length

gave over the attack, saying, "Who knows, but maybe he's a fairy or a leprechaun from the hills." In truth, he was more like the cub of a Bengal tiger peeping out of its wigwam. The scene was now fast closing – not without dramatic effect – the full moon seemed to review with more than lurid light the departing meal-mongers as they entered the inn yard with bandaged heads and sore bones; while the red bog stuff and the white marl of the damp road gave them all the appearance of a piebald group; the village stream, too, reflected a hundred bright porringers and spoons, with little children devouring "crowdy;" while in the centre stood the pride of the village, the good old oak tree, around which blazed with glowing heat the "ring fire" of victory, thanks to the "great bog," on which might be seen "swinging and singing away," some dozen of old kettles, and the ever to be cursed "praty pots;" while the women stood over them with small sticks in their hands, dubbing the oatmeal in, with a more joyous chorus than the witches in Macbeth over their cauldrons, for they had already forgotten –

> The toil and trouble
> For bubble, bubble!

From *Dissuasive Warnings to the People on Street Warfare* (1839)

Alexander Somerville

LETTER II

However honest the intention, and useful the purpose, of those who write for the abolition of popular error, there are few persons more liable to be accused of sinister motives, or at least assailed with suspicion. If you do not go with the popular opinion, that opinion goes against you; and if you would control, or in some measure direct it, and would study to be fair and reasonable in argument, not loading those with whom you differ with abuse, there is another assortment of individuals who accuse you of insincerity. The author of these letters is accused by certain persons, of being a scribbler hired by the enemies of popular rights: while others assert, and by the assertion have scared some Newsmen from selling this publication, that it is a disguised attempt at instructing the physical force men in the use of arms, and the performance of street tactics.

That the object of these letters may not be misunderstood, let the following plain statement declare their purpose and plan.

The purpose is to dissuade the Chartists from the use of physical force. The plan is to carry conviction by argument and demonstration, so far as demonstration can be carried in writing.

To admit the honesty of purpose that actuates the leaders, and the earnestness and unquestionable courage that would be exhibited by the people were they to rise in insurrection, but to shew that whatever their honesty, earnestness, and courage may be, that they cannot possibly carry conquest on their side, while the mighty odds of cannon-balls, shells, rockets, cavalry, infantry, sovereignty, aristocracy, and all the influence of wealth from the peer to the shopkeeper is against them.

To depict what insurrection must be while it exists; what uncontrollable crimes it must authorize; what commercial ruin it must spread; and what social wretchedness it must leave as its memorial.

To effect this, Macerone's defensive instructions were quoted in the first letter, and are now about to be tested by a sketch of street warfare supposed to be raging in the town of Birmingham. It is necessary to make that populous town the foremost in these supposititious sketches, as the *means* of insurrection exist there to an extent beyond all the other towns of England put together. The timid reader must not be alarmed at seeing a stout, and in some instances for a time, a successful resistance made against the military. He must remember that Birmingham is able to arm every inhabitant who chooses to take arms in his hands, and that in these sketches it must stand in rebellious superiority, high above those towns where the manufactures are *soft fabrics*, and where the arms are innocent pieces of iron called pikes.

To test the power of a military, against an insurgent enemy, let the following correspondence be pondered well; it is such as would be written by an impartial observer of the events:-

Birmingham, (Date uncertain.)

"You will have heard in London, ere this reaches you that the long dreaded popular commotion has at last burst in Birmingham. Of the condition of the neighbouring towns, we know nothing; but so far as we are concerned the outbreak realises the worst fears of one party, and the highest hopes of another. It is now six o'clock, P.M., and since mid-day a continual rattle of musketry, overborne at intervals, by the bomb-thunder of the cannon, has been kept up in the principal streets.

"Such is the consternation among those who remain neutral, and the impetuous energy of those who are taking a share in the hostilities, that nothing can be learned of the precise incidents that led to the first blows. Even rumour, at other times so prolific of information, stands petrified in dumb affright; all, from whom information could be had, being so completely astounded by the strength of the insurgents, or so closely mingled with them, that no talking is heard.

"I believe, however, it was an assault on the police, who had apprehended some of the more violent-tongued agitators, that brought on the collision. One thing is certain, the police and a large number of special constables were forced to a hasty and disorderly retreat through Smallbrook, and Edgbaston, from Holloway Head, and pelted with bricks and other missiles from many of the windows of those streets. They made a halt and attempted to form in the Bull Ring, but simultaneous with their appearance there, a mob issued from New Street and beset them on the rear.

"For some time confusion was all that presented itself to those not mingling in the affray; but there is reason to believe that heavy blows were dealt out with fatal effect by both parties, even at that early stage of the conflict. The Riot Act was read, but the voice of magistracy had no sound amid the clamorous din of the excited assemblage. Flints and fragments of brick were hurled at the police, while the cries of 'Now's the time' 'Out with the cannon!' 'Up with the barricades' and similar expressions, made, with the hootings and hurrahs, an overwhelming noise. Some firearms were discharged, but by whom, or with what effect, is uncertain. I have no doubt however, but some of those more impatient spirits, who have been for weeks past, calling for immediate action, were foolish enough to fire first. But the question of, who drew the first blood, is lost in its insignificance amid the destruction of life that ensued and now rages.

"The cavalry made their appearance at a hard trot with *carried* swords, in Dale End, Moor Street, and Park Street, simultaneously; having broken off into separate detachments of a troop each from Coleshill Street, which, as you know, is the way from the barracks to the scene of outrage. Another troop was dispatched from the barracks to clear the streets adjacent to St. Phillip's Church and keep the churchyard clear, as it was apprehended that it might be made a stronghold by the mob.

"Meantime a detachment of the Yeomanry also made their appearance in Bordesley and Deritend, having been assembled, as I understand, somewhere on the Coventry and Warwick roads, ready to march into any of the towns where riot might first appear, as a tumult in Coventry has been also expected for some days past.

"I believe that considerable forbearance was manifested on the part of the dragoons; particularly in Park Street, where they were most roughly assailed by a shower of those round hard stones, which you know form the foot pavement of most of the Birmingham streets, and which had been taken up for the sole purpose of levelling the heads of the police: but a report I have just this moment heard, says, that the first blood was drawn between the military and the populace, by the former running some of the latter against the railings of the Nelson monument, and that several shots were fired from some of the adjacent windows, which, killing a horse and wounding two or three dragoons, were deemed by the commanding officer a sufficient aggression to warrant him in firing on the rioters in return.

"It is evident that the physical force part of the inhabitants have been prepared for this; for no sooner did shots issue from the carbines of the cavalry than the windows in every direction emitted volleys of musketry. I understand several attempts at barricading were made in those streets merging with the space around St. Martin's Church, but unsuccessfully, as the military kept charging in all directions. The populace however held possession of the church for some time, how they got into it I do not know – perhaps they had been prepared to force it in accordance with their instructions in street warfare which lay it down as a primary object to obtain possession of all churches; – but they did get in, and as I am informed, made considerable havoc among the military before they were overcome. They were overpowered by a party of infantry, who with fixed bayonets, and ball cartridge in their muskets, rushed on and killed or took them prisoners. This was the first time that the celebrated pikes had a trial with the military and the event is worth particular notice.

"The party who held possession of the church, were most of them armed only with pikes, the greater part of those with firearms having chosen to take their station at windows and in streets less exposed to the military; or it may have been, that running to their homes or the broken up warehouses to obtain arms – for even that Parisian expedient has not been dispensed with here – they found the approaches to St. Martin's occupied by the dragoons, and were thereby obliged to leave it in the keeping of the pikemen. The pikemen on the other hand, were not generally armed with firelocks in consequence of the recent practice of carrying the pikes beneath their clothes to the public meetings; and they in the church having taken possession of it immediately on the first appearance of the military, either deeming their pikes sufficient to protect themselves or being unable, in the emergency, to procure other arms. But had they been well supplied with firearms and ammunition, they would have made a very different defence from what the pikes enabled them to make.

"These articles being a species of short sword, somewhere about two feet in length and in the centre, an inch and a half in breadth, are of little use in encountering any enemy superior to a policeman and his baton. In attacking the police, they are most formidable weapons; and it is to their use in that respect, that we are indebted for the war that now rages in the streets, – but against the military they are innocuous. The soldiers with their loaded muskets, and bayonets fixed on the muzzles, overpowered and disarmed the pikemen with comparative ease. Those of the latter who had pistols, made a short resistance, and it is said that a few of the soldiers were killed by pistol-shots as they entered the church; but an instrument two feet long, or even the best sword that Birmingham ever produced, stands a sorry chance in such a mass of confusion, before the soldier's loaded and bayoneted musket. The bayonet has had many deeds ascribed to it which it never performed – particularly the fudge of hand-to-hand combats in the field of battle: but in such cases as that of attacking the pikemen in St. Martin's Church it is eminently qualified. A soldier could then

108

shoot his man and stab another; and if necessary, another and another without the victims being able to strike one effectual blow in return. This was done in the church and a wounded soldier, whom I have just seen, states, that he observed several of them wound themselves by the sharpened point which abuts beneath the handle and which is intended to cut bridle reins or some such thing.

"The military having gained possession of St. Martin's are making it, I understand, a centre of operations, and have also made it a prison for those insurgents or part of them who have fallen into their hands.

"I must not omit to tell you however, what happened with some of the prisoners who were taken in the church and conveyed to the Public Office in Moor Street. They had been secured –

"Half Past Eight.

"Excuse the last sentence not being finished. An awful bombardment is now raging. I had thought the rattling musketry and the occasional cannon shocks of the afternoon, were the climax of the strife; but the battle may be said not to have begun until about seven o'clock – an hour and a half ago. At that time the insurgents held St. Philip's Church – the church-yard, and the adjoining approaches. They had several pieces of cannon in the church-yard and it is now ascertained that the shocks heard in the afternoon were from those pieces. The adjoining houses were all in the possession of the populace with every window lined by sharpshooters. Temple Row, and the streets and lanes connected with it, were barricaded, and the barricades defended by rifle, and pike men, and a piece or pieces of cannon at each. The line of Bull Street and Snowhill had been traversed by the cavalry; and several detachments of infantry had been stationed along that line: but every attempt to expel the insurgents from the locality of St. Philip's proved fruitless. The loss in attempting to force those defences is said to have been severe; for the insurgents, well sheltered, repelled the military with fearful effect.

"The events, however, of seven o'clock have altered the complexion of that district. A rocket troop made its appearance, but being fired on with deadly rapidity from the windows, it was some time before it began operations. Seeing this, the General commanding the troops, gave orders for the artillery to be brought up and open a fire of shells at once, the guns of the artillery having been up to this time firing stray shots more to intimidate than to do execution. A nine pound shell was thrown into the rear of one of the barricades as a beginning, which on its explosion scattered destruction and consternation on all sides, as a friend who witnessed it, tells me. Another followed, which exploding, as these missiles are intended to do, at about four feet from the ground, added to the slaughter and confusion. At the same time a rocket, the first fired, made its direful course over the heads of those at the barricades, and dashing into the thicket of human bodies in the church-yard threw many of them to the ground from which they will never rise. In a few seconds this was followed by another which was not quite so destructive to life, as it was rather higher than the proper level: but it showed its great power with dreadful effect, it having come in contact with a tree which it shivered as effectually as the stroke of a thunderbolt would.

"Two guns throwing six and nine pound shells respectively, continued their operations for some time and demolished several houses which the insurgents

109

were fortifying. It is astonishing with what precision these projectiles can be thrown into any given space; but the most astonishing performance of all, and what seemed to strike the insurgents with profound stupor, was a shell thrown from a mortar which fell, as it had come from the moon – entered the roof of a house – sunk through the garret and upper floors, and exploding in the third story bursted the walls and set the house on fire.

"This was thrown by an eight-and-a-half-inch mortar; and you may figure to yourself what like the explosion of a thirteen-and-a-half – of which you see so many in Woolwich, would be. But you are perhaps not aware how the mortar is used, – I will tell you. It is used for short distances, and for firing on objects of which, you cannot, or do not wish to obtain a view. For instance, if you are at the back of a street, the front of which is fortified, or so defended by sharpshooters that you would be instantly shot – you charge the mortar with a shell, and elevating it almost to the perpendicular, it is fired. The shell bounds high into the air and comes down on whatever spot you intended – the degree of elevation towards the perpendicular, together with the quantity of powder which constituted the charge – ruling the distance. This shell falls with such velocity, that it would sink through all the floors of any house were it not to explode in its progress; but the science of gunnery is brought to such perfection that it can be made to explode at any given point of its descent. But not only are shells from a mortar used for bursting or burning houses; – the Shrapnell shell, or spherical case as it is technically termed, can also be thrown by mortars. *Its* sole object is to destroy human life. It is charged with musket bullets, which, when it explodes, it scatters in conjunction with the fragments of its own body, in all directions, with a slaughterous power, dreadful beyond any other instrument of death. This shell is however, commonly thrown from field artillery, particularly when the numbers of an enemy are multitudinous. I am not aware if any of them have been used this afternoon, I believe not; but two or three tin-cases were fired, which in certain situations are awfully destructive:– these are what, in former times, used to be called canister shot. I am informed that two or three of them were discharged in New Street, but am not certain. "Neither am I able to tell all that was done in St. Philip's Churchyard with the shells. From the singular appearance of the rockets – they have attracted more attention from onlookers, and spread more terror among the insurgents than any of the other projectiles. You have seen a powerful steam engine letting off the steam; the steam which rushes out with such velocity and noise, resembles the rocket, which being ignited, bounds off with a curve through the air and dashes itself murderously into a crowd of persons, if so directed. It is a straight pole of about seven feet in length, is tapered to half an inch in thickness, from two inches, or two and a half. Attached to the heavy end, is a composition invented by Congreve, from whom the rocket takes its name, which no nation but England has yet been able to avail itself of, and no individuals in England, save those who make them in the Arsenal, are acquainted with.

"I should give you more particulars, but at present nothing can be depended on save the general fact that the destruction of life and property is immense, and that the populace are fighting most inveterately. From all quarters the rumour which now begins to float brings tidings of disaster. It is said that some entire families whose houses were made the scene of strife have been destroyed. A young lady, daughter of the eminent brass-founder Mr. – was shot dead early in the afternoon at the drawing room window, while imploring her brother, a fine youth, whom I hear is also wounded, not to join the insurgents. One of the cannon balls from the insurgents, entered a house and killed two old people, it is said, and two of their infant grandchildren. But these particular incidents must remain untold until another period. Yet I cannot refrain from telling you one extraordinary occurrence of which I am just informed. The lady of – Esq. who lives near the Hen-and-Chickens, gave birth to a child at eight o'clock this evening, and the doctor and one or two others were actually killed at that very moment by a rocket from the Royal Artillery which seems to have been fired into that house by a mistake. I was not aware sooner that the rockets had been used in New street, or I might have gleaned some more particulars.

"Just this moment heard that the railroad has been destroyed at several places to arrest the transmission of troops and artillery from Weedon. Other reports say that a large number of shoeing smiths and farriers who were thrown out of employment by the coaches being run off the common roads, went in a body, and taking the opportunity of insurrection in Birmingham, broke up parts of the railroad. I am inclined to believe this report.

"It is said that in several streets the populace have fired the houses. I am informed also that the warehouses and residences of some obnoxious manufacturers are burning by the hands of the incendiary; but this may not be true, as I think it more likely the fires have been caused by the rockets and shells of the artillery.

"A dreadful circumstance has just occurred:– a quantity of rockets fell into the hands of a section of the insurgents who are said to have made a most gallant onset and defeated a party of infantry that acted as coverers to the rocket troop. With these rockets some of the people, more bold than skilful, began to fire on the military, when the capricious instruments being improperly understood by those whose hands put the match to them, dashed rearward among the insurgents and made awful havoc. This, you may perhaps be aware, occurred two or three times with the French in the Peninsular War, when they had the misfortune to capture some of these mysterious things of death. More recently too, in Spain, the Carlists captured some of them from the English Artillery, and attempting to fire, slew a large number of their own infantry: – this, as you know, I was an eye witness of.

There are two extreme currents of rumour meeting each other, now that the first affright is over, and I find it very dangerous to come within the influence of either, unless I abandon myself wholly to one and go headlong with it wheresoever it may carry me.

"One tide of opinion carries on its surf the greatest heroism and glory in favour of the military, and every thing that is vile and savage against the insurgents.

"The other tells of the inhumanity of the military in uselessly destroying life in the streets: in causelessly blowing down houses with artillery; and in many instances that are mentioned, retreating before the insurgents in a most cowardly manner: while the same confluence of rumour proclaims the general valour of the populace and the individual heroism of many of the persons taking a lead or fighting in the ranks of the insurrection.

"I need not say that both sides have their faults and their virtues; that both have their heroes and their cowards; both their deeds of honour and dishonour; and that both, in relating their history, will have their exaggerations.

"Much, it is said, was depending on the hope that the military would not fight against the people, or that they would partially turn their services in favour of the insurrection, if not actually join the insurgents. This hope was founded on delusive suppositions. A soldier talking to a civilian, and telling what he will do in the case of a popular outbreak, is no authority on which you can found an opinion on the fidelity or infidelity of the army; he may be a thinking man, but whatever his individual opinions are, he is carried to the execution of his military duties, by the mindless mass of which he is in himself a powerless atom."

A continuation of the foregoing extracts will appear in the next letter, and will give minute details of the conflict on both sides.

LETTER III

"Midnight.

There is a lurid glare shooting over a portion of the southern sky at intervals, which is said to proceed from the houses adjoining Mr. –'s manufactory, the factory having been set on fire by the populace; but with the exception of these and an occasional musket shot, which bursting out in such a night as this may be likened to death speaking in his sleep, all is subdued, obedient to the dominion of midnight. The street lamps in many districts remain unlighted, which circumstance, with the moonless sky and the drizzling rain of the lowering clouds, augments the natural horror arising from housewreck, pillage, murder, and twelve o'clock. But there are darker things around us than the lampless night. Men's minds are dark; and the uncertainty of our to-morrow's fate is the darkest of all.

"I am now in possession of several particulars which may be interesting to you, and which, as I may not survive to-morrow, shall now be committed to paper, to be forwarded at some future time, we being now, by the breaking up of the railroad, entirely cut off from any direct communication with London.

"In the first place, there are about five thousand armed troops in Birmingham; seven hundred of these are regular cavalry; fifteen hundred yeomen cavalry; two thousand infantry; and the remainder artillery. It is said that several more yeomanry and detachments of militia are expected here by the morning light.

"But in the second place, against all these we have in Birmingham from twelve to fifteen thousand men armed with musketry, nearly all of whom, there is reason to believe, were actively engaged yesterday; and it is unquestionable that ten thousand more would be found with arms and actively engaged should there be any likelihood of speedy success on the side of the insurgents.

"Between those two parties then, the battle will be fought that is to decide the physical force struggle, and as a matter of course, now that the struggle has begun, it will decide the fate of the charter; and that is, because no other town but Birmingham can arm its inhabitants in any degree suitable to hold out against the military.

"You will perceive this the more plainly by the perusal of the details which follow.

"About six o'clock a party of foot lancers armed in the Macerone style charged down New street, having emerged from one of the adjoining streets to carry the position occupied by a nine-pounder and a company of infantry near the Hen and Chickens. Those lancers came on most boldly, quite in accordance with their instructor's injunction, when he says "*Infantry and artillery must be charged so as to render their fire comparatively useless by preventing its being repeated;"* and also when he adds, *"Be prompt and you will destroy them; hesitate and you will be destroyed."* In strict accordance with this injunction, those foot lancers dashed down the street; led boldly to the charge, and as all who saw them testify, they wore a most formidable appearance. At first they seemed so regular that the officer commanding a detachment of infantry, considerably in advance of the position held by the artillery, was uncertain if they belonged to the insurgent force. But the discovery of the long lances soon told what they were, and he opened a fire of musketry on them.

"A few fell by these shots; but the effect was trifling save by the wounded men causing some confusion with the unwieldy lances when they fell before or among the feet of their comrades. They went on. A retreat sounded for the infantry. The skirmishers fired and joined their ranks. Double quick was heard, and the soldiers at its sound seemed to flee; emboldened by which the insurgents rushed more fiercely onwards, and raised a loud and soul-uplifting shout as they rushed. "They flee!" "The soldiers flee!" "Charge on the red-coated cowards!" were the cries of the foremost, and the echoes of those in rear. But in a few seconds more, the order *"Subdivisions from the centre, right and left shoulders forward!"* was the loud command of the officer heading the entry; and that instant, his men opened out towards the two sides of the street, making room for a nine-pound gun to send a tin case into the front of the impetuous insurgents. It went; and oh God! what havoc! It had but forty yards to scatter its bullets, and there, ripe as the harvest, was its prey. Front men fell. Rear rank men ran against those in front, the latter doing more mischief by the foolishness of being six men deep, than even the canister bullets did. Men fell biting the stones in death's agony. The lances tripped up others who stumbled unhurt by the shot, and their unwieldy length, with the suddenness of the disaster – it occurring at a moment when the regular troops *seemed* flying before them, but when the regulars were in reality alluring the insurgents to destruction – caused a confused halt, and that halt, though a small space of time, was long enough to allow the dexterous gunners to repeat their charge. They repeated it, and with the infantry, showered death on the daring band – a band as daring – as truly brave, though foolishly equipped and incautiously led on, as ever shed their blood for or against a royal cause.

"They retreated, that is, those who could; but several were taken prisoners, and a large number out of the whole, were left wounded, dying, and dead. Had cavalry attacked them immediately on receiving this disastrous arrest to their impetuosity, few or none of them could have escaped. And, supposing them to have been more formidable in numbers, and to have approached closer to the gun, then the infantry were there and formed ready to cover it. Besides, there might have been two or three pieces of artillery as readily as one, so that we see these foot lancers, in this case, had more contingencies in their favour than against them.

"The foot lancers were, however, tried on another occasion, sometime during the afternoon, and had a fairer trial of the weapons than those in the case just related. They issued from some of the inferior streets into Lionfield street, where, meeting a party of infantry and special constables, they gave battle, and clearing that thorough-fare with little difficulty, as the opposition offered was weak, they remained in unmolested possession of the whole district, including Steelhouse-lane, Colmore-row, and St. Philips, as far as Ann-street, for nearly an hour. At last, three troops of cavalry galloped into that district, by Astonroad, and immediately put the lancers of the insurgents to the test. The latter were well prepared, having crossed the street with a bristling front to the amount of six or eight men deep, supported by musketry from the rear and the windows; also by plentiful discharges of brickbats, tiles, bottles, jars, crockery, and many other moveable and throwable things, which hands, directed by impulses provocative of slaughter, laid most readily hold of.

"'Charge the chartist blackguards!' was the cry of the officer commanding the cavalry – 'Trample the ruffians to the earth!' and he tried to do so, but the cavalry could not. He retreated; and the shouts of the insurgents drowned even the din of their own arms.

"'The cavalry are coming on the other side!' was the succeeding exclamation, an exclamation so immediate, that it mingled with the shouts even when they were loudest. And most truly, the cavalry were coming. They were coming from the direction of Dale End and Coleshill street; and coming in numbers so powerful, in motion so rapid, and purpose so well concerted, that none could doubt but this locality was to be subdued at all hazards, and with all possible dispatch. 'They are coming; but stand to your guns my lads! there are barricades between us, a cannon on each, and pikes and pistols in your hands to keep the murderous hirelings off,' was the responding address, half command, and half admonition of Davis, the steel-ring maker, who, from his knowledge of military tactics, and most unquestionable personal courage, had been put in command of the barricades adjoining Lionfield street; 'Stand to your guns, and be steady,' he again said, in a voice that emulated the trumpet, and his men *were* steady! They were more – they were ready; and what with lances, rifles, cannon shots, and a considerable quantity of roof and window missiles, the soldiers were again compelled to retreat.

"Inspirited at this successful resistance, a party of insurgents, with the brave Davis at their head, dashed forward each with his pike, lance, rifle, fowling piece, pistol, or whatever arms he carried, and determined to close up the lines of Bull-street and Dale-End; and if they could form a junction with the insurgents who held the Railway depot, or were supposed to be holding it, but who had been expelled by rockets and bomb-shells thrown from the barracks, it was believed, and not without probability of success, that they might be gaining possession of that and the space towards Deritend, assist their brothers of insurrection in that quarter, prevent the entrance of reinforcements by breaking down the different canal bridges, and it might be, make a movement on the centre of the military operations, which was, as mentioned formerly, in the locality of the Bull Ring.

"Davis's orders were for those carrying long lances and pikes, to take the front in scouring the streets, so that they might the more readily shew an impregnable array of pointed steel, when they were, as they were certain to be, assailed by cavalry. It was not an easy matter, however, to put such an order in force. The rule of action among the insurgents was the measure of their enthusiasm. A soldier on the other hand is ruled by being of the right or left subdivision; of the first, second, third or fourth section; by being a right or a left file; first, second, or third of threes; right or left hand man of divisions, subdivisions, sections and so on: and he is powerful only in his capacity to perform all or any single duty required of him in his position. By his keeping his position and attending implicitly to the words or notes of command, the officer, can form or execute plans, with a body of such men, as if that body had but one mind. Not so the commander of a body moved by impulse and ruled

114

by their measure of enthusiasm; they may be courageous, but their leader cannot execute plans. Each man has a mind, and being uncontrolled by discipline, the whole, in the absence of concentrated design, become exposed to contingencies.

"Several leaders of the insurgents, as well as Davis, but he particularly, discovered the error of men being led by mere impulse. He had ordered, as already mentioned, that those bearing long pikes and lances should keep steadily in front, and that those having only firearms should form the rear ranks, so that they might, when necessary, halt and form across the street, a front, impenetrable to cavalry.

"But the soldier rushes to the thick fight impelled by his animal nature. If destructive, he is impelled by the mere desire to slay the enemy. If combative, he rushes on from the desire of indulging that prevailing faculty. If possessing the love of approbation, he is foremost that he may be seen. If possessing the last faculty, in conjunction with a large share of cautiousness which begets fear, he makes a dangerous soldier at such a time as an insurrection, where he is not compelled to obey a leader's law. Suppose such a person to have a musket, and no pike, it would have been his duty to make one of the rear rank; but in charging along the street, his love of approbation would force him forward so long as it was a run, and no opposition; while his cautiousness would take alarm the moment he saw the cavalry presenting a front; he would then fall back, displacing those who might have kept their places properly, and making a vacancy, in a place, and at a time when there ought to be none, and when a disciplined soldier, under the control of severe law, would not have dared to displace himself.

"Other predominating tendencies in individuals would equally derange the assailing insurgents: – combativeness and destructiveness combined, or, perhaps united with love of approbation, would make a pikeman outrun all order; and if with these qualities, he carried self-esteem, it would be impossible to convince such a man that he ought to keep in the ranks; he would be wiser than any one else, and by running forward, his insane excitement would, by an onlooker, be called courage. But real courage is manifested, when men perform, in any situation, any order. These observations were eminently verified by the results of several insurgent charges, and ultimately in that headed by the courageous Davis.

"Emerging from behind one of the barricades, his party, lancers and long pikes in front, went forward, causing a company of the – light infantry to retreat. But men, whose places were in the rear, got up to the front, while others who should have been in the front with their lances, fell to the rear. Men, who from a sense of duty, remained in their rear rank places, pushed forward those who had fallen back with the lances. These last, in some cases, run against the men in front; at which one or two who ought not to have opened their mouths, but who could not resist the desire to speak, swore at those who were thus blundering, and some of the blundering men being persons who would not take a reproof of any one swore in return. An old soldier, who had been at Badajoz, – and who recollected that many of the English, employed in that assault, were killed by their rear rankmen, while forcing their way in crowds and disorder, with bayonets on their musket's muzzle – was calling to mind also that many colonels, all those, indeed, who had seen the disorder once, would not allow bayonets to be fixed, when making an assault where order could not be preserved, until the men were on clear ground – on the ramparts, or about to encounter the enemy; this old soldier, was calling these circumstances to mind, and most heartily disapproving of any pointed instrument being carried save by the front rank, when all his fears were verified by a charge of cavalry. It came so suddenly, that the insurgent leader had only time to give the word 'Halt!' – and add 'Prepare to receive cavalry!' Yet to those words of command, the most of the pike and riflemen gave instant obedience by dropping on one knee, and had all been moving in complete order, they would have presented an irresistible obstacle to the dragoons.

This irresistible obstacle was destroyed, however, by some of the pikemen carrying muskets slung over the shoulder in accordance with the Macerone instructions, and which, as any soldier knows well they would, prevented them from closing up, and occupying the small space which is absolutely necessary for men to occupy on such an occasion. And moreover many were out of place. A man with a fowling piece was in the place, where one now two or three yards behind him, should have been with a pike. This man attempted to fall back, on observing which, the pikeman next, him not having heard the command distinctly, or not having been drilled so well as some of them, perhaps being more weak in the nerves, or having the origins of cautiousness much larger than those necessary for such an emergency, attempted to fall back also. This occasioned an unsteadiness among those immediately behind, and was nearly creating a panic such as happened once to a regiment in the battle of Busaco.

"The cavalry galloped up and fired their carbines, which in a few instances took effect on the front pikemen. The latter in most cases kept firm, with their knees on the ground pressing the butts of their lances, and holding them slanting upwards, while they attempted to fire pistols at the dragoons with the other hand. The folly of supposing that a heavy dragoon would not make these lances of the kneeling men fly aside by a parry of his sword was soon apparent. They were knocked aside, and an entrance instantaneously made into the insurgent ranks. But even this was not requisite to enter the ranks; openings sufficient to admit the dragoons were made by the mistake of men armed only with fire-locks having taken the front.

"The strong right arms, and the stout hearts wielded their weapons as well as the most sanguine physical force advocate predicted they would. But alas! there was a power against them, and an unfitness of weapons with them, that men making speeches at public meetings neither understand nor suffer themselves to be informed of. Trusting to the Macerone instructions, some had made the shafts of their pikes of the 'American pine,' which was shivered by the parries of the dragoons, as any one knowing what American pine is might have known much earlier. Others found that though their lances were strong, and would have readily run through a dragoon or his horse, had either come against its point, they could do nothing with it, for having missed the thrust when the dragoon was at the pike's length they were overpowered by him dashing his horse forward, and trampling, or hewing them to the stony street. In this havoc, the insurgents who carried short pikes – those of the sabre fashion – did some execution. These articles are calculated to kill a horse and perhaps a rider, when the conflict is desperate, and the slaughter dealt from hand to hand, but wielded by a man on foot against a horse-man, it is impossible such a weapon can continue effective. Men of the names of T – n, D – n, D – h, and others whose names I am not informed, are said to have fought most gallantly. But a remnant was only saved, by the fury with which the people at the windows showered down stones and tiles, and as some say, boiling water, on the cavalry, which arrested them in their slaughterous pursuit of the retreating insurgents. It was from this, and a few similar defeats that the leaders of the populace resolved on keeping within the houses, and firing from the windows, fortifying public buildings, and so on, which, as was remarked in the fifth paragraph of what I have written since mid-night, warrants the expectation that the military will have a much harder task to perform than they would have had, had the insurgents continued to act on the offensive. The retreat of the populace to the houses, they being nearly all in possession of firearms, warrants me to conclude that the heaviest of the insurrectionary battles will be fought in Birmingham, other towns being differently situated as regards weapons, and no weapons being so suitable for indoor fighting as firearms.

"The magistrates are sitting in council, and are conferring with the military authorities as to what terms ought to be offered to the leaders of the insurrection to avoid farther destruction of life and property; but nothing can be concluded on that point until instructions arrive from London. Meantime the military authorities have determined to blow down, progressively, every house fortified by the insurgents – there being a sufficiency of artillery for that purpose, without again exposing the soldiers in the streets.

"And now, the mind searching into the future, asks, What will be the result of this broil? But in vain we seek for conclusive certainties. Are other towns in insurrection? If they are, is the opposition to the military as strong as in Birmingham? If the government cannot put down the insurgents, who will govern? Where will the funds, and the banks, the commerce, the manufacturers, the foreign possessions, the home wealth, the aristocracy, the mansions, the estates, the clergy, and the churches and the church lands go? If the insurrection is put down, who will be hanged? Will there be wages, or work, or food? or, will there be hungry, houseless, fatherless, husbandless, survivors of cruel warfare and its more cruel successor the triumphant and avenging law? Will a Lord Eliot come from some foreign country to intercede for mercy to the prisoners of *English* civil war? Will the merchants of London and Liverpool, see any 'blot on the map of Europe,' by putting prisoners to death in England, as they did in the case of Spain? Where will be the end of this beginning?"

To these doubting interrogations, the future letters of this series will afford a very probable solution. In the meantime the Birmingham correspondence is left off, to describe the panic in London, which must be occasioned by the news of provincial insurrection. This panic, with news from the north, will be the subject of the next letter.

LETTER IV

The following extracts from newspapers the dates of which are *at present* uncertain, combine interest and instruction relative to the progress of insurrection.

From the fourth edition of the T –

"City, 12 o'clock

"As we expected, the intelligence from Birmingham published in our first edition, has disordered the money market to an unprecedented degree. It would be useless to quote the prices of stock, for so great has been the consternation and so few the sales that no quotations can really be made. One irrepressible feeling of strong, deep, broad universal indignation pervades the merchants and citizens, an indignation that we trust will, without one day's delay discharge itself on the culpable ministry, whose criminal forbearance has brought this vast empire, with all its mighty interests into the vortex – no, not vortex, for thank God there are yet the means of preventing that – but the jeopardy of a revolution. It is asked, and we reiterate the questions, – why were all the Chartist leaders not, long ere this, arrested? Why were those which were arrested not all brought to trial? why were those whose trials took place not condemned? and why were the condemned not executed? Offended justice scorns the false humanity with which a vile political philosophy attempts to answer these questions. If O'Connor's head had been, long ere this, stuck upon some 'Northern pole' instead of his treason being tolerated in a 'Northern Star' we might have seen the north purified of his odious influence. Had the trunkless craniums of Vincent and Frost adorned respectively the market places of Monmouth and Newport: had Baillie Craig's swung over his haberdasheries in Kilmarnock, with a few dozens of Doctor Taylors, Flemings, McDowalls and their villainous associates throughout Lancashire and Yorkshire; not omitting to have had Hetherington and Cleave on each side of Temple Bar, the nation might have been saved from the disgrace of insurrection and its wealth from the hazard of spoilation.

"But though late, these things must now be done. The merchants in the city ask indignantly, why the rebel prisoners taken yesterday were not instantly put to death? Is the pusillanimous whig radical town council of Birmingham to hazard the existence of this great commercial nation by interposing its spurious humanity between crime and justice? No, not a traitor must live to have his crimes cavilled at by lawyers; off with their heads in every street, and every town, and we will answer for the effect."

From the S – – of the same evening

"In a late edition last night, and in our morning edition of this day, we gave intelligence of the insurrection, which yesterday, in frightful reality, broke out in Birmingham. We now publish additional, and to a considerable extent, exclusive details, which will be found in another column.

"Amid the alarm which prevails and the uncertainty of many contradictory reports, we might incline to with-hold our comments for at least another day; but though we are not in possession of aught that can, even by any twisted constriction administer to the peace of the public mind, and though it might therefore be better not to augment the general consternation, we cannot refrain from administering a corrective to some of our Morning contemporaries, whose second, third, and fourth editions, have, during the day, poured forth high pressure wrath on all and sundry, who have at any time, in any way differed in opinion from them.

"A morning paper, self celebrated as the leading journal, demands an instant, unhesitating and unlimited effusion of Chartist blood. It asks, why were the heads of such and such persons not stuck on poles, and market-places, and shop doors, long ago; and why was the law not put in butchering execution. It

118

informs us also, that the merchants of the city are full of indignation, because some prisoners, taken by the military, and rescued as report says, by the insurgents, had not been instantly put to death. We doubt not but the merchants and many more than the merchants will cry for instant execution. It is one thing to hear of military murders in a foreign country, and another to have an interest in perpetrating them at home. It is not long since Lord Melbourne was admonished by those citizens of London and Liverpool, who do not love his lordship's politics, to interpose for the prevention of the military executions of Van Halen and Cabrera in Spain; yet the same parties, in and out of parliament, extenuate the same crimes in Colonel Prince, the Cabrera of Canada. They have some interest in the severity of Canadian military law; they had no interest in that of Spain, therefore they could be political under the guise of humanity. But what will it – must it be in England? the interest is immense. Can wealth, titles, law, religion, and royalty, verging on one common jeopardy, afford to be humane? No, they cannot even afford to be just – they will have blood, legally if they can – murderously if they must.

"But a word with the Tory party and the Tory press. What measure has so much incited the poor against the rich as the New Poor-Law? Who are they, that to thwart and annoy their political opponents have chosen even to foster the discontent of the poor, thrown their shield to a man who counsels the factory-workers to 'march three deep and save each other's heels' – extended their sympathy to, and adopted as a martyr, a preacher, who inculcates as a sacred duty the necessity of arming against the work-houses and the cotton-mills? who, we ask, to defeat political opponents, have thus tampered with the elements of rebellion? The answer is the Tories and the Tory press! but we say, beware, Tories: you have rich fields, and woods, fine houses, and great wealth in stored treasure and daily income; take care of all these, for in the battle of poverty against wealth, hunger against fullness, industry against idleness – the distinction of Tory and Whig will be left to the historian."

The same paper goes on to remind the leading journal of its 'brick-bat and bludgeon' doctrines of seven years ago, and the defiance then given to military threats; and quotes from it the sound and forcible argument which it put forth on the 24th May, 1832, namely, that "each individual, admitted to the suffrage, makes the noisy mob one less in number; and that the more general the admission, the less danger will there be of the door being forced."

The following is from the government organ.

"Ten brigades of artillery have left Woolwich this afternoon for the North. Five of these have gone by sea, to be landed at Hull, and from thence to proceed into the interior of Yorkshire, where urgency may most demand.

"A Cabinet Council was called at the unusual hour of twelve last night, on the express arriving from Warwickshire; and a Privy Council was in consequence summoned and met at the early hour of eleven, this morning. A proclamation, declaring the town of Birmingham under martial law, was issued. We hear also that the question of sending a strong force of Guards to the midland counties and the propriety of sparing them from London, was entertained, but, as yet, none of the Foot Guards, and only one regiment of Horse (the blues) have received orders to march. The latter go direct by railway to Warwickshire."

On the following day the morning papers contained additional information to the effect that –

"Disastrous reports continue to reach the metropolis. The troops on their way to Birmingham, yesterday, were arrested by the breaking up of the railway, near Dunstable. It is broken in several other parts, but that was the first encountered, and the disaster was dreadful. Three trains loaded with detachments of cavalry, infantry, and artillery, were overturned in one complete smash of wreck. So well was this planned, that for miles along the line no person but those interested in the disaster had been permitted to approach, lest they might discover the design. A correspondent remarks, that besides the great advantage gained by the insurgents in thus obtaining a battleless victory over the military, a few hundreds of them, had they been there and prepared, might at the time of the shock killed every soldier, and taken the arms and ammunition without being opposed."

The same paper with all the others of that evening, contained the following intelligence.

RUN ON THE BANKS, AND COMMERCIAL FAILURE.

"From the excitement of yesterday considerable apprehension was felt for the holders of paper to-day. However, the demand for gold was for a time moderate, owing, no doubt, to the prevalent opinion in the city as well as over the whole metropolis that the outbreak in Warwickshire would soon be subdued, or that though the insurgents might hold out for some time, they could not by any possibility succeed in establishing themselves in power at the expense of the laws, such ample means being at the disposal of government. But a circumstance has occurred, trifling in its origin, yet most alarming in its consequences. The house of W.W.R. L. & Co. stopped payment, and though its liabilities do not amount in the whole to 60,000£, it was, from its known connection with houses in Birmingham, looked on as the first crack of a coming crisis. It has proved so. During the latter part of business hours, the demand on the banks has been immense, surpassing anything we have seen since 1825. The alarm taken at this trifle, which in all probability would have occurred though there had been nothing wrong at Birmingham, was augmented by the reports of the railway being broken, and the troops, not only arrested in their progress to suppress the insurrection, but their numerical efficiency to a great degree destroyed, there being no less than sixteen officers and upwards of two hundred rank and file, with twenty two horses killed, maimed, or rendered unserviceable. The report of this occurrence on change with the other just mentioned and the rumour that such intelligence had reached government as would cause the proclamation of martial law to extend to the whole of Warwickshire with the counties of Leicester, Nottingham, Worcester, Stafford, Lancaster, York, Durham, Cumberland, Edinburgh, Forfar, Fife, Lanark, and Renfrew, spread the alarm to such an extent that the rush for gold became overwhelming: and it is feared that to-morrow the announcement of several failures will increase the panic. Meantime the bank and several eminent capitalists are affording secret assistance on the most liberal terms, and that, it is said, not more from their own desire, to subdue the panic, than by the special and secret interference of government, to all respectable houses who have any fear for their liabilities. This however will have little effect. Public credit is shaken, and we see, that while civil war in former times, was in England as it would be in most other countries yet, a matter of mere military strength and political intrigue, it is now subject to the operation of other influences more powerful, than the numerical strength of armies, the munitions of war, or the positions of encampments. At this moment a merchant of the city of London, or a jobbing capitalist on the Exchange may with pieces of paper throw the whole country into a greater convulsion that ever the boldest rebel Lord could, even with half the kingdom for a retinue. In the olden time the fields with little cultivation, fed, and clothed the population:– When the war was over its locality was again cultivated, and all went on as it was before. Not so will our modern commercial system if cracked by insurrection; it is too artificial to withstand the shocks of civil war; for though the land was once the wealth, it will be found that now the landlords are too intimately dependant on commercial stability to survive even a commercial revolution. But we wander; – a political revolution, involving the whole landed, funded, and trading wealth is now in active progress and we must to its events devote ourselves.

* * * * * * * * * * *

Further extracts from newspapers are for the present omitted as it is intended to give succinct narratives of the insurrectionary events of different towns with all their consequences. To begin these, the following from Glasgow is adopted; it is written by an observer and to a considerable extent a sharer of the hostilities that have laid waste such a large portion of that great commercial and manufacturing city.

"It was on the 16th, that we heard of the insurrection in Birmingham. Previous rumours had prepared us to hear of an outbreak in Newcastle and the colliery districts; but few people expected, though it is undeniable that many desired, these rumours to be the heralds of any important occurrence. We had, like all other towns where the Charter had any supporters, a meeting to pass resolutions of remonstrance, in consequence of the contemptuous treatment of the National Petition, and the members who presented it, in the House of Commons. This meeting was held, as all our great assemblages are, on the Green, and was swelled by numerous deputations, from Paisley and the populous towns and villages forming the neighbourhood of Glasgow. The rumour of an outbreak in the north of England was confirmed to us by certain information, much about the same time that we received the startling intelligence of Birmingham being in the heat of an insurrectionary street warfare. The news was electrifying. The timid among the working people, and the rich mill-owners and merchants were electrified in a degree of exact reversion from the great body of the people; so were of course, many of the shop-keepers and tradesmen whose easy circumstances make them take unto themselves a superiority over the men of the hard hand, and the fustian jacket. But among the vast population from whose industry, ingenuity and sweating toil the wealth of Glasgow is produced, a loud and continued burst of acclamation rang in approval of the populace of Newcastle and Warwickshire. The speakers grew more animated: the speeches took colour and strength from the southern news; and instead of one meeting; one platform and one speaker at a time, meetings took form and action to themselves in a dozen places, where the rejection of the Charter, and the insurrections in Newcastle and Birmingham, with the rumoured rising of the shires of York and Lancaster, were energetically discussed.

A committee was appointed at the large, or as we may call it the parent meeting, to draw up resolutions, sympathising with the English insurgents and pledging the people of Glasgow to support them with their hearts, their purses, and if need be, their hands, to the last extremity. These resolutions passed, it was then proposed and warmly responded to, that the whole procession of trades and deputations from the country, instead of moving from the Green in a state of dispersion as had been intended, should now proceed once more to the streets, through which they had processed in the morning, and exhibit their vast physical strength, rend the air with their plaudits, express their satisfaction at the intelligence from the south, and appal the hard hearts of their own own hard work masters.

"Meantime the authorities, with a mixture of energy and affright took counsel among themselves as to what had best be done to keep the commotion within the bounds that Birmingham and Newcastle had over-stepped. Some advised that no shew of military should be made, because, however noisy the demonstration might be, if it was not impeded, or the people irritated, the whole might pass harmless to all, save those, who measuring their riches and recalling to their minds the source from whence they came, balanced that wealth with the strength of the hundred thousand right hands uplifted in the streets, and found conscience and cowardice – twin attendants of guilt – stinging them with retributive apprehension. It was decided, however, that the military should be called out and stationed at the various approaches in the neighbourhood of the Green, to prevent the procession from entering the town. Moreover, the Peace Association which had been formed, in accordance with the injunction of Lord John Russell to the Lord Lieutenants of countries, was summoned together and had its numbers apportioned to several positions, of which St. Andrew's church, the college, Campbell's warehouses in the Candleriggs and the jail, were the principal. Boxes of muskets and barrels of ammunition were secretly conveyed from the barracks to those places, as well as to several other parts where the military were stationed, and where, should collision ensue, it would be necessary to form military positions. These were at the jail, to command Hutcheson bridge, the Saltmarket, and the Green: at the bottom of the Stockwell, to command the Old bridge, Stockwell street, Briggate, &c.: at Jamaica-street, to command the New bridge and communicate with the others from the Gushout-house eastward: at Barrowfield toll, as a centre of operation for Bridgeton: at bridewell, George's-square, the bazaar, Royal Exchange, and in many of the manufacturers' warehouses, throughout the city and suburbs.

"Though these preparations were secretly made, it was not long before the populace caught the rumour of the Peace Association being armed, and also that a large number of them were in St. Andrew's church. The knowledge of this, inflamed the already excited people more than any other single circumstance could have done: more by far than the appearance of the military and the stoppage of the procession: more indeed than the terrors of military array, of horse and foot present, and artillery expected, could subdue. An universal burst of indignation broke from the multitudes, which was succeeded by a deep murmuring noise, a noise made up of voices, planning ulterior measures, assenting to and dissenting from warlike propositions; some proposing a dispersion to meet again with arms; others to set the cotton-mills on fire: many urging by argument the propriety of remonstrating through a deputation to the Lord Provost against the military being called out to stop the procession; but all, by voice and gesture, by oath and vow, denouncing the armed menace of the Peace Association. The police, the military, the meetings dispersed, the procession prohibited, anything seemed tolerable but the arming of one portion of the citizens against the other – that they swore to be avenged on, and it was not long ere summary and fearful vengeance was executed.

122

"It has been mentioned that a party of the armed citizens was stationed in Campbells's warehouses, and that the bazaar, which is adjacent, was also a military depot; we should rather say it was intended to be a military depot, for on the flags being hoisted on the Green, exhibiting in broad letters, the words, 'WE MEET HERE AT SEVEN O'CLOCK!' and the cry being raised of 'seven, at night, for the meeting on the Green,' a vast concourse of persons proceeded to the cross, and filling the Trongate, Salt-market, King street, Candleriggs, Bell street, and adjoining thoroughfares, with, in some places a wedged, and in others a moving multitude – the forces, military and civil, stationed in the bazaar, were ordered out to make a clearance of these streets. Whether the massive doors were burst open, or had been left open; or whether in that case any force was left to protect the place, and had been overcome is now uncertain, but the bazaar was speedily filled by the mob. This movement gave an aggressive impulse to the multitude, and in five minutes more, they were in undisputed possession of all the police buildings. The prisoners that had been made, were lodged in the jail, and consequently no precaution had been taken to have any superior force at the police office. At the same moment, Campbell's warehouses, garrisoned by armed men, and containing an immense quantity of valuable property, as all acquainted with Glasgow know they do, were discovered to be on fire. By whom the torch was applied, at what time, or at what part of the buildings, is uncertain; a dense column of smoke and a growling burst of grey flame was the first indication of the incendiary. The cry rose for the engines, with counter cries of 'No! let them burn! down with the warehouses!' added to which were many imprecations on the garrison of Peace Association men, who were now attempting to escape, and calling loudly for the engines. Whether the engines might have saved the property is a question never to be answered. The mob had possession of the police buildings in which the engines were lodged, and a fiat of popular will, forbade their service to the firm of Campbell & Co. not so much it is believed, from these gentlemen being of the high Tory mercantile aristocracy, as from their having made their houses the position of a force armed against the populace. The flames crackled; the throng inside having barricaded themselves against the mob could not escape. Shouts of savage derision greeted them as they danced wildly at the windows and on the roofs imploring succour from the mob below. 'Throw out your muskets, and your bayonets, and we'll help you down', was called to them and many of the poor wretches sought to purchase life by doing so, which act, however, had no other effect than the furnishing of a score or so of the mob with firearms. The fire, the smoke, the destruction, the despair, and the death, mingled and spread. It over-grew all possibility of control; and as the dragoons with drawn swords bore down the crowd through the Candleriggs and Bell street to make room for the police, who hastened to save this populous locality from ruin, the scene of wreck grew frightfully sublime. Men women and children, old and young, were trampled by the kicking horses. The crowd rushed before them towards the bottom of the street, and were met by a counter current of retreating crowds chased by an infantry from the opposite direction. Their centre was opposite the Bazaar and the burning pile; and there, immovably wedged, crushed, suffocated, roasted, stood the involuntary victims of an accident, the accident of being in the Candleriggs at that particular time. They screamed, they fainted, they prayed, they swore; their faces livid with suffocating heat, and the hue of the red fire; the impotent hands waving a signal or making a menace; the last sight of the last wretches falling into the gulph from which they had vainly and hopelessly retreated; the swords and the helmets glancing and the horses snorting and kicking, still pressing the crowd inwards; these made up a scene to which imagination, revelling even through the regions of the infernal, has rarely found a parallel.

LETTER V

Dreadful as was the kicking, and trampling, and rushing, and fainting, and crashing of burning floors and roofs, described in the last paragraph, there was a height to which terror had not risen, and an excess to which disaster had not extended, even within the compass of the swelling flames that consumed the corner tenements of Bell street and Candleriggs. Behind the warehouses that were now at ruin's meridian, there was a small square, or, as it is called in Glasgow, a close. In one corner of this close there was a large cellar, occupied by a whiting merchant, that is, a dealer in the stuff used as size colour for the common whitening of common houses. In a haste, while the first symptoms of noisy crowds shewed themselves in the neighbouring streets, the ammunition barrels which were being conveyed from the barracks to the several other military positions, were deposited in this cellar. It is more than probable that those who put them there perished ere they could give any warning of such a contingent danger; at least nobody seems to have given warning of them; and no alarm of gun powder was spread. It exploded! and ere the terror produced by the rebound had allowed the formation of even a vague conjecture, broken tiles, slates, stones and fragments of fiery wood rained death and wounds, as it were from angry Heaven, on the heads of the striving multitudes.

Those who mingled in, or overlooked the Candleriggs supposed the strife they saw was the centre of conflict; so thought those whose accidental locality was somewhere else. In Dunlop street, a fire, evidently lighted by the incendiary, raged in uncontrollable violence before even the timid in other parts of the town had thought of taking fear to themselves. How this fire should have been so early kindled is not easily answered. Perhaps some of the persecuted showmen, who had been incarcerated by the manager of the theatre for indulging the Glasgow fair goers with penny theatricals, had scratched a lucifer. Or it might be some outworn wretch, whose cowed spirit nightly shrinking beneath the imperious tongue, clenched fists, and twisted face of the great Aleck, took courage and crying revenge, let slip the friction on a quick match. Whatever it was, the earliest lighted fire in the unhappy insurrection was the T – R –, Dunlop street. Like other fires, it crackled and blazed, and gave a crash, and crumbled into wreck: but unlike all others, it burned and went out, unmourned and unregarded – we might almost say unnoticed by all, save one, and that was poor Aleck himself. He stood in posture suitable to the solemnity, and with that oath which has been uttered by him for the millionth time, namely, "Gracious God!" he began the fruitless enquiry, not at any bystander, but at himself, of "Who has done that? All my splendid property gone! all gone! gracious God!"

Thus we see, that even in the very earliest stage of riot, there are some people who depart from the spirit of the commotion to carry out private revenge on particular persons. Mr. – was no political man, but he is a despot whose

124

property would need a double hazard insurance whenever a riot comes within his neighbourhood.

It has long been a custom with Glasgow mobs, when sufficiently excited, to arm themselves with stobs and palisadings, torn from the Green. In this case the iron railings which have supplaced the wooden stobs, were used, and most formidable weapons they were. A propensity which the youth of the city have ever indulged in, when any tumultuous excitement prevailed, was also exercised in the early part of the commotion – that was, the tearing down of scaffolding, masons' sheds, and such like, to make bonfires. This is, however, only worth mentioning because of a soul thrilling incident related to it, and because of the events which these beginnings gave rise to.

Some tar barrels had been seized, and a journeyman baker in the employment of Mr. Thomas Goodwin, head of High Street, had in a moment of enthusiasm, got one of them burning on his head, and had placed himself in the front of a procession. With this blazing above him, and followed by the cheering multitudes, he marched into the Trongate. He had proceeded towards Argyle Street, when just about the time that the military scoured that thoroughfare, and when the approving shouts were loudest, that end of the barrel which rested on his head being loosened by the flaming tar in the interior, gave way, and the burning mass fell down encompassing his body. Whether he might have been saved by speedy assistance is only an enquiry: as it was, no one could assist him. The military at a hand gallop, and with drawn swords, were forcing the procession from its rout, and every person at the time was rushing along mindful only of his personal safety. The poor baker, some of them thought, had thrown down the burning barrel: but it was as has been stated, for half an hour after, the fragments of his body and the ashes of the barrel were found together.

All the mill-masters are by no means such monsters as the over-charged harangues of the Oastlerian school would represent them: nor do they come under the description of the coarsely caricatured cotton baronet in Mrs. Trollope's 'Factory Boy:' they are, in many cases, persons whom circumstances other than their natural constitution have placed in a position to which few of the labouring millions who would aspire can possibly attain; and who, be they merciful or overbearing, just or unjust, have but one reputation – a reputation grafted on the system of labour, not on their individual merits – that is the reputation of being tyrants. We say there are many individuals who are excellent exceptions to that character, and believe there is not, and never was a being such as the creation of Mrs. Trollope; but though not unnatural and distorted in every phase of character as that personage is, there are tyrants to be met with among the mill-masters and tyrants who are such by nature, and independent of the system. Of these, there is one, or rather was one in Glasgow, on whom the imputation rested with peculiar fitness. A rather coarse but perhaps appropriate chorus became common, and was often sung by the workers as they emerged in their crowding hundreds from the immense factory in which they had wrought, and sweated through the long day's unhealthy vapour. This chorus spoke the sentiments of public esteem, in which its subject was held, and was, as nearly as can be rendered into writeable language, as follows:-

"You're a devil on earth, Jock T – dd. Jock T – dd!
You're a devil on earth, Jock T – dd. Jock T – dd!

You're hated by men and despised by God!
The devil will get you, Jock T – dd, Jock T – dd."

Such was the song of the children, the women, and the men as they found themselves released from the day's toil, in the mills of the tyrannical T – dd; and it will perhaps not startle the readers of this narrative to hear that those mills were the first of the cotton piles that sent up their broad crest of flame to the scowling sky on the evening of the 16th.

It now became evident that if the working population of Glasgow were not armed as well as some of their southern brethren of the physical force ranks, they were not without a pre-arranged purpose as regarded the tinder-box or the lucifer match. But even as regarded arms, they had not yet been proved – no actual warfare having occurred on the first day of their commotion. There was much galloping about of dragoons, and marching of infantry; a few collisions with the police and a great mustering of yeoman cavalry. There were dispatches sent off to Leith Fort, and Stirling Castle for reinforcements of artillery. The chief authorities planned measures of defence: and men, not the foremost on the platform or the hustings, planned measures of bold aggression. There were some who having sworn to be first in the hour of danger now shrank into dumb inactivity; while men of the loom, the anvil, the awl, the needle, or the cotton-mill, who had never vaunted of their prowess or their wisdom, were now in the busy front of secret preparation. The military prevented any meeting from assembling on the Green, as had been intended for the evening; and night, at first, scared by the red fire of the falling flames, now saw the embers die and the tumult cease; and dismissing her winking attendants to take a sleep in heaven or meet her in some other world, she called silence to the elements, bade Clyde lie quiet, and breathing blackness on the troubled city, left it to repose.

But there was no sleep in Glasgow. A waking night-mare sat upon the darkness, and distorting the realities of the present with visions of the future, dispensed its influence over the minds of men, filling all parties, alternately, with hopes, fears, easy peace, and startling affright. Whispers, were the words – even weak whispers; but the thoughts were strong, and strong men bethought themselves of what should be done.

All was yet dark and soundless, when, about the hour of two on the morning of the 17th, news from Edinburgh, by express, gave information that Dundee was, the previous evening, also on the verge of insurrection. Scarcely had this intelligence been delivered by the messenger to the authorities, for whom it was intended (to induce them to take the most hasty precautions in the west), when a cry rose, that the great cotton-factories, near the cattle market, were on fire. At the same time shots were heard from that direction, and bugles sounded, "Turn out the whole." It was an electrifying burst of new life. A large party of police and special constables, under the efficient command of the active but ill-fated Captain M –, started from the Tentine buildings, and at a quick run were making their way up the Gallowgate, when suddenly a shower of stones was hurled on them from near to where the thoroughfare, forming King Street Calton, joins the Gallowgate. To their surprise, here, they discovered, in attempting to attack, and take prisoners, the parties who had thrown the stones, that this branching thoroughfare was barricaded by upturned carts, logs of wood, and other impediments. Captain M –, however, not daunted at this, sent forward his force to the Graham square fire, under some of his superintendents, and with a section of his men made an assault on the barricade. The staves of the police and the stones of those behind the barrier for some time rattled about, no one knew how, where, or what at; but at last, the Captain, grappling hand to hand with some of the Caltonians, (for it was the inhabitants of Calton, who were making this a position of insurrectionary strength), placed a pistol to the breast of one and demanded his submission. "Fire that pistol and you're dead!" was the hasty exclamation of a mechanic, who, in turn, presented a musket to the breast of Captain M –. "Villain! down with that musket!" said a sergeant of the police, who suddenly sprung behind the mechanic, and at the same time levelled him to the street with his truncheon. "Murderous rascal!" uttered a dozen voices at some yards distance, for the party of police were now in possession of the barricade, having been so soon successful as was supposed because of the people's unwillingness to shed the first blood. "Murderous rascal!" as we have already said, was the exclamation of a dozen voices, and at the same time a pike, the first stained with blood, did the first deed of this day against the legal forces. The sergeant was stabbed through and through; and groaning some prayer or curse, he staggered and expired.

"Fire! men, fire!" was the instant command of Captain M –, for the police were armed with long horse pistols, for this occasion, in addition to their common staves. They fired! He fired! and fire was returned from those whose tremulous hands and panting hearts had up to this with-held the beginning. But the cry of "fire!" "down with the blue-coated villains!" was now heard distinctly and earnestly from the men in the fustian jackets; and so obedient were those of them who were armed to the call, that the din of musketry instantly drowned all other sounds. "Wretch! ras–rascal! – devil!" was the half-choked utterances of a strong pikeman, with whom Captain M – had grappled, and whom he was crushing against a wall, choking him with one hand and wresting the pike from him with the other:– "Wretch! villain! Kate help me." Hearing which, a female exclaimed, "Oh my gracious! our John will be murdered!" and immediately uniting in the fray, attempted a rescue. Two policemen assisted the Captain. Three mechanics came to the help of John and his wife; and hard hits were dealt about by all of them.

"Peggy White! what are you about? put up the window for heaven's sake and break their heads with the axe, or the poker, or the tongs – oh my goodness, our John's down!" was the cry of Kate, who addressed some one that made no answer, and who now laid on the shoulders of a policeman most prodigiously, with a sawyer's hand-spoke.

"My eye! here's the trump o' the beaks in trouble, Bob!" said a well known professor of the light-fingered art, who had had many a time to take the earth when hunted by the keen scented M – ; who now recognised that chief functionary for the first time during the fray; and who was addressing himself to a brother freeman that had as much reason to shun the torch of the Captain! "Strike me dead! but the trump's beak's catching it now, and no mistake!" he continued; and then pausing a moment, added, "give me that Queen's messenger! I'll do for him!" and in a twinkling a gun was discharged among those who still grappled with each other; but the shot did not hit the Captain, though intended for him and though fired within a yard of his breast. John had a moment before been dragged from his position against the wall by his amazonian wife, and was just in the place to get the bullet intended for Captain M –. He got it, bled, staggered, let fall his pike, groaned, died; and Kate, like a tigress, as she was, flew on the already exhausted chief of police. It was over with him. The most daring, dextrous, and useful police officer that ever did

127

service to the citizens of Glasgow, died in conflict by the hand of a woman. The merchant citizens have since done honour to him by a public funeral and a monument in the Necropolis: he deserved the honour. Peace and respect to his memory.

This encounter which lasted altogether about a quarter of an hour now ended by the police being fairly defeated. Some of them were left wounded and dead, though not so many, as was at first supposed, for several of those who escaped hid themselves in their relatives' houses, and were never seen for the next five days.

The military were now scouring the streets in all directions as they had done the previous evening; but frequent assaults of stones from people stationed at windows, and now and then, a shot from the same stealthy assailants, told them that the spirit of insurrectionary aggression was rising.

As soon as daylight enabled the eye to make the discovery, bills were seen posted in every quarter proclaiming the city, the suburbs, and the countries of Renfrew and Lanark under martial law: decreeing instant trial by courts martial to any person taken with arms in their hands, which crime was punishable with death.

At the same time bills were scattered in every direction containing the following –

NEWS!   NEWS!   TO ARMS!   TO ARMS!
AND NO COMPROMISE!

"Birmingham is triumphant! An express this morning informs us that all Lancashire and Yorkshire are in arms! Dundee and the whole north-east coast of Scotland are beginning! Edinburgh is ready! The troops in the south and west of England are all called into London! The Banks have stopped payments! Now is the time, sons of the factories! Triumph or Revenge!

And shortly after, another bill appeared which contained –

"Up with barricades in every street; no robberies, no more fires; reserve the torch to the last extremity, we shall triumph. The brave O'Connor has fallen at the head of the patriot forces in Manchester. Let those who emulate the noble sacrifice resolve to avenge his death! Men of Glasgow, do not hazard the cause by a battle on open ground. Let every window have its sentinels, and every sentinel his rifle, pistol, stone, brick, bottle, boiling water, melted lead, vitriol, or whatever life-destroyer he can lay hold of. Women of Glasgow! put the infants to bed; and make those who are able, gather stones; Stand you by your husbands, and help your sweethearts!" "GOD SAVE THE RIGHT"

Then there was a counter declaration signed by the Magistrates, and several other parties who commonly profess to be the friends of the people. It stated that –

"The rumour is false! No town in the kingdom is in insurrection but Birmingham; and there the people are giving in. Ten pieces of artillery are now on their way from Edinburgh to destroy you; and by destroying you, to level our lovely city to the dust. Refrain from

128

violence and all prisoners hitherto taken will be pardoned; proceed, and they will be executed by sentences of a court-martial every half-hour."

To this, other announcements from time to time succeeded.

The district of Calton soon bore the symptoms of a locality, formidable for insurrection. Every thing that could be found moveable was piled as barriers at different parts of the streets, principally at corners where one line joined another. The barriers raised at the corners of Green Street, and King Street; Green Street and Kirk Street; Green Street and Great Hamilton Street and Main Street; and Kirk Street; with all the intermediate lanes and closes, were such as effectually opposed the police; the military being mostly employed in the mercantile districts of the town, a very severe trial to carry the defences of the Caltonians was not made during the 17th. The most formidable barrier of all, however, was that thrown across the Gallowgate near the Molindinar burn. This cut off the communication between the eastern districts and the city most effectually. It was maintained until the arrival of the rocket troop from Leith fort on the morning of the 18th; but more of that hereafter. In the meantime we shall describe the dreadful scenes that ensued in Charlotte Street, where, as also in St. Mungo Street and other lanes leading from the Gallowgate towards the London road, barricades were erected to prevent the ingress of forces from the Green.

Charlotte Street, in order to make the barrier at the Gallowgate bridge tenable, was a most important position, and it was quickly under the centre of insurrectionary operation. By daylight, a party armed with rifles, fowling-pieces, pistols, pikes, sabres, bars of iron railings, handspokes, hatchets, pickaxes and many other varieties of weapons for fight, and implements for work, took hasty and unceremonious possession of the houses in this street. Materials were wanted for the barriers, time was pressing, and smash went the doors and in went the insurgents. Barrels, boxes, benches, and whatever could be laid hold of most readily were speedily applied. Two companies of infantry from the barracks having been opposed in their progress westward, at the Molindinar barricade, were for a time exposed to a rear fire from the end of this street, as also to a pelting with stones and an irregular window firing from houses in the lower part of the Gallowgate. One company of these succeeded in establishing itself in the houses by which it as effectually prevented the insurgents from proceeding eastward beyond the barricade, there being another barrier erected and strongly defended at the turn of the rising ground half way between the Molindinar burn and the cross, so that the intermediate space was a strong position and effectual stoppage to the communication with the barracks and the city, or with the city and the Calton: this company took and held possession of the low part of the Gallowgate, while the other attempted to force its way through Charlotte Street, to come round by the Green, to join the forces that held the Salt-market.

But Charlotte Street was not so free a passage as they had supposed. A hastily designed, loosely formed, yet, for a time, efficiently obstructing barrier opposed them. The fire from the immediate rear of this, was heavy, yet by no means so smart as the fire from the windows of various houses in the Street, from which windows, though the shots had to take an oblique direction, the messengers of death and wounds were plentifully discharged.

"Oh save us! save us!" was the cry of some poor woman whose domestic sanctuary was thus early broken in on by armed men – "Oh save us! what's this we have lived to see?"

"Fire on my lads; take a good aim, never mind tears, and cries, and prayers to-day! take a sure aim: One shot that tells, is worth twenty that only makes a noise," so said old Watty Brock, once a non-commissioned officer in the 26th Cameronians, a man who had seen service, and who now commanded, or seemed to command, a party of insurgents in Charlotte Street.

"Open your door Mr. S –;" was the demand of another party, who attempted to get admittance into a house which as yet had its door closed.

"No, you blood thirsty villains; I'll suffer my house to be burned about me, ere I will let a set of thieves, robbers, murderers, down-right murderers into it: I'll suffer martyrdom first;" was the reply of its owner, an old man, from behind the door.

"That sledge hammer, and the pickaxes, bring them here; burst the door: that's the way: another blow: there it goes: now up stairs. Hurl all the boxes, chests and bedding outside. Put the mattresses to the window to screen you from the musketry, for *now* we'll have hot work of it."

"Why do you halt! pull the old superannuated idiot out of the stair! *that's* the way my boys!"

"Oh father! father! give them all they want if they'll only save your life! give them everything!

"Young lady," said one of the aggressors, "We want nothing of you but the use of your house. We are neither robbing nor murdering; killing we may be, for while the bad cause is supported by blood, the good has no alternative."

The young woman was proceeding to tell that she had an old infirm aunt in the house that had not moved from her couch for many years, that she hoped they would not molest her; and that she saw a man among the mob that had entered, who was once prosecuted by her father, and who had in consequence threatened his life: but she was stopped short by the tumultuous rush that was made into the house from the outside, which rush was caused by the appearance of a troop of yeoman cavalry at the head of the street, where as yet the barricade was imperfect.

And now there was din and disaster. The yeomen at the head of the street fired; the infantry at the bottom fired. Every window vomited fire, smoke, and thunder. The upper barricade gave way. The yeomen came down; and the insurgents retreating, forced an entry in spite of bolted doors, fainting screams, threats and entreaties, into every house. Bullets struck up, and bullets struck down: bricks, stones, pots, crockery and every moveable missile was hurled on the heads of the Yeomanry.

The Revolutionist (1840)

Hath any one of our readers beheld, with unmingled pity and horror, the paraphernalia of a state murder – hath he looked with unsparing eye, on the formality, and heartless manoeuvring, characteristic of royalist government assassins, about to carry into effect the last awful sentence – pronounced on an erring, but it may be, an honest culprit, who hath, by the wisdom of our ancestors and the legality of modern "justice," been doomed to die? If so, hath he felt with the keen pang of one who can look with sympathy on the misguided actions of a weak mortal about to be hurried into eternity, for an offence which the philanthropic proves to be rather an error of frail humanity than a predetermined crime?

If we had the supernatural power of calling up the past, and again producing the realities of D'Orsey's execution,* our readers would at once have been attracted by the appearance of a young man who stood alone amongst the assembled thousands, like himself, straining their visual organs to bursting, with all the anxiety of interest, to catch every look from the benevolent sufferer, and every movement that marked the proceedings of his murderers. The prepossessing appearance of the onlooker would have excited the attention of a casual observer: he was tall, and somewhat of a light make; the finely chiselled features and classic curl of his dark brown locks, of themselves would have endeared him to all who make the outward man their test, and physiognomy a guide to the stature of the man. His dress was that usually worn by the artisans of Paris; it was, however, incomplete, as the hurry of excitement had torn him from his toil *minus* his upper garment; the sleeves of his shirt were of snowy whiteness, vieing with the occasional paleness of his face: one sleeve was rolled up to the elbow, betraying the wiry muscles of one who had been born to labour for his daily bread; both arms were folded across his breast, and he gave no outward evidence of life, save the violent heaving of his chest – the straining blood-shot eye – and the perpetually changing blush of his naturally pale cheek.

When the prisoner made his appearance, guarded by the minions of despotism, the Operative – for such is the most fitting name by which we can designate him – turned his head aside, and tears of manly sympathy were seen gushing down his dark expressive eyes, affording ample scope for the observer to admire the warmth of his affection for the Apostle of Liberty. All eyes were fixed on D'Orsey, as he uncovered his noble brow, and deeply interesting were the expressions of feeling for the Poor Man's Friend; but when the Count de Sombreuil was observed to approach his victim, a general groan of hatred burst from the spectators. The Operative caught with a frenzied grasp the powerful arm of a friend who stood beside him. "Will they dare to murder him?" he emphatically ejaculated; "can they be really so blind to his virtues as to desire his destruction?" But the response of his neighbour was unheard, unheeded, or the neck of D'Orsey was now uncovered, and now might be marked the concentrated movement of the troops surrounding the scaffold, and the

* D'Orsey is the republican hero of the prequel to this story. He is executed by his arch-enemy the Count de Sembreuil in the early stages of the French Revolution [ed.]

portentous addition to the numbers who surrounded the Republican. A pause of momentary duration ensued, and the prisoner knelt at the block – his lips are moving, and his prayers ascend on high; but can they disturb that sacred moment with such unfeeling haste? – the shining instrument is now exalted – for a moment it is suspended in the air – and now, O God! D'Orsey is murdered!!! The patriot's soul is borne to its haven – the home of the righteous – the oppressed.

What a cowardly want of decision stains the character of the people – of the multitude! All is now silence! – nought is heard but the sobs of women and children; nor can aught be seen save the glistening cheek of the weather-beaten, hardy veteran! How strange! that the men who are first on the path of danger, should weep; yet true it is. Those men were the friends, the companions of D'Orsey, in his struggle for American liberty, and yet how calm they are. But hark! O no! it cannot be. They have no arms! What signifies a mere tumult? it is an every-day occurrence – and amid a host of soldiery! and yet it is true! There is a movement – an universal heaving of the mass. What can be their aim? surely there is no intention of rescuing D'Orsey! No, no; the bloody tragedy is finished – THAT cannot be their aim.

For a time there could be no apparent aim with the "rabble." But where is our hero, the Operative? he is gone! nor can our eye distinguish him amongst the assembled thousands:– there he is, flying to and fro, amid the dense mass. How well adapted he seems for such an arduous task! he is here, and there, everywhere – now in front of the instrument of death, facing the soldiery – then, again, forcing his way to the extreme rear of the multitude; and, again, returning to the centre, he is easily identified: none so busy, nor yet so conspicuous as he is; none oppose his endless wanderings – *he must be a favourite*. There would have been no difficulty *now* for an isolated spectator ascertaining that all was not "right" with the populace, for the soldiers now faced the crowd, their burnished arms glittering in the sunshine, and their firelocks "ready" to commence the work of death. Once, only once, did the mob, as if impelled by some unseen power behind, rush in amongst the troops: it must have been at some opportune moment, as the rush is well sustained. Now the ranks are broke! the military are divided into three parties – nor is it possible they can regain their former position, for thousands of the unarmed crowd prevent their consolidation! wide and more widely separated is each group of the royal troops from its fellow. The main body is headed by the Count de Sombreuil, whose uplifted arm and shining blade is continually visible. Vainly does he command and threaten the subordinates. The pressure still increases and confusion becomes more and more apparent amongst the trained warriors. There is the Operative, with stern fixed eye upon the Count, – now he approaches the "noble" de Sombreuil – he is beside him, and few could discern that movement of the Operative; he has pricked the flank of the Count de Sombreuil's steed – it rears and plunges, and even now has left its fellows, and is dancing amongst the "rabble." The indefatigable artisan is still beside the Count. At this moment a few of the soldiers charge amongst the crowd, and regain their lost leader; foaming with passion at his steed, he seeks scope for his unbridled resentment, by striking at all around with his sword. The demon seems to possess him: he has given orders to the soldiers to fire upon the mob! Too subservient to the will of a tyrant, they did fire, and many a widow and orphan is left to mourn the treacherous act; but our hero has escaped amongst the fortunate few, immediately surrounding De Sombreuil, with the speed of lightning. The Operative grasped the murderous arm, and, quick as thought, hurled the despicable wretch from his horse. All is the work of an instant. None of his subordinates are prepared; and few of his minions are ready to sell their lives for such a worthless "noble." He is now completely at the mercy of the infuriated people. By some mischance a neatly folded document fell from the breast of the Count during the struggle; one of his guards, for he had guards enough NOW, *good, new and true,* lifted the paper from the ground, and gave it to the Operative, who still clung to the side of the "noble." It was addressed "To the Count de Sombreuil, in haste." The contents were written in a hurried business hand, as follows:– "It is our will and pleasure, that D'Orsey suffer the full penalty of his rash conduct. The rapid increase in the number of those turbulent orators demands that instant, and effective means must be adopted to crush the spirit of rebellion in its birth, or witness the noble fabric of our constitution utterly and for ever destroyed.

"Let your exertions be wholly applied to the attainment of that object, the importance of which we endeavoured to impress upon you at our last interview. Spare neither titles nor gold, nor any means whatever, to effect your purpose.

"Should it so happen, that the enthusiasm of D'Orsey is really sincere – that his attachment to Republican principles cannot be tampered with – then he must die.

"You will, as a matter of course, procure an ample and efficient military force on this occasion; and as there is a probability of some insane attempts to rescue D'Orsey, encourage it for a time, that you may procure an additional number of examples, that will afford a beacon to warn all and sundry who may in future dare to question our justice – our authority.

"Knowing your attachment to our interests, and aware, also, of your ready assistance on emergency, we may add, that circumstances may occur, which, on your part, require additional exertions and zeal in our behalf more than we have anticipated; if such circumstances should occur, we would only add, that you are left to act entirely as you consider necessary. And should it so happen, that our affairs require immediate and decisive steps to promote our interests, or add to our power, spare neither age nor sex."

The Operative finished its perusal, and seemed for a moment lost in thought; he again looked at the document; it bore no signature, but he observed that upon the wax with which it had been sealed there was an impress of the secret and confidential seal of Louis XVI!! Alas! the fact was too apparent, the finger of royalty was visible on the murderous scroll; the WILL of the sovereign was evident. The infernal policy of a king had penned the harrowing lines – "As there is a probability of some insane attempts to rescue D'Orsey, encourage them for a time! that you may procure an additional number of examples; that will afford a beacon to warn all and sundry who may in future dare to question our justice – our authority!!"

Almost suffocated with the surprise and horror consequent on reading this damning sample of crown-craft, the Operative handed it to a young man who stood beside him, with orders to "read it to the multitude;" no sooner was the desire expressed, than the young man was elevated on the shoulders of two brawny plebians, – men formed by nature to be useful to their fellows, and well adapted for the honest, though humble, rank of labourers. While these royal instructions were being read, Count de Sombreuil motioned to the Operative, as if desirous of speaking to him. Unwillingly the artisan approached – "You hear the princely offers of his most sacred majesty to your infatuated friend

133

D'Orsey – 'spare neither titles nor gold;' these he blindly refused; had he accepted of them, he would have been still alive, and ready to be received as an equal by the wealth and rank of Paris:– these terms I now offer you on this condition alone, that you forthwith assist me to escape from the power of these vulgar brutes," sneered the Count, pointing to the crowd by whom he was surrounded; "nay, more, I pledge my honour, as the second noble in France, to procure not only wealth and titles to you for this one act, but I also assure you, in all certainty, that you will be received by his most sacred majesty as a friend; and also that you will be rewarded for this service from the treasury of your sovereign, and created one of his majesty's privy councillors." He looked at the Operative with the eye of a courtier desirous of marking the progress of his treacherous villainy.

"No, count, no," exclaimed the Operative, "you mistake my character, I am poor in means, yet I would fain be rich in honest worth; it suits not my character to share with a crowned thief in plundering honest industry; I have no ambition to become the fawning slave of a king, nor the tool of a brothel keeper; I hate the robber who filches a poor man's last morsel, and I scorn the rank and titles of the worthless who riot in luxury at the expense of the widow's sorrows and the orphan's tears. For years, even from boyhood, have I longed to wrest the power from the grasp of kings, and their worthless coadjutors; Heaven points the way; the hour hath come, and I swear by all that is sacred in heaven and on earth, that I shall never rest from my labours until universal liberty is firmly established, and until the labourer receives the fair and full reward due for his toil, and tyranny is utterly and for ever purged from our earth." So saying, and darting a withering scowl of contempt on the Count de Sombreuil, the Operative turned his back upon the Count, who now betrayed evidence of his hereditary "nobility" by attempting to bite the hands of his guards, tear his clothes, and perform some other antics only known to his caste in the hour of danger; which failed not to excite the merited contempt of his more "humble" adherents.

The attention of the Operative was now wholly engrossed in devising means to ensure the success of the "rise", by distributing trusty messengers to watch and report the movements of their enemies; procure arms; and electing competent and faithful leaders. Many of the citizens were now armed; these were selected and stationed opposite to the different streets that led to the great square, in which they were assembled. A council of thirty-six was then elected and empowered to act as the executive; these, with three leaders, (the first of whom was our hero the operative) formed the entire legislative power of the vast assemblage. Delegates were deputed, and sent to all the different quarters of the city, and acted as politic missionaries on their route, rousing the citizens wherever they appeared; and successfully did they perform their undertaking, for the strength and numbers of the rebels were continually increased and argumented by the addition of fresh volunteers, and an occasional supply of fire-arms procured from the different gunsmiths' shops throughout Paris. We have been thus minute in describing the character, plan, and operation of a French revolt, as we are well aware that many of our readers have no means nor opportunity of ascertaining more of the characteristic features of republican France than what the pleasure or policy of a government paid "historian" may condescend to grant. But to our tale: The trial of the Count de Sombreuil now engaged the attention of the executive council. After a strict and unprejudiced examination of facts regarding the conduct of the Count, the members unanimously affirmed "That Count de Sombreuil, after a most careful examination of facts, sworn to by his own soldiers, and many respectable civilians, has been found Guilty of Injustice, Tyranny, and Murder."

This decision having been made known to every human being in the assemblage, the council then demanded, "What punishment should be awarded to Count de Sombreuil?" The multitude unanimously voted "That Count de Sombreuil be punished with the same instrument, and in the same manner as our immortal Patriot D'Orsey was murdered! and that this sentence be instantly carried into execution."

The Count, who presented a most miserable appearance to the multitude, having by the violence of his terror nearly lost his reason, was borne to the scaffold, with the aid of a window-shutter, on the shoulders of four young men, where having fainted, he was restored to his senses by the timely arrival of a most benevolent medical gentleman, and staunch republican, who administered some restoratives to the despairing "noble". The council having consented to the request of the "rabble," viz., "to see Justice duly administered to the Count de Sombreuil," sent for a priest, one of the most popular favourites of his "class;" a most generous and humane man. The holy "father" was soon beside the poor "noble;" but the moment he was perceived by the Count his ears were assailed with the most horrid and blasphemous imprecations on the "hoary headed –!" as the aristocratic oaths of Count de Sombreuil signified. The venerable instructor, shocked at such behaviour in a human being in so trying a situation, retired to a corner of the scaffold, and relieved his bursting heart in freely giving vent to his overpowered feelings.

The executioner approached the Count, who screamed and struggled to avoid his iron grasp, till worn out by terror, he became an easy victim, and shared the fate he had too oft prepared for others. He died unwept for – unlamented.

Messengers arrived, who informed the Operative that immediate steps were about to be taken by the government to suppress the tumult; and also that the troops that had left the ground might be looked for every moment, with double their own numbers, and a reinforcement of cavalry under the command of the most experienced officers.

Nothing daunted by the fearful intelligence, the leaders instantly commenced operations to prevent the success of any sudden attack. Those who possessed arms were formed into detachments, and distributed so as to command the avenues leading to the great square. That portion of the "mob" who possessed no means of defence were ordered to disperse, and, if possible, gain positions at the windows and house-tops in the neighbourhood, and desired to procure as many missiles, in the shape of brick-bats, stones, &c., as would afford a temporary assistance to their comrades in molesting the troops that might be stationed underneath. All were implored to act in small detached bodies, so as to confuse the "regulars," and prevent the consequences of a "charge" on the part of the royalists. This injunction was obeyed willingly, and all now anxiously awaited the attack.

In a short time the rumbling of heavy guns, and the regular "tramp" of foot soldiers was heard more and more distinctly, until at length they made their appearance in one of the main entrances to the square. On entering, they marched directly to the scaffold; but great was the consternation, and loud were the imprecations on the perpetrators when the body of Count de Sombreuil was discovered. Shortly afterwards two regiments of cavalry joined them; and the appearance of such an assemblage of troops, at such a time, and in such a place, would have elicited a multitude of enquiries from a stranger. What was their intention? Whom did they fear? for all seemed peaceful and square; not a human being except themselves was to be seen: all around, north, east, south, and west, presented an appearance of quiet; yet the artillery were actively engaged in preparing their guns; the infantry were drawn up in solid squares, their muskets loaded and ready. The cavalry were arranged in flank, their burnished sabres gleaming in the air, and officers and men were all hurry and preparation for some hidden danger, some foe unseen.

The pomp and heraldry of war reigned triumphant for a time. This mighty army acquired new vigour, new bravery from the non-appearance of an enemy; they began to wax valiant, in their security, their victory! Now the "noblest" blood of France led the van! and now commenced the "gallant" strutting and "parade" beneath the windows of the peaceful citizens. Had any of our poor Chartist brethren beheld that puissant army, marching and countermarching in their newly acquired "glory!" it might have afforded food for their bare bones, and wholesome nourishment to their rebellious spirits; but we are digressing; – to our tale: For awhile the tramping of war steeds, and the heavy regular tread of the "warriors" was amusing enough, but in the end, even to themselves, became monotonous, and they prepared to retire with "honour" from the field of fight, each officer to receive the personal thanks of his sovereign, and the applause of court beauty! While the subordinates, the "men," were picturing to themselves their share of "honour," and the substantial reward of a sixpenny silver medal!!!

After the preliminary arrangements necessary in preparing for the march, our royal army then commenced its retrograde movement. In front were some twenty or thirty horsemen, followed by the artillery and a few lumbering field pieces; these were followed by the infantry, and the rear was borne up by cavalry. Altogether, it was one of those imposing sights that are only reserved as a boon to the "loyal" subjects of magnificent royalty.

Determined to banish every spark of rebellion, by this displaying of such an "invincible" force, the commanding officers had chosen a somewhat oblique route homewards, that the troops might excite the gaping wonder of the *canaille* at the grandeur of their appearance; for this purpose, they entered a narrow street (the houses on each side of which are inhabited by the labouring – the "lower" classes) that described a straight line of some two miles in length, leading from the great square. To give effect to their martial appearance, and partly from the nature of the ground – the street being paved on a slightly inclined plane – they commenced a slow march homewards. No impediment, no obstruction seemed to await them; all bore evidence of the same deceitful calm, and onward they progressed, by every step nearing the end of the street.

The small shops on each side were shut, no human face was visible. All was silent, until they reached about half a mile from the top, when suddenly the horsemen in front perceived about a dozen civilians, armed with firelocks; without awaiting "superior" orders, the front row of cavalry fired their carbines, and one or two of the civilians fell; their comrades disappeared. The troops then halted; those in the rear not having witnessed any cause for the firing from their position, immediately crowded to the front, and officers and men, horse and foot, were indiscriminately mingled *en masse*, each more anxious than his neighbour to ascertain the cause; none were obedient to the shouts of the commanding officer, but all lent their aid to the oft-repeated enquiry, "What is it? What is it? Who fired?" and none seemed able to supply the necessary information. Confusion prevailed for a time. Looking behind, to the bottom of the street, they perceived all avenue for retreat cut off in that quarter. During the confusion, one of the *macaronie* leaders, with a body of sturdy helpmates, had contrived to barricade the lower end of the street with weighty bales of goods, large stones, and heavy wooden rafters, torn from the bread-bakers' cellars, &c; though temporary, it presented an effectual bar to the egress of the soldiers in that quarter. Above, at the upper end of the street, the soldiers perceived a strong body of men busily engaged in some process of a similar kind with those beneath; seeing the perilous situation in which they were placed, the soldiers were about to follow the "command" of their officers, and were forming into columns, when they saw a large waggon, such as are usually employed in Paris for the conveyance of goods from one quarter of the city to the other, propelled by the mob towards them. It was filled with stones; the trams were kept trailing on the ground, by means of heavy weights attached to them; increasing in speed as it neared the troops in its descent, it rushed amongst them, and dealt terror and death amongst the soldiers in its progress, till shattered by the velocity it drove against the shop windows on one side of the street and was dashed to pieces! Driven to madness with the peril of their position – seeing their comrades hewn down by this new and powerful enemy, the soldiers thought of nothing but their own safety, and attempted to employ no means of defence save that which promised the only chance of escape from certain destruction – an immediate retreat! Impressed with this feeling, they began a retrograde "quick march," and were confusedly hurrying to the lower end of the street, when lo! another foe appeared, in the shape of a second waggon, similar but yet more formidable in its appearance than its predecessor. It was still larger, and had large planks of wood tied cross-ways behind; the planks protruded some four feet, on each side, over and behind the wheels, and in its downward progress swept every obstacle along with it from both sides of the street. Fearfully did it perform its part. Horse and rider offered no impediment to its monstrous embrace. All were crushed beneath or borne along by the gigantic engine, till, reaching the bottom of the street, it burst open the barricades, and hurling across Great Square, drove up against the scaffold, erected for the execution of D'Orsey, and, tearing the wooden fabric from its foundation, fell in pieces amid the ruins of this scene of death!

The remainder of the troops – those who had been fortunate enough to escape the doom of their brethren in arms, by clinging to the walls for protection from their merciless foe – were now assailed from the windows above, by myriads of their *living* enemies: stones, brickbats, and missiles of every description were literally showered upon them. Gathering courage from the imminency of their peril, they threw down their burdensome and now useless arms, and sought their only protection in flight! The last of the scattered "host" were fast disappearing, when a body of the triumphant *canaille* appeared, marching in regular files, and headed by the Operative, and another bronze-complexioned youth; he was a short, thickset figure, of military "bearing;" and, though apparently younger than the Operative in years, his authoritative commands seemed to have their due influence with the artisan and his adherents; for the instructions he gave were obeyed by all; and truly he was well-fitted to instruct, as few men at his age could boast of his experience. The Operative and the young stranger (for he was unknown by the Parisians, and his accent bespoke the foreigner) were evidently known to each other, as they might have been observed, even at that trying moment, to interchange the many little kindnesses known only to those who are intimately linked in friendship's firmest bonds. With their followers, the two leaders – for such they were – marched down the middle of the street, where they halted – at this time many of the mob were engaged in picking up the *lost laurels*, or rather the *left muskets* of the "*warriors,,*" and others were seen breaking with sledge-hammers the carriage portion of the forsaken heavy guns (once in possession of the royal artillery, but now, by the common usages of war, the property of the victorious "rabble.") These guns were miraculously saved from the ruin done by the waggon, on account of their diminutive stature; thus permitting the *macarone* war chariots to pass over them without damage to either.

While the bulkier portion of the mob were congratulating each other on the success of this their first real trial of strength, some workmen were busily employed erecting a temporary platform in the centre of the street; this was soon finished, and three large old-fashioned chairs were placed upon it; one of them was ominously covered with black cloth. The Operative and his young friend were each conducted to a chair, amid the shouts of the surrounding multitude.

It was truly a heart-stirring scene! and no sincere advocate of popular liberty would have felt disappointed with such a reward as that which our two friends now obtained – the warm affection of a grateful and now joyous people! The Operative and his colleague were scarcely seated, when a young maiden, barely entered her teens, approached; she was fair, and possessed the light blue eye that told of colder climes; young though she was, the face possessed mature attractions that few could look upon without admiring; it was lovely, and yet not beautiful; but possessed in the general portraiture an expression indicative of the internal existence of that noblest, heaven-born gift, that wins the channel to the most callous heart, Benevolence. In her hands she bore three chaplets of flowers; they were bright and blooming, and might have afforded the poetic genius of a lover an appropriate semblance of herself. With the assistance of some of the stalwart youths surrounding the platform, she reached the Operative, and delicately encircled his head with one of her wreaths.

The artisan raised his eyes to the face of his lovely visitor, her eye caught his, and the blush of maiden modesty o'erspread her fair cheek, as she faintly said –"Accept of this as an humble but sincere token of esteem, for real merit and honest exertion; less worthy aims are paid by the worthless in gold; live and learn to estimate the true value of the one and the other: reward to the brute, and commendation to the man." Then turning to his friend, she in like manner placed a garland on his brow, and said – "Good and brave men seek no return for their labours but the gratitude of the liberated captive; no recompense for exertion, save the thanks of the honest and true." Her voice faltered, and her eyes were dimmed with tears as she approached the third chair; it had no occupant, and was still covered. Fixing the remaining wreath to it, in the fervour of her feeling, and the true spirit of her faith, she knelt down at the foot of the chair; and while the large tears dropt heavily on her pure vestments, she breathed a prayer to the God of battle for the soul of the departed leader, who had fallen at the first fire of the soldiery, ere the commencement of the attack by the populace. It was a solemn scene. All around the platform were uncovered, and seemed imbued with the same holy feeling; many of those immediately surrounding the young maiden knelt down also, and poured forth their gratitude to the Divine protector for their signal deliverance from the fangs of their mercenary enemies.

The maiden arose from her kneeling posture, and glancing with a look of ineffable benevolence on the pale countenance of the Operative, retired, amid the blessings of the assembled crowd, to her home, in one of the wings of the Great Square.

After a few minutes had elapsed, the Operative arose from his seat, and stepping to one of the sides of the platform, commanding a full view of the lower end of the street, addressed the multitude as follows:–

"Frenchmen, – proud am I to acknowledge in your presence that we have this day witnessed the dawn of a new day in the history of our country! that we have been common participators in a struggle for the freedom of our enslaved countrymen! and that our success informs us that a cheering prospect yet awaits the virtuous endeavours of the patriot, to confer the blessings of liberty on oppressed and broken hearted France! With an unarmed, undisciplined, body of men, we have this day read your oppressors a lesson that time shall never eradicate; and we have proved to our high-born "nobles," that success depends not on the arms, nor the number, but the hearts of those who wield them! Continue, therefore, to act with prudence, but determinedly. Let wisdom guide you in your councils; secrecy and firmness in your decisions, and your country will speedily own that, to do your duty, you only require to know it. In our conflict to day, we have been much benefited by the wisdom and experience of a young Corsican, whose personal coolness and ready stratagems were mainly conducive to our ultimate triumph. He is one of yourselves, and he pledges himself to live only that he may exact vengeance from royalty for its manifold tyrannies." Then taking the hand of the young man, the Operative led him to the end of the platform amid the deafening plaudits of the immense multitude; he then continued his address: "Be not dispirited, whilst ye know that one honest heart beats for your happiness – your freedom. Time and circumstances demand that we bid France a temporary adieu. In our absence, see that you are linked each to each in sacred brotherhood; and we shall return to lead you on to victory or death! In the meantime, permit me to caution you against acting in large bodies; this is the cause of your defeat in your past struggles, as it affords an easy victory to well trained, well-armed soldiers. Swear to me, then, that you will obey me in this; for the lives of my warm-hearted countrymen demand that you should swear." Here he paused, until satisfied with the number of those around him, who shouted, in the enthusiasm of their already bursting hearts, "We swear, we swear, we swear." The Operative cried out, "I am satisfied." Then raising his eyes to heaven, he murmured a prayer of thanksgiving for their success and their safety; and throwing his arms out, as if to embrace the assemblage, he shouted at the full pitch of his naturally powerful voice – "Adieu, Frenchmen, adieu;" then leaping from the platform, accompanied by his young friend, he hurried through the crowd, amidst sobs and blessings, and with his companion speedily disappeared.

Thus ended the first Parisian real trial of strength; it proved a triumph, solely through the wisdom of the leaders; and conveys a great moral lesson, both to the ruler and the ruled. Who or what the leaders were, we cannot positively determine. The following quotation will perhaps afford some intelligence regarding one of them. It formed a suppressed passage from both French and English editions of *Count Las Cases' Journal:* –

'In less than fifteen years from the present time," said the Emperor Napoleon to me one day, as we stood viewing the sea, from a rock which overhung the road, – "the whole European system will be changed; revolution will succeed revolutions, until every nation becomes acquainted with its individual rights. Depend upon it, the people of Europe will not submit to be governed by these bands of petty sovereigns – these aristocratic cabinets. I was wrong in re-establishing the order of nobles in France – but I did it to give splendour to the throne, and refinement to the manners of the people, who were fast sinking into barbarism since the Revolution. The remains of the feudal system will vanish before the sun of knowledge. The people have only to know that all emanates from themselves, in order to assert their right to a share in their respective governments. This will be the case even with the boors of Russia; yes, Las Cases, you may live to see the time – but I shall be cold in my grave – when that colossal but ill-cemented empire will be split into as many sovereignties, perhaps republics, as there are tribes which compose it. The states and principalities of Europe will be in a continual state of turmoil and ferment, perhaps for some years – like the earth heaving in all directions, previous to an earthquake – at length the combustible matter will give vent – a tremendous explosion will take place – the lava of England's bankruptcy will overspread the European world, overwhelming kings and aristocracies, but cementing the democratic interests as it flows. Trust me, Las Cases, that as from the vines planted in the soil which encrusts the sides of Etna and Vesuvius the most delicious wine is obtained, so shall the lava of which I speak prove to be the only soil in which the tree of liberty will take firm and permanent root. May it flourish for ages! You perhaps consider these sentiments strange and unusual – they are mine, however. I was a Republican, but fate, and the opposition of Europe, made me an Emperor; I am now a spectator of the future."

The Insurgent Leader (1840)

He was wandering through the leafless forest, hiding himself in the shadow of the shelterless trees.

The clotted blood froze over an unhealed wound upon his brow; his garments were torn, and soiled, and bloody; the bleak wind pierced through his bones; the continual snow lay upon his bare head; he was feeble from exhaustion and long fatigue; he was perishing with hunger and cold: a keener cold was at his heart.

He dared not seek relief in the villages; he was a vagabond and outlaw; a price was set upon his head; and the first wretch who should meet him would murder him, to obtain a reward, gold and infamy.

He sank down in the snow, to await the coming of death, the only thing which was not his enemy: he was alone and in agony.

A few days since he had a happy home, a fond wife, beautiful children, and loving friends; he was a man of genius and virtue, loved and honoured by all who knew him.

His countrymen were enslaved and injured: goaded into desperation by the long-sufferance of intolerable wrongs, they took arms to redress their grievances.

He was not too selfish to sympathize with them; nor hypocrite enough to prate of pity and withhold aid; he did not stay to calculate consequences to himself; his benevolence was not posted in his ledger: was this a crime?

His fellow-men were in arms, and needed his assistance; their cause was his own, and the cause of justice: he was neither a traitor nor heartless; he became a leader of the people.

Therefore his house was burned to the ground, his wife and babes destroyed within it; his friends, some lie unburied in the place where they were murdered, some pine in loathsome dungeons against the day of the gallows.

Victorious tyranny lamenteth but one thing: that he, the rebel leader, dieth unbeholden and unmocked.

They have hanged his corpse upon the gibbet; brutally they insult the nobility which, even in death and ignominy, is more glorious than their bloody and infamous triumph.

The Maid of Warsaw,

from *The Romance of a People* (1847)

Ernest Jones

(Jones's tale of the Polish uprising of 1830 concludes with the retreat of the defeated Polish army into Warsaw. Zaleska (the 'maid of Warsaw'), Wladimir, and Tsartsima join the retreat, pursued by their Russian arch-enemy Orloff)

In vain Wladimir implored Zaleska to fly – in vain he exhausted every means of persuasion – her only answer was:

"When country and liberty are lost, love and death remain."

Time sped – her resolution was unshaken. Precious moments! The pealing bands and heavy tramp of the Russian columns fell on the ear as they marched across the centre of the city, but few streets off. The path of flight and safety was intercepted.

Zaleska smiled a sad heroic smile. At that moment the sound of four guns was heard, in slow and irregular shots. Like the burst of a volcano the reply of a hundred cannon came shattering through the town.

"Brave souls!" cried Wladimir, his face kindling with enthusiasm – "let us die with them," – and bearing Zaleska onward, he hurried in the direction of the fire, and presently they beheld a small group of soldiers rushing away from a dismantled battery of four guns, and Russian infantry pouring after them. A large old church rose behind the retreating Poles.

"To the church! the church!" cried the voice of Tsartsima, who waved his sword in signal to his comrades – and the gallant troop retreated within the pile. The last volley covered their retreat, and amid its smoke the great doors of the church were closed in the face of the Russians, and securely barred.

The enemy thundered without – they beat at the portal with the butts of their muskets – the massive planks resisted. Meanwhile, thick, fast and hot, came the fire of the besieged – and as fast flew the reply of the besiegers.

"Bring the cannon!" shouted the voice of a Russian officer – it was Orloff – and the artillery was pointed towards the doors.

All waited for the effect of the discharge. It came – and the strong portals were shattered to atoms, while the balls entering the church, tore up the marble floor, and sent the splintering fragments in all directions.

At the farther end of the sacred edifice the tapers still burnt on the high altar, as calmly as though nothing but peace and silence reigned around them. Before the altar were ranged a group of two or three men – the last survivors of that gallant band – the rest lay stretched dead or dying on the pavement. Among the few survivors were Wladimir and Prince Tsartsima. Between them stood Zaleska.

In that last hour all enmities had been reconciled – love alone, pure, holy, perfect, survived the wreck of passion. A funeral chaunt pealed from the altar – it was Poland's national hymn – a fit and hallowed requiem for dying liberty.

When the Russians saw the sacred tapers gleaming – when they heard that mournful solemn chaunt – when they saw that Maid of Warsaw like an angel come from heaven to save the conquered city, the stoutest paused in awe upon the threshold.

"Onward! and exterminate the rebels!" cried the voice of Orloff, and the obedient soldiery advanced with levelled muskets.

The Poles had exhausted their last cartridge – but they stood with bayonets fixed. There was that despair in their attitude, that the Muscovites cared not to confront it closer.

"Fire!" again exclaimed Orloff.

"Let us die together, Zaleska!" and Wladimir drew her to his side.

"And I – I too – claim one smile in dying" cried Tsartsima.

With a sweet seraphic smile the Polish maiden stretched one hand to Tsartsima, who, sinking on one knee before her, pressed it to his lips, awaiting death.

"Stay! Stay!" almost shrieked Orloff, who at this moment recognized Zaleska and Wladimir, and wished to have his victims living in his power.

But the words came too late! At that moment the volley rung – and the bodies of the dead lay dropping along the marble steps of the altar.

"Accurst! They have escaped," cried Orloff – advancing to the dead. But before he could touch the body of Zaleska, a sudden cry was raised.

"Fly! Fly! the church! the church! It rocks! it falls!"

A dreadful crashing was heard overhead – a shower of mortar and fragments came dropping down from the roof – a cloud of dust enveloped everything – and one deep toll from the bell in the tower on high rung with a fearful sound.

"The tower is falling!" roared a thousand voices outside – while within the Russian soldiery with frantic haste rushed to the door.

"Stand! make way!" shrieked Orloff, trying to escape. But a life struggle respects no persons – his troops blocked the way – and ere he had passed the centre of the nave – with the crash as of an earthquake, the great tower of St. Aloys fell!

Loosened by the fire of the Russian guns during the siege, the lower walls had not been able to support the superincumbent weight – and the last support had been destroyed by this final onslaught.

The falling tower buried all beneath its ruins, and the bystanders, when the dust cleared away, saw a new element of destruction at work. Thin blue wreaths of smoke came winding through the crumbled mass. The church had caught fire, perhaps from those very tapers that shone so quietly upon the altar. In the chaos of victory none cared to stay the flames, and the mighty element destroyed alike each vestige of the victor or the victim who had been compassed by those walls.

Nationalism,

from *The Romance of a People* (1847)

Ernest Jones

(Wladimir Scyrma, the Polish hero of the story, is press-ganged into the Russian army, where he becomes a successful officer, and moves in court circles in St. Petersburg)

The winter palace in St. Petersburg was the scene of gaiety – a court festival was being held – and in a country where the crown is the absorbing element of wealth and power, radiated back again, it is true, through an overgrown aristocracy, almost irresponsible to any law save the will of the emperor, festivities like these are pageants such as realise the two extremes of barbaric splendour and western luxury. All that art and science could achieve was gathered round that northern throne – from the light grace of music and painting to the massy grandeur of architectural magnificence; from the fine inspirations of the poet to the rude achievements of the warrior. All was vast, great, surpassing; yet science could feel no joy, poetry no enthusiasm, war no chivalry – for all was cast prostrate beneath one iron will – all was spread beneath one frowning eye; and he who moved along that soft, elastic floor could hear no cheering sound; laughter was no laughter – mirth was no mirth, – it was but the whirring of the wheels of life, through which was heard the jar of jealousy, the tremulous motion of fear, the oily gliding of slavery or the under-working of ambition, all hid beneath the same smooth face, while the hands of tyranny pointed the hours of life. And at times, between the pauses of the music, it was a piteous thing to hear the low icy wailing of the wind without, that respected not the revelries of kings, and to know that that same blast had chilled with death the hearts of shelterless peasants; that it had lifted the rag from the cold breast of the starving mother, and frozen the nourishment on the lip of the dying child; that it had blown over the fireless hearth of poverty, and through the cell of imprisoned despair; that it came big with the moan of a prostrated people as it blew over the mighty wastes of one man's dominion; that it came from where every holy feeling had been trampled under foot; from where every gentle hope had been bitterly crushed; from where every manly energy had been trodden down; and all to swell that pageant, and to make the greatness of that man.

To think that for every jewel sparkling on those wanton breasts, the eye of the exile had grown dim and blind; for every tissue rustling round those worthless limbs the sighs of childhood had deepened into eternal silence; for every order flaming on those military trappings, murder and treachery had been at work, and bones were bleaching on far fields, ashes were lying in far villages, and orphans and widows were moaning with hopeless sorrow in deserted homes through the wide breadths of that vast empire; and then to see the brutal boast of might, the truculence of power presenting its cannon and its bayonet at every turning, pluming its carnage with the crest of military glory, boasting of its murders with the name of law, and flaunting its blasphemy as a right divine: it was enough to make manhood, taking the alarm, cry, Havoc! in its heart; and humanity, that gentle advocate of peace, indignant at the parade of the brute force to beat it down, for once cry, "Torch and sword!" to smite the smiter, and to slay the man of blood.

But, alas! tyranny does not often appear in its full deformity; – it has the beautiful at its command to mask its hideousness; the bright fascinations of life are gathered manifold around it:– music mingles with the death-groan on the battle-field; carnage turns glory, by a touch of chivalry; slavery assumes the name of valiant devotion; cruelty slinks behind the flowing robes of priestcraft; and despotism takes the awful semblance of divine delegation. Thus, once within its vortex, the eyes of inexperience are blinded, – and we may hardly wonder that the young, the ardent and the honest, should fall into the snare.

In one of those brilliant saloons, a young man, whose noble mien gave augury of better things than being the willing votary of power, was listening to the voice of the most admired in that gorgeous circle. Had nothing else made him an object of notice, being marked by that of the Princess Neva, the most beautiful and influential lady of the Russian court, would have been sufficient to challenge attention; but there was another circumstance that raised for him the estimation or the envy of others – he had been distinguished by the imperial favour; a common soldier in the army, he had saved the life of a Royal prince, justly forfeited to the outraged honour of a subject; but though the doom was deserved, his gallant spirit could not brook a murder in the dark, and he had struck down the assassin at the decisive moment. This gained him notice and promotion; – the eye of power being on him, attracted him to deeds of daring; despotism, that is ever ready to recompense military prowess, since this is its most deadly weapon, singled the young soldier forth as an example to others – he rose rapidly in rank – emulation added its impulse – the triumph of outstripping titled competitors had its fascination – (for an autocrat weighs not the rank, or the descent, but the usefulness of its slaves) and *that* was accomplished which harshness or authority could never have achieved: a few years had changed, for a time at least, a young, aspiring patriot into the bold soldier of a despot. This soldier was Wladimir. And now another element was added to temptation. The notice of the princess flattered his mistaken pride – her beauty kindled his imagination – and thus he leant over her chair, drinking in the rich music of her voice, that with its sweetness half opened the gates of his heart to her arguments. And she – the courtly intriguante – if there is truth in looks – she loves him! She – wily diplomatist, from whose thought, men said, all passions had died, and who lived like a beautiful statue amid a world of forms – can it be, that true feeling has awakened in that breast, and won, at least, the confidence of him, who had none other to whom he could confide his secret doubts and hopes; thus making her companionship a dear necessity, and – perchance – screening inconsistency beneath the mask of friendship? But thus it was. He had unbosomed his thoughts to her – the Russian soldier was still a Pole – and the armies of Russia were ordered to march against his country. It was the eve of insurrection, and he might have to charge with the destroyers against the ranks of his countrymen. Blinded as he was, he revolted at the thought – while the bright logic of the princess combated his arguments. Did she fear to lose him for ever, or did early prejudice pervert her judgement? Whatever the cause, she listened to words of daring freedom, that had been treason if overheard, and that challenged her admiration, while she met their truth with all the showy sophistry of conventional philosophy.

"You spurn what you call despotism," she said, "you cling to nationality. Free your great soul from the narrow trammels of conventional society – cease to look to a people – look to the collective race of man. Cease to deal with an abstract theory – deal with a great practical good."

"But how can that be good which causes misery, violence, and death?"

"Listen: – Under this autocracy is a great amalgamation of conflicting interests. Bound by the hand of power, they harmonise. Give them freedom, and have anarchy. One will extends the tranquillizing sway of order over turbulent and savage hearts – your boasted nationality is a relic of barbaric discord. Your class systems breed wrong in *one* community – so national distinctions create evil in the great commonweal of mankind."

Her glittering sophistry verged closely towards truth, and dazzled even the freedom-thirsting spirit of Wladimir.

He, too, hated class distinctions – and he forgot that the impersonation of class-rule in one man perfected its despotism – leaving its evil and divesting it of its weakness.

Something like this may have flitted across his mind when he said: "But your laws are written in blood and upheld by violence – the scaffold, the mine, and the bayonet, win the obedience of the people."

"Blame them, not us, for this. If their savage prejudices drive us to bloodshed, the fault is theirs, not ours. Granted that sordid officials, with their mean, petty passions, tyrannize and oppress, did we bid them do so? We *make* the law – they *abuse* it. You blame Russian tyranny in Poland. Would not Polish officials do the same, were the position of the two countries reversed, and yet neither government might be to blame? Rest assured, Captain Scyrma, while laws have human instruments, they will be perverted."

"Then it proves that the administrators of the law should be responsible to the people; for, were the democratic power there, the functionary dare not exceed his authority among those from whose very hands he received it."

The princess was silent. "And is not all here," continued Waldimir, "trodden down beneath the iron heel of power – Every noble aspiring, every free and gallant impulse checked, crushed, congealed?"

"How say you?" resumed the lady. "Ha! ha! for the follies of men! It is not amusing to hear you say this – you, who, were you free as you call it in your country, would be an abject serf, trodden under the heel of an overgrown aristocracy – pariah of a caste, from which you could never rise, since the brand of your birth follows you to your grave – nay, even in it. Presume to love a noble-born girl in Poland, and see what response you will meet," added the beautiful princess, whose bright eyes had read every secret in the heart of Wladimir. "Presume to speak for the rights of your country, and mark how you will be listened to – no! that is the privilege of your aristocracies! but here, you, the serf, the pariah of Poland, are the favourite of the court of Russia; all know your birth, and all honour you the more; you are the companion of royalty and princedom, of great warriors and statesmen, of the rulers of the earth, and every position and preferment lies open before you. Now, serf in Poland! where is tyranny? Now, freeman in Russia! where is slavery?"

Wladimir was silent. He felt that in one sense the words were true; and the crowning despotism overlooked all smaller distinctions; his impetuous spirit was roused at the recollection of a Tsartima – at the fancied scorn of Zaleska, and he fell into the error into which democracy has so often fallen, of choosing the lesser out of two evils – oligarchy and monarchy, instead of rejecting either as a worthless mockery of common sense, and thinking, acting, ruling for itself. And Wladimir, in his choice, true to human nature, inclined to that which wounded his self-love the least. It was, therefore, with new feelings that he listened to the words of the princess, –

"Oh, Captain Scyrma! Wladimir! a noble career is yours – perhaps in you I behold the man, who, once risen to great power in Russia, may do more for the real good of Poland than ten thousand Scyrmas dying in its ranks, as die they must if they resist us. A bright, bright destiny is yours – a happy one – do not, do not cast it from you – and, crowned with glory, should you love a Russian maid, were she a princess, she will never ask for prouder patents of nobility than those on which your own great actions shall affix the seal."

She rose to leave the room, and, as she passed, fixed her large black eyes upon Wladimir, with a look of – oh! that must have been love! Her sweeping garments touched him as she passed – close – oh! close to him – her breath fanned his cheek – he stood as one entranced – she was gone!

"Fate take me!" he cried, and rushed from the room.

147

'A Midnight Rising',

from *De Brassier: A Democratic Romance* (1851-52)

Ernest Jones

(De Brassier is a renegade aristocrat who becomes leader of a mass political movement purely in order to spite his own class. In order to consolidate his power, he calls a Convention in which other leaders are accused of treachery, and the movement is slyly encouraged to undertake an uprising which De Brassier betrays to the authorities.)

It was a dim, moonless midnight. The stars shone, but a dull, heavy canopy of smoke and mist hung redly over the city – reverberating the lurid glare of the lamps. The town was silent – more than usually so. Even the steady footfall of the policeman on his beat was unheard. The customary stragglers, generally seen returning about that hour from belated orgies, were missing. A vague, depressing solemnity seemed drooping over the scene: in fact, the projected insurrection had got rumoured abroad – and fear held the doors of the wealthy classes closed – while the working population, unwilling to engage in the desperate venture under unknown leaders, kept sullenly aloof.

To judge from appearance, the government was perfectly unprepared, and about to be taken completely unawares. Not only were the police, as already observed, withdrawn, but no signs of military were to be seen. The town seemed abandoned to the riot. But it was far otherwise. The living trap stood waiting although viewless. In the barracks whole regiments of horse and foot, were under arms. To pass by their closed doors, and unrevealing walls, no one could have dreamt of the pent-up hurricane within, for not a light was in the windows – not a voice floated over the gateway and not a footfall sounded in the court-yards. The town-hall, the churches and the public buildings were full of soldiers and constables. Cannons were ranged within the quadrangles – the mansions of wealthy and obnoxious individuals were garrisoned with troops – floating reserves lay moored along the bridges – ready at a moment to be conveyed down to any quarter where their aid was needed. The corner houses of imperilled thoroughfares were filled with infantry, to open a deadly cross-fire on an advancing crowd – while artillery was placed at the further ends of streets, to shatter them with fatal salutations, and throw them back recoiling from the volley, on sudden charges of the cavalry hurled down against their rear. The whole city was a network of military posts. Wherever the rising broke forth, (and the authorities well knew the plan), it was sure to be surrounded on all sides. Wherever a knot should gather, in the wealthier portions of the city, it was certain to be severed from the rest. The field of insurrection, seized beforehand in a hundred places, was lapped all round by a destroying force. Another great drawback resulted from the secret conspiracy, which is unfelt in an open moving of the masses, in the face of day – it was this: that the conspirators would have to throw themselves first into the poorest parts of the town, for there only did their anticipated supporters live. The dwellings of the rich would therefore, be safe, and the authorities would fight under great advantage – for the desperate weapons of fire and torch would be unavailing in the hands of the insurgents; there was nothing to gain in burning their own houses – while their enemies would not fail to retaliate, and, if needs be, burn them out of their strong-holds, or force their way by blowing up the streets, since they would consist only of the dwellings of those against whom they were fighting.

Such was the posture of affairs – when groups of men might have been seen here and there, issuing cautiously from low and obscure houses, in different quarters of the city, and hurrying onward to appointed stations. Mostly muffled in large coats or cloaks cautiously concealing the arms they carried, starting and swerving at every passing sound, they looked more like thieves running away with their plunder, than like patriots marching on to liberate an empire.

At last most of them had reached their appointed positions without molestation, and, as they thought, in secret. They little knew that thousands of eyes were watching them unseen – they little knew that the still churches, and the sober-looking houses, past which they stole unheeding, were crammed from threshold to roof, with eager and resistless foes – they little knew that silent footsteps were gliding after them like their shadows, in the distance, noting their every movement, and that a network of telegraph was in motion over their heads, conveying from steeple to steeple, from roof to roof, the tidings of their progress and their numbers – High above them those signs were passing in the darkness, – as nightglass, or concealed light-signals, kept talking to and fro – yet under and amid this vast machinery, crept through the streets the living fear, and glided the desperate resolve. So disproportioned were the powers, that one could almost smile at the terrible preparation of the government, were it not that insurrection is an inexplicable game, in which the sudden turn often baffle the expertest calculations.

Thus the conspirators moved on in unsuspecting silence. We will follow one of their detachments – it was led by Hotwing – a fiery young tailor – who had armed himself, with two horse-pistols, nearly as big as himself, and a huge old cavalry sabre, the point of which stuck every now and then between the pavement, so that it seemed a doubtful question, whether he would drag the sabre on, or the sabre would hold him fast. However, he was boiling with enthusiasm – and ever and anon he gasped with white face, "The universal republic – eternal death to all tyrants" – he was in the midst of a sublime, undertoned peroration, when a staggering heavy step was heard coming towards the party, and presently a drunken man appeared before them:"Hallo! Stand and give an account of yourselves!" – cried the reveller.

"Oh Lord, we're lost!" – "we're discovered!" – "we're taken," exclaimed the conspirators – and the one slunk here – the other there – while Hotwing was compulsory brave, for in his effort to get away, his sabre stuck between the stones, and pinned him fast to the spot.

"We won't go home till morning!" hummed the drunkard, and passed on.

"Death to all tyrants!" – cried the tailor, drawing his sabre, and rallying his party, who came back when they found the alarm was false. "Where did you run to? – always face a danger, and it flies from you – had it been a real enemy I would have cut him down thus – you see!" he said, flourishing his sabre – "as it was, I let him go! Now on! to victory!"

And on they went. Strange, that conspirators are so frequently the most cowardly of mortals, and that the most timid will sometimes dare the boldest venture. True, though at present, unaccountable contradiction of the human character.

At last, the preconcerted points were occupied – the groups stood waiting. The signal was to be when the cathedral bell struck twelve. Ominous and fearful pause! The feelings of the young recruit upon the battle-field, when waiting in momentary expectation of the first thundering volley from the opposing battery, is nothing to those of conspirator so placed, uncertain of support, challenging so terrible a power, and, with no outlet of escape or safety, if defeated, about to take the first open step of insurrection.

At last, heavily and mournfully, the first stroke pealed from the grey gigantic tower that loomed over their heads unseen amid the gloom, their reverberations pealing above them like the solemn voice of some great spirit in the air, dooming them to death.

Every man started, and a universal shiver ran through all the scattered bands, save one, where the Poacher, who seemed to drink a glorious joy from the scene, had rallied around him some friends, as desperate as himself and scarce more sane.

"On – death or liberty!" gasped Hotwing.

"To arms! – To arms!" cried his nine followers, and rushing down the street, to where others had kept groups of the most desperate assembled, under various pretences, in public-houses and elsewhere, firing their pistols and cheering, they began to draw after them the leaven that were intended to ferment the whole.

"To arms!" – came in a louder voice, as distant shots were heard answering the signal, telling them their comrades had succeeded in gaining their posts, and beginning the movement in their respective quarters.

"To arms!" – rung in a cheerier tone, swelling with added numbers – as standing before a warehouse, the first thin curls of smoke wreathed from beneath their hands.

"There'll be a torch to light the path of freedom!" cried Hotwing – and struck his sabre against the door steps, that the sparks fell showering at his feet.

"Look there! do you see that light?" and he pointed over the housetops, where the street sank down a hollow, to a distant quarter of the town.

"Yes! the lamps!"

"Yes! the lamps of liberty! – that's burning lads!"

And sure enough the glare broadened, deepened, and soon a huge column of black smoke rose majestic and bent sullenly down over the devoted city, while sharp, bright tongues of flame, were darting into it from below, as though trying to eat a way through the mighty mass.

"See the reflection there!" – cried one, pointing to another quarter.

"No reflection that! – fire! fire! the artillery of insurrection is beginning to ply! Well done! colleagues, on and at them, boys!" – cried Hotwing – who was beginning to kindle with the inspiration of the scene. His countenance glowed – his stature seemed to enlarge – and the poetry of his nature being roused, something – ay! even of the hero! seemed to enter the heart of him who had been but a coward so short a time before.

Verily, circumstances change us wondrously! As yet, no opposition had appeared in the streets – the authorities seemed paralysed. In six different parts of the city, the conspirators had commenced operations simultaneously. Six great fires were glowing, spreading, and waving over the sea of houses: the plan was well conceived – those fires lured the people forth, as a candle lures

150

the moth. The conspirators had calculated in the almost certainty, that the report of the city being fired, would draw the populace into the streets – and, sure enough it did. All the doors and windows had been closed – but presently, as the glare came flashing thorough the casements, sash after sash was thrown up, door after door was opened, by the curious or terror-struck inhabitants, to see where the fire was, what part was endangered, and how it progressed Presently they wanted further tidings – they came into the streets, the crowds swelled – curiosity attracted them nearer and nearer to the scene of conflagration – the tide kept setting steadily from all parts towards these luminous centre-points – and soon, despite the precautions of the real leaders of the democracy, and without the slightest intention of taking part in an insurrection, almost the whole of the working classes were out of doors. A busy, anxious, murmuring hum undulated along the immense multitude – rumour after rumour rippled across them like a breeze – and, tossed by vague surmise, doubt, fear, and expectation, the pulse of the population kept beating faster, – they became restless, feverish, excited – dangerous – and lightly to be impelled by any accidental circumstances.

Verily, curiosity is the recruiting sergeant of an insurrection.

Meanwhile, the shop-keepers in the threatened quarters had sent deputation after deputation to the mayor and the general commanding the district, for assistance and support.

The authorities returned courteous and reassuring answers, but withheld the requested succour none the less. They contented themselves simply by moving small detachments of police and infantry to the immediate scenes of conflagration, to prevent its spread – making a few almost harmless charges in the crowd, and merely protecting the operations of the firemen.

Their line of conduct is explained by the mutual correspondence between the secretary of state and the local authorities.

The latter had informed the government, that they had discovered a conspiracy and projected rising, and could at any moment seize on all its leaders – but had abstained hitherto from doing so, in order to glean more information. They received the following answer:

"You are requested not to interfere with the conspirators, since it is deemed advisable they should mature their plan and attempt its execution – as by that means only His Majesty's government will be able to secure all the mainsprings of the insurrection, and prevent any similar attempt in future. You need entertain no alarm as to the safety of the city, for such overwhelming forces will be placed at the disposal of the general commanding the district, as will render groundless all feelings of apprehension."

The secret instructions given to the government agents, were as follows:

"We do not wish the rising checked. We wish the people to be implicated. Take your precautions, and then give up the streets to the rioters. Probably, the people will be disinclined to join in the attempt – since it is originated by a small knot of desperadoes only. Impunity will bring them out – Therefore, do not interfere. When the working-classes are fully implicated – then put your forces in motion, and crush them to atoms. Spare neither sex, nor age. The object of government is to draw the people out, to let the lesser portions of the populace commit sufficient outrages to disgust and alarm the middle-class and then to give them so terrible a lesson, as shall prevent, for another century, any repetition of the attempt. This rebellion must not be nipped in the bud – it must be crushed in full bloom." The local military and police authorities issued instructions to their subordinates in accordance, and added:

"As it is possible that some of the leaders of the people may throw themselves among the crowd, to *dissuade* them from violence, and exhort them to go home, – *shoot these men as soon as they appear,* since these are the most dangerous. But if, on the other hand, you see men leading and urging the populace on, *don't touch a hair of their heads* until you receive fresh orders.

"Since it will be necessary to satisfy the inhabitants that we are doing something for their defence, you must here and there make charges on the rioters – but take care to issue forth in small numbers only – to hurt as few as possible, – and *to get yourselves beaten,* and retire within your barracks and stations.

"Should you find the populace slack to take part in the riot, you must irritate them, attack them without provocation, and so lure and entice them into a reprisal."

In accordance with these instructions, while a power was everywhere held unseen sufficient to crush any rising in a moment, the riot, as stated, was permitted to progress unimpeded. But the people seemed to be enacting merely the part of spectators. Ever and anon, a desperate group kept passing here and there, through the masses, waving red or parti-coloured flags, and shouting "To arms!" "Liberty or death!" but the crowd received them either with sullen silence, or derisive laughter. The flames of the conflagration were beginning to die out, a gloom and coldness was smiling on the movement, the populace were subsiding into quiescence, curiosity was satisfied, and fatigue wanted to go home and sleep, when, here and there small parties of police, might be seen sallying out of their stations, and without a word of warning, drawing their staves, and with gross insulting language, knocking the crowd about most shamefully.

The people, guiltless of any outrage, at first submitted, then murmured, then resented, then resisted. The authorities had intentionally sent out small unsupported parties. The blood of the mass once roused, to quell it was not easy – the police fought with fury and desperation, but their isolated knots were soon surrounded – passion rose – anger got the mastery – a series of fierce desperate scuffles ensued, – and soon the beaten guardians of the peace, lay trampled in their blood, – wondering, when dying, why they had not been supported,

The people were compromised at last!

"To arms!" – cried the conspirators.

"To arms!" – shouted the multitude – and like a living artillery, the gathering deafening roar, clashed from tower to tower, and rolled reverberating over the myriad roofs.

The insurrection was fairly engaged!

Still, the government forces were kept back – sufficient only being put forward to maintain the irritation, carry on the skirmish, and give confidence to the insurgents. Thus the night passed – a constant surge rushing and undulating through the streets – while higher and higher rose the barricades, louder and louder pealed the cheer, shriek, groan and imprecation, – the stray but quick succeeding shots, the occasional regular volley, telling how the desultory work of death was going onward on either side, – and the constantly renewed conflagration, bursting out from point to point, like phantasmagoria lights flashing on the darkness, soon extinguished by the strong hand of power, that

152

feared the conflagration's reaching the rich portion of the city, and breaking forth anew, added a ghastly and uncertain interest to the tremendous scene.

One thing was to be noticed – it was, that every effort of the insurgents to penetrate into the aristocratic quarters of the town, was vigorously and easily repelled, and that the two bands of conspirators, who had attempted to raise a conflagration there, had been instantly arrested. The insurrection was confined to the poorer parts, and allowed to rage and spread unchecked within those limits.

At length, the morning dawned upon that dreadful night, and then, first, the inhabitants began to entertain an accurate notion of the true posture of affairs. The whole lower portion of the town was in the hands of the insurgents – almost the whole of the working population had been drawn into the movement, and there it stood – the stalwart labour of that vast tide of industry – defenceless, angry, impotent, lapped round by death on every side – but fierce, triumphant and exulting, a ready but unconscious prey, waiting but for the signal of destruction to be issued.

In the interval of that night, moreover, the precautions had not been taken by the insurgents, to which prudence pointed. The leaders being utterly incompetent, no strong positions had been fortified, – the time had been spent by the active portion in drunkenness, plunder and debauchery, while the real democracy, the real working-classes, acting without leaders, merely upon impulse, had done nothing but crowd the streets, and repel the petty assaults which kept up their irritation, and, by so doing, also prevented them from going home.

Fresh orders were now issued from headquarters. The time for striking the intended blow had come. The prey was ready trapped – the last scene was approaching. One chance of salvation was still offered to the people; with the first break of dawn, Latimer* appeared among the crowd. He had seen through the plot of the government – he had hurried up to town – and, hastening to the scene of danger, came to warn the victims. He urged them forthwith to disperse to their homes, told them an overwhelming force was coming down upon them, and warned them of the hopelessness of resistance. His words were having weight, when suddenly, the doors of a church, near to where he stood, were opened, a rush of constabulary took place, and despite the efforts of the crowd, whose action in Latimer's defence was paralysed by the very words he had just spoken, the assailants succeeded in carrying off their prisoner.

"I was urging them to disperse – and to obey the laws! I have had no part in the rising!"

The officials smiled contemptuously. That was just the very reason why he was arrested!

The first grey hour of morning, when the damp falls chilly around, – is always dispiriting. Even the veteran soldier feels it on the dawn of a battle-day – much more an undisciplined and unarmed crowd. The authorities, too, had chosen their time well. They had to let the populace exhaust themselves by a night of excitement and vigilance – some weakened with hunger, others overcome with intemperance – and now, when the first sobering gleams were falling on the feverish mass, they selected the moment for attack.

Uncertain what to do, the leaders of the conspiracy were marshalling the

---

* Latimer is a Chartist leader opposed to De Brassier. See 'The Convention,' included below.

153

masses – there was not one commanding mind among them – and, indeed, had there been, they never would have allowed the people to rise at a time when the government was prepared to receive them, and the utmost strategy and statesmanship of the leaders consisted in keeping the people where they were, as flocks waiting for the slaughter.

Presently the border skirmish ceased – the police were withdrawn. Hotwing noticed the fact – he thought the authorities were exhausted and that now was the time to push on to the wealthy quarters and seize the seats of the municipal government, when his attention was pointed to the following object: the great infantry barracks crested a hill on the south side of the city, overlooking its streets. The huge gates were seen to open, and a black stream to issue downward from the chasm. The troops were marching. Four abreast, those fatal gates kept vomiting forth that long, dark, narrow line, the tall fur caps of the grenadiers nodding and undulating like the sable plumes of some gigantic hearse – while their grey coats and brown guns, with bayonets yet unfixed, left not a single gleam relieving the funereal mass. They marched in utter silence, and even their dull measured tread was unheard on the wet ground among the mist – coming down like a phantom-death upon the crowd. An involuntary pause overcame the latter – every breath was hushed – every eye was fixed – the cheer died on Hotwing's lips – as he stood watching which way the portentous march would turn. Right towards the centre of the crowd it came. A tremulous, uncertain motion seized the mass. Should they fly? Suddenly, the low muttering of a drum was heard in the rear – it was taken up on the left, it was repeated on the right – the troops were bearing down from every side! Where should they fly?

Anon, the ear of the most practised caught an ominous sound. It was like the rumbling of fire-engines in the dead of night. "The cannons! the artillery!" – whispered voice to voice – and a deadlier whiteness stole over every face. Still the men stood – not from courage – but from paralysing panic – they did not know where to turn for escape – and so they stood – like a worm that stops beneath the lifted heel.

At this terrific moment, too, not a leader was to be found, save Hotwing and the Poacher – the latter with a smile of demoniac delight upon his lips – the recklessness of the maniac and the courage of the desperado.

Not so with Hotwing – he had mounted an eminence whence to address the crowd, when the march of the troops had first been pointed out to him – he still stood there – speechless – his eyes first fixed on the advancing line – his head then turned from side to side, as from side to side the successive tones of the ominous drum smote upon his ear. He was evidently vibrating between abject craven cowardice and the courage of desperation. The old, rusty sabre had sunk with his unnerved arm by his side – his glance began to wander, hurried and uncertain, through indefinite space – he was evidently on the point of gliding down among the crowd in abject pusillanimous self-abandonment – when, suddenly, the full band of the guards burst pealing from their head – his startled ear drank the invigorating sound, he turned towards them – the first rays of the morning sun fell on the hillside they were descending; and as they moved, as though in reciprocal salutation to heaven's glory they flung out their noble banners to the wind – and like magic, at the given word, the glittering fringe of a thousand bayonets leapt up like flame above their heads, sparkling, shifting, and flickering in magnificent contrast to the sable mass that bore them onward underneath.

Hotwing's eye brightened. "Men!" he cried, "stand firm! this day shall try our mettle!" and, waving his sabre, he led on the boldest to the barricade that crossed the head of the street up which the troops would march.

Thus the turn of a pulse can make a man a coward or a hero!

Few followed him – and those that did, grew fewer every moment, – while, behind, the living wave swept away to the remote side of the great space in which the crowd had gathered – trying to flow off into the distant streets.

But up those streets came nearer and louder the roll of drums and the hoarse roar of clattering guns, and presently the flashing lines of infantry, the high plumes of horse, and the black shapes of the deadly ordnance, broke startling on the view.

Back ebbed the human flood, in wild and frantic tumult – trampling on each other, they rushed once more into the open space – penned in for slaughter by the stern and breathing barrier that closed in on every side, more narrowly with every moment.

There was a deep and painful silence, merely broken by the hoarse hurtling of the weltering mass, and the stifled cries of the weak, of women, and of children, trampled under foot amid the wild, inextricable crash. It was the pause before the thunder.

Meanwhile, the columns of infantry had entered the square from the streets, and deployed along its sides, rank shifting before rank, like clouds widening outward for the storm.

The hush became complete for a moment – fearful expectation stayed even the struggle for life among the crowd. Every ear could hear the dreadful words: "Present arms – fire!"

Like the touch of a single hand upon the key of death, in one sharp volley, without one lingering shot, came the terrific crash, and one gush of fire issued simultaneously from full 2,000 muskets. The distant streets felt the shock – the glass fell shattered from the windows – the ground rocked underneath – but louder than the deafening roar came the shriek and groan, and imprecation from 200,000 voices, – father wept over child, child over parent, husband over wife! One vast lamentation rolled loud, and long, and lingering up to heaven! but before it died, again came that deadly volley, and closer and nearer, onward and inward pressed the flaming, cloudy line – while not a single unit in its ranks was hurt in return by the unarmed, helpless people.

The brutality of the attack seemed to change terror into fury – the cry of fear altered into frantic imprecation, the courage of a mad rage seized the people, and a terrific struggle began on both sides. One hideous form, above all the rest, was seen leading and cheering on the mass – it was the Poacher – and, with a redhot iron in his hand, destruction marked his path, as he rushed mad and blindfold among the very bayonets of the troops. None now talked or thought of flight, – indeed they saw it was impossible – compulsion forced all to struggle, from the natural instinct of self-preservation – and, despite the efforts of the officers, to preserve the ranks of their men unbroken, the frenzy of the people was so resistless that they got in between their lines, and the soldiery were parted into isolated knots. From sheer dint of numbers the people were actually getting the better in the struggle – the troops were breathless – the tide was turning. Then all the bugles sounded the recall, the scattered groups of soldiery fought their way out of the crowd – the people were astonished at their achievement – a loud, thrilling, glorious cheer burst from every lip – the wounded, the dying, the broken-hearted, even, joined in it over the bodies of their slaughtered dear ones. "Revenge! Revenge!" burst the simultaneous cry – the very lips of love echoed it in their bitter sorrow, and on, after the retreating troops, disordered, headlong, bleeding, rushed the furious crowd!

Steadily the troops fell back, – rank closing on rank, as they extricated themselves from the pursuit. "They fly! they fly!" was the shout of the pursuers – when lo! they halted – they opened – and through the chasm, up at full gallop rushed the batteries.

Pity draws a veil before the picture. For one full hour, from every side, grape and canister flew shattering amid the close-wedged throng – like a ball bandied to and fro, from battery-range to battery, from front to rear, from side to side, the populace were hurled, recoiling from each volley, fewer each time remaining standing on the field – while one convulsive pavement of writhing, bleeding, limbs was trampled at their feet.

At last the carnage ceased, for few remained to murder. The hot sun had climbed high in heaven – but he shone not – for the thick packed smoke hung with a heavy reek of blood close over the scene. The sound of struggle died down in one deep, universal groan, and the reformed lines marched glittering across the field. In one part of the space alone resistance still was offered. One hand alone held a white flag aloft – on it was inscribed in red letters, the word "Liberty." Still it fluttered bravely amid that sulphurous gloom – and around it some dozen men yet lingered.

An officer rode up to them:

"Surrender! and you shall be spared."

"Never," said Hotwing

"Your life shall be safe."

"My life – there lies my wife, shot by you through the heart! – there lies my child, trampled to death! My life! THERE *lies my life*! Come on!"

The officer was moved – his savage, drunken soldiery levelled their guns and aimed – he made them desist.

"Come – take my advice, my poor friend! Surrender, I will do my best to get you pardoned." Then seeing that Hotwing made no sign of submission, he was mercifully about commanding his men to retreat, unwilling to have that gallant blood upon his head – when Hotwing suddenly rising from the stupor of grief which had succeeded his last words, raised himself proudly aloft – and turning to his comrades, exclaimed:–

"None have submitted this day – we have been entrapped and butchered – but not conquered – there they lie! our dead – we'll not disgrace them, living – charge, boys, charge! the People's battle is not over yet!"

A faint, mournful cheer rose from the gallant group – as they marched onward – right onward against the proud, strong column of infantry that came moving across the field – like reeds before the torrent down went the weak resistance – straight over the people passed the royal march.

At last the white flag had fallen – the gallant hand that lifted it was cold – the conflict was over – loitering pickets alone maintained the ground – the military music died in distance – but that eternal trumpeter, the wind, lifted a mournful paean on the field – the cloud parted – and an isolated gleam of sunshine dropped, by a strange coincidence, upon the spot where Hotwing and his band had perished.

Peace and honour to his memory! Contemporary annalists may ridicule the poor young tailor – he was but what the world had made him – the mould of heroes is often marred by the die of society – and whatever his weakness or his

156

fault, at least, ridicule him as you will, he vindicated the honour of democracy to the death! Verily! the People's battle is not over yet!

THE OUTCAST (1839)

W. J. Linton

"Thou rascal beadle, hold thy bloody hand:
Why dost thou lash that whore? Strip thine own back.
None does offend, none, I say, none."

Shakespeare

God is good! Our appetites were not given for our destruction. Why do we abuse the good gifts of Nature? why do we thwart the pure instincts which should lead to healthful enjoyment? Because a man swears falsely that he is called by God to superintend the morals of society, does it follow that honest folks should allow his pretensions to interfere between them and their happiness? Because a man tells a lie, does he thereby acquire power to sanctify vice, or to license virtue? – Rose Clifford might not have argued to this conclusion; she might not have *thought* all this; but she *felt* it, and acted in accordance with her feelings – she did not call them convictions. Because she was a woman, Society cursed her, and tore her heart out. She was branded with a fouler mark than that of Cain, and unrelentingly scourged to death.

Rose Clifford's father was a respectable shop-keeper in a country town. His family were remarkable for their harmony and good behaviour. Rose was a beautiful girl, affectionate and gentle-hearted, and possessed of as much sense as falls to the lot of the generality of human beings. She had strong feelings, was what is called a child of nature, that is, was innocent and pure-minded, not suspecting offence, and truthful as she was trusting. No one, who knew her, could call her otherwise than modest, though she was too much a creature of impulse to act always with what is considered propriety by the immodesty of prudes. She did not pretend to strength of mind: those who educated her, did not think that she would ever need such a thing. Such I knew Rose Clifford, a very few years ago. Since, I have lost sight of the family, having settled myself in a shop, in London. I was then what is called a hawker; though, I believe, I was quite as respectable as I am now; since I do not find that I am a whit more honest for keeping a shop.

One night, some little time ago, I was returning home when I was accosted by one of those unfortunates who are licensed to sell disease and vice in the public streets, as a means of poisoning society and prolonging their own fearful existence. She was reeling along, uttering the most obscene language. She looked like the incarnation of most filthy lewdness. Her eyes were sunken and bleared and bloodshot; her face was furrowed with premature wrinkles, and wasted by disease, so that it was horrible to look at. I shrunk loathingly from her impudent leer; but had not reached the end of the street, when I was stopped by hearing a dreadful shriek. I turned: for though I do not approve of men foolhardily thrusting themselves into unnecessary danger, yet I cannot think any man justified in sneaking away from the assistance of a fellow-creature. She was lying on the step of a door, unable to rise, and moaning piteously. I learned from one of the crowd – so sure to collect to gaze upon misery; as if it were a rare thing in cities – that "some *gentleman*, whom she had insulted," had knocked her down: some libertine rather, (for none else could have done it,) who did not lose his temper, the scoundrel! when he insulted the victims of his selfishness. But I am losing my own temper. – Well, I helped to carry her to the hospital; and, feeling an interest in the poor creature, I called, the next day, to inquire about her. She was dying. The coward's outrage had only hastened her admission to her last earthly refuge, the hospital. I was allowed to see her. She thanked me very much for my poor kindness. With much difficulty, I obtained her name: it was Rose Clifford. In an after visit I learned her sad story.

It appeared that a young man, apparently estimable, and of good connections, had paid his addresses to her. She did not know why she loved him, but that his attentions were agreeable and she felt a need of some one to love. His person, too, was handsome; and she was not sophisticated enough to suspect so fair an appearance. It is natural for us to love a beautiful person: for, were not nature falsified by the torturings of social artifice, a fair form and aspect would ever be the index of a lovely soul. But enough that she did love him – as intensely as her nature was capable of. Her father disapproved of the match. It did not appear that he knew anything of the man she loved; but he had chosen some one else for her husband. Perhaps, *his* father had chosen for him: and slaves grow into tyrants. She was ordered, on pain of her father's displeasure, to prostitute herself in "holy wedlock" with a man whom she could not love. Instead of obeying, she eloped with him she did love. She was now in her lover's power: and, clinging to him for protection; heart-avowed to be his, for better, for worse; too simply loving to conceal her affection; her naturally ardent feelings, the embraces of the loved, time and circumstance, all ministering to her passion;– what wonder that she forgot – to ask a stranger to read her an indecent homily on the physical purposes and effects of the love of man and woman? I have said she was modest. It is not to be thought that a modest woman in the arms of her lover would find time to think of a stranger – whatever the penalty. Men and women in such circumstances do not reason: perhaps it is not desirable that they should. Besides, if a father's sanction was not indispensable, surely the sanction of a stranger might be disregarded. What was her offence? An offence against those passionless beasts who would have men and women brought together, at stated times, by certain overseers whose business is to superintend the marriages of God's children, as a farmer *manages* the instincts of his cattle. What was her offence? *Truthful action* – a virtue: Is this a punishable transgression? She was sufficiently punished in the loss of her self-esteem – for she believed the world's *lie*. Yet, she had confidence in the man to whom she had given her heart. Was she to doubt him? She *knew* he would protect her. Alas! he only loved himself. I do not blame the act, but on account of its world-ordered punishment. He was bound to shield her from *all* evil. Yet now, when she had a claim to his gratitude as well as love, he pitifully deserted he. His *love* was but the expression of a sensual desire; that satisfied – he left her. He might still, perhaps, have "married" her; but had not courage to see *his* wife pointed at – even for her virtues. She was left friendless – almost penniless. She applied to her father: he refused to see her or to help her. What could she do? With much difficulty, she obtained a menial situation; but was discharged when it was found that she was with child. She told me a wretched tale of her confinement, and the privations of herself and infant. I had not thought that human nature could endure so much. But, at length, Famine laid his gaunt hand upon her child; and the mother saw no resource but to sell herself for her child's sake. She endeavoured to find the deserter; and learned that he was "married" to another woman – one less loving. Again and again she appealed to her family; but received for answer, that she had disgraced them, and was not entitled to their assistance. "Oh!" said she, when she came to this part of her story, "they knew not what they doomed me to. They bid me starve; they hardly meant that: but, if they could have foreseen what I have endured – I have passed long nights in the open streets, wanting food almost without clothes, pinched with cold, drenched with the winter rain. I have borne the brutal scoffs of the heartless passers-by; the more brutal insolence of vulgar selfishness; – and, Oh God! – the foul charnel embraces of drunken lust –" and she shuddered at the recollection:– "How my heart sickened; and my flesh would creep! – to be the property of every foul thing, diseased or drunken, that would pay the price of the poison which I drank in very desperation, to forget my infamy, though it only maddened me to dream of things that made me desire rather the keeping of the grave-worm."

Poor victim of other's heartlessness! thou art at rest. She died, in dreadful agonies, a few weeks after her admittance into the hospital. She had only just completed her twentieth year.

Preachers of a morality you never practise! ministers of Evil, who write the name of *Reverend* on the front of your hypocrisy! tell me, if the Hell your devilish malice has invented for the punishment of the worst blasphemy, holds worse tortures than this woman's misery? tell me, what blasphemy can exceed this pollution of the holiest temple of the Spirit of Love? Ministers of Religion! you will say, "We are not answerable for this: we do our utmost praying and preaching daily, to cure this Misery; but it is a necessary evil." Whited Sepulchres! Specious Liars! – Every man, who upholds a system which he knows to be productive of wrong, is answerable for that wrong. Every one, who holds out the hand of fellowship to the libertine, is an accomplice in his worst crimes, and guilty of their worst consequences. Shall men be absolved from the foul sin of a life's profligacy, because they pander to their selfishness, by supporting Magdalen Hospitals? or, shall a worn-out profligate, a crawling nuisance, be the cherished guest in *noble* drawing rooms and *respectable* homes, and the wretch's companions be irreproachable? Let those, who tolerate the evil, share the reproach! Good God! that a filthy thing, whose body is one mass of disease, the obscenity of whose mind is, if possible, even more diseased and disgusting, whose heart is rotten – should be the favoured companion of an innocent woman! that *delicate* woman should prefer a jaded libertine, marrying him to reform him! These are the *females* – call them not *women!* – that sneer at the pure who is content with her purity; that fiercely trample upon her whose only crime is a want of immodest hypocrisy. Out upon their unshamed infamy! There is but one name to fit them: and that not bad enough. These are the mothers of slaves, of male and female prostitutes. – Were the *life* of a Man of "Pleasure" laid bare, the world would shrink back with loathing from a monster whose hideous deformity is now veiled by the hypocrisy of *gentlemanly manners*. If any must be cast out from society, let them be these, the purveyors of infamy – not their compelled prey; let them be these, the depraved – not the truthful; let them be these, the willingly prostituted – not the betrayed and unwilling victims!

All that I have written is true. Alas! it is but a faint transcript from not the worst page of the scroll of daily evils. As many are the *Right Honourables* of society whose lives are more abominable than the lives of the many Outcasts. I ask not for their punishment: but I ask, of them, *Charity for their less guilty sisters*; I demand, from all, JUSTICE FOR THE DESPERATELY-ABUSED!

THE OUTCAST IS ONE OF MANY.

The Free-Servant (1839)

W. J. Linton

"Next to governesses, the largest class of female patients in lunatic asylums is Maids of All Work." – *Harriet Martineau*.
"Britons never will be slaves!" – *National Song*.

Jane Stephens was the daughter of a ploughman. The Legislature, in its benevolent wisdom, had decided it was for the good of the community that Richard Stephens should be condemned to hard labour without hope of improvement, for the term of his natural life; and Sir Thomas Jenkins, who drew large rents from the produce of the fields on which Stephens and others laboured, was decidedly of the Legislature's opinion. Indeed, Sir Thomas was one of the "collective wisdom" or House of *Commons*, and as such had voted that it was just and necessary that one in ten of these condemned labourers should be shot or cut in pieces to preserve this beautiful constitution of society. Stephens only thought there was no beauty in slavery: but what mattered what a ploughman thought when the landlord and government, and of course the clergy, chose otherwise? – but my business is with the ploughman's daughter. Jane was the eldest of a large family. She was soon useful: nursed the baby, took her father his dinner, kept the house in order, and was both the assistant and companion of her mother. She was a fine healthy girl – would have been called beautiful, had she been born "a lady"; good-tempered and loving; industrious and ever ready to help any who were in need. When she was about fifteen, her father not being allowed to support his family, it became necessary that she should go to *service*. It was a hard thing to part from home and all who were loved and loving, to go among strangers, to be alone – for her mistress allowed no "followers", thinking servants had not the same affections as others, or, if they did wish to see their friends, there was no time; and to work like a mill-horse – but that she did not think of – in fact, to sell herself for five pounds a year. But then, she would be helping her mother; and anything was to be endured for that:– so, with a cheerful countenance Jane engaged herself to a *mistress*; and exchanged the old cottage in the fields for a dirty house in a narrow street in London, nearly two hundred miles from her native place. Here for three years she laboured as under-housemaid to an arrogant woman who had "no idea of being spoken to by *a servant*;" one who wondered servants' instincts did not teach them how to adopt immediately the habits of every new place, how to humour the ever-varying caprices of possibly a fretful mistress: – but I must pass to her next situation, as maid of all work, procured solely on account of her excellent character from her last place.

And maid of all work she was. Her master was the owner of a manufactory and, consequently, from home the greater part of the day, coming home for his meals. His family consisted of himself, his wife, a son and daughter nearly grown up, a boy eleven years old, a girl rather younger, and an infant in arms. The house was let out to lodgers. An artist had the first floor; an actor had one room on the second floor; and three noisy and not very clean Germans shared the remainder of the second floor and an attic; the family occupied the other attic, the ground floor, and the kitchen. At this time I was acquainted with Jane's master. He was a worthy man, good-hearted, and very kind to Jane. His wife was, I think, as well-meaning a body, but rather warm, and a little bit hasty; and poor Jane seldom passed a day without some opportunity of understanding her mistress's disposition. The son worked at his father's business. The daughter assisted in the light work, but left the laborious part to her mother and the maid. To do Mrs. Simpson justice, *she* was never idle: always working, and muddling as she worked, so that Jane often wished her mistress wouldn't help her. The children were not much less troublesome.

Soon after Jane went to them, Mrs. Simpson was laid up with a bad bilious attack. The daughter had enough to do, nursing her mother, even with some assistance from Jane, on whom the work of the house entirely devolved. She had to scrub and sweep the house, to make the beds, to cook for the family, and the first-floor lodger (who sometimes had company), to wait upon all the lodgers, to answer the door (the knocker had just discovered the perpetual motion), to run errands – marketing &c., to look after the children, and, in her leisure time, to wean the baby. Amid all this, for which she received eight pounds a year, Jane was assiduous and good tempered; and though not happy – for she had not forgotten her home, and pined for the green fields and old country friendliness – still she never neglected her work. At length, her health gave way: she was obliged to leave her place; and a long illness was the result of the over-tasking of her strength. Slowly she recovered, to find herself in the desert of London without friends or money, almost without clothes – having been compelled to part with them during her illness.

From this time I lost sight of her. God knows what became, or will become of her. Perhaps she was reduced to beg her bread in our very Christian streets; or perhaps – for she was beautiful – destitution and despair may have conspired with villainy to force her into that lowest deep of degradation, the life – Oh, no! not the life, the horrible wretchedness of prostitution; or perhaps she may have been fortunate enough to procure another situation: fortunate enough! Is it good fortune to be worked to death, either without or with kindness? (The Simpsons were kind: the rigours of her servitude there arose more from ignorance, which renders people careless of others' sufferings, than from any wilful cruelty.) But, even if she were *fortunate* enough to get another place, what must be the result? Continual toil, unbefriended and without hope, till at length, too old for service, she is compelled to seek a precarious subsistence as sempstress or char-woman, hardly living in some miserable garret; and when that last fortune fails her, she may die of cold and starvation in the streets, "a natural death;" (How dare men so lie? Well-fed jurymen, reconsider your verdict!) or she may have the comforts of a workhouse hospital. Oh! there are but too many who bear this doom. What has become of girlhood's hope and gaiety; of the woman's beauty and lovingness? Did not they deserve a better destiny? Domestic service, indeed! – domestic slavery! Respectable philanthropists! can you not prescribe any remedy?

Now I am well to do in the world: but I keep no servant. My wife and children wait upon me, and I help them. We know nothing of command and obedience: for we take a pleasure in serving those we love: – and I would recommend rich folk and gentlemen, if it be only on account of their own comfort, to discharge all their servants, and be served by those who love them, taking their turn in the work most fit for them. But, even if they are not wise enough to study their own good, let them be just to others, and not condemn their betters (perhaps) to slavery, merely because their laziness or pride – I don't care which: they may settle it between themselves – will not condescend to *menial* offices. Nothing is menial to Love.

"But what shall we do without servants?" says the fine Lady. Do what honester folks do – wait upon yourself! Why should other people be sacrificed to your selfishness? – Poor Jane Stephens! there are many such as thou wert; as worthy of good, and as ill-used: – I can write no more. It is too horrible to think of.

The Young Seamstress (1847)

The incidents narrated in the following sketch took place prior to the formation of that excellent Society, at the head of which stands, as patroness, Her Majesty the Queen Dowager – we mean the Society for the Relief of Distressed Needlewomen. This philanthropic association must have the good wishes of all humane persons, and the last cannot evince or set forth the sincerity of those wishes better than by aiding the Society's funds. Much good has been done, and it is to be hoped is still doing, through the medium of the charity in question; and, as a necessary consequence, an increasing treasury will cause the sphere of benevolence, like the ever-widening circles put into motion by a pebble cast into a lake, to be in a constant state of progression and enlargement.

In the district which extends east of the Minories, famous for its colony of Jews, and not far from the busy region of St. Katherine's Docks, there is a long straggling street composed of remarkably high houses; as if, however, to counterbalance the privilege of being nearer the heavens than other domiciles, these ancient houses are built so close to their opposite neighbours that the men can almost shake hands or exchange blows across the way.

The houses are nearly all of one description, as may be surmised from the uniformity of the placards displayed in the windows. Each floor, single room, and back attic, is dedicated to the service of lodgers, the ground apartments only being reserved for the master or mistress of the establishment. The prices vary on every flat, diminishing in proportion as you ascend to the highest region, where, though the danger, in the event of fire, is the greatest, you have the advantage of being farthest removed from the noise, and the small puddles of water lying stagnant in the street; while in some positions, you may catch a glimpse of the Thames, a breath of free air, and in the summer, a gleam of sunshine.

In one of the topmost rooms of a house in this street a girl was busily employed with her needle. She was fabricating sundry shirts, of coarse blue check, such as are worn by sailors. The apartment was clean, but miserably devoid of furniture. The single table that served for her work and meals was of coarse deal; the three ricketty chairs might not sustain a greater weight than that imposed on them by emaciated beings who are usually found in this locality. The floor had no carpet, but it was carefully washed, and sprinkled with yellow sand. A mattress was rolled up in a corner, and a closet, ventilated by a small window, displayed a second bed composed of bundles of straw, covered by rough sacks. From this might be inferred that the girl, labouring at her needle, was not the only occupant of the room.

Seated as near to the paper-patched window as he could get, was a man about sixty years of age; his garments were worn to the last thread, yet darns which, from their countless number and neatness, could have been accomplished by none but female hands, prevented them from falling into rags; his hair was cut neatly, being parted on the forehead, and his hands and face, scrupulously clean, were not those of a common artisan; yet dull as the light was, it proved sufficient to reveal in the expressionless lines of the pallid countenance, and the vacant stare of the glassy eyes, that the mind of that man was a wreck; that the fine invisible chords, uniting the soul and the brain, were snapped; and that for him, at least in the present state of existence, the light of truth, the universe without, and the world of the affections within, existed no longer.

Near the moping idiot who was the father of the fair girl, two children were at play; the old man did not seem to heed them, though the boy shot his marbles between his feet, and the little girl placed her doll upon his knee. His eyes were fixed on a few ears of corn, a potato and a turnip, which he turned and turned in his hands, uttering over them meaningless words. The source of the singular pleasure experienced by the unhappy man may be traced to memory – he had known better days.

Mr. Melford had been a small farmer. At a short distance from the ancient village of Norwood, in Surrey, and on the left hand as you ascend the hill, you may perceive several little cottages nestling in most rural and picturesque positions; one of these had been his own, together with a garden, an orchard and several acres of land. For many years he had enjoyed the freehold, when a distant relative, a griping miser, discovering some flaw in the deed by which he held the tenement, claimed it for his own property. A law-suit was the consequence; the miser won his cause, and Mr. Melford was a beggar. "Misfortunes," says the old adage, "never come single:" the houseless man lost his wife, and these two great calamities destroyed his reason.

Caroline Melford was eighteen years of age; the idea of resigning her father, whose idiotcy was of a perfectly harmless description, to a lunatic asylum, and her young brother and sister to the workhouse, was repugnant to her nature. She resolved, without hesitation, to support them by her own hands. They moved from place to place, the fair girl battling with poverty, yet hoping, struggling on, until we find her and her charge occupying, as described, a room in a squalid house in one of the most wretched regions of the metropolis.

It was now about three o'clock; the young seamstress had not broken her fast for the day; but the two children and the idiot had devoured for their morning's meal the last piece of bread which the cupboard contained. She still plied her needle, striving to forget in that activity, the hunger that was gnawing within. She hoped in a few hours more to complete her task, and then her employer, Mr. Jenkinson, would pay her for the making of six shirts: these sailor's shirts had already taken her twenty-four hours of unremitted labour and when completed would have occupied her two full days. What was her remuneration? Mr. Jenkinson was considered a very liberal man among the slop-sellers, and so he paid two-shillings per dozen shirts, the workwomen finding their own thread. Generous Mr. Jenkinson! who allowed twopence legal coin of the realm for the mere sewing and hemming one man's shirt – two silver shillings for only fifty hours' labour! We will not say one disparaging word of a gentleman so merciful, liberal, and considerate, as Mr. Jenkinson.

"Now, when are we to have our dinner?" said the little boy, suspending his game of marbles, and running up to his sister's table. "I am dying of hunger and so, I'm sure, is father."

"Dinner! dinner!" said the idiot, catching the welcome word, as he played with his potato and his turnip. "But ye shan't eat these; I shall plant them in my farm next year. Dinner! ay, quick – I'm hungry." And he stared with vacant but wolfish stare toward his daughter.

The little girl joined in the cry for food.

"Now, hush! my dears," said Caroline, without suspending her toil. "I shall not be able to buy you anything until I have finished my work. However, I shall not be long now."

166

"Not long? And what do you call 'not long'?" said the boy in a sullen tone. "I can't wait."

But the little girl seemed to know their relative positions and misfortunes better; for she kissed her sister, and asked if she herself did not feel hungry having eaten nothing for the day.

"Dinner! dinner!" again muttered the idiot from his corner.

Another half-hour passed; solicitations for food became more urgent, until the impatient cries of the three half bewildered her by whom their wants had been supplied so long, that they scarcely deemed the necessaries of life could proceed from any other quarter. But the shirts were not completed, and Caroline knew it would be in vain to apply to Mr. Jenkinson for payment of her work until the last stitch was sewn; and to raise money by pawning was no longer possible – nothing remained to be pawned. A thought, however, struck her; she would not keep them famishing any longer; accordingly she hurried from the room. With hesitating step the girl approached the apartment on the ground-floor, occupied by the woman who kept the house.

"And what do you want, Caroline Melford?" said the worthy lady, whose face was very red; for she had just dined.

"Will you oblige me so far, ma'am, as to lend me for a very short time –"

"Lend you, Caroline Melford?" interrupted Mrs. Gubbins in considerable surprise, glancing from some fruit and a bottle of spirits at her elbow to the intrusive applicant, and back again.

"I shall receive this evening money from Mr. Jenkinson. I only ask until that time for sixpence to purchase something for my father and the children to eat."

"Only sixpence?" said Mrs. Gubbins, elevating her red eye-brows.

"Only sixpence? Bless my heart! one would think by you that sixpence was no coin at all. What a face, what impudence some people have, to be sure! Young woman, I'm surprised at you!"

"I am sorry if I have given you offence, ma'am."

"Ask me to lend you money, and silver too!" pursued the lady in virtuous indignation. "You owe me already just a fortnight's rent. I must say this is rather too bold – too bad."

"I expect some better work next week, and then I will certainly pay you the half-crown due for the rent." "Expect? You are always expecting, and never getting. Hark'e, young woman: 'expect' is a word that doesn't suit me; I give you one week more, and if the cash, which will then be three shillings and ninepence, ain't a-forthcoming, I shall seize the sticks you have up-stairs, and bundle you out, father and children. Now, leave me."

Mrs. Gubbins slammed the door upon her young lodger, and returned to her fruit and spirit-bottle. Caroline ascended the stairs slowly, and in tears; yet her fruitless negotiation and the indignities she had suffered were not sufficient to crush her hopeful, persevering spirit. As well as she was able she silenced for a short time longer the clamours of the hungry three, and determined to complete her needle-work, and so receive the money from the slop-seller.

"Sister, haven't you done yet?" said the boy. "We shall all die of hunger if you don't make haste to Jenkinson's!"

"Dinner! dinner!" still growled the old man with the hollow wolfish eyes.

"I am going," said Caroline. And a few minutes afterwards the girl was on her way to the shop of Mr. Jenkinson.

The slop-seller was standing at a small desk inside his counter, busily engaged with his letters.

167

Caroline had placed her parcel on the counter, and waited several minutes before he deigned to address her. At length he spoke in abrupt and short sentences.

"So, you are come, are you? What's in your bundle?"

"I have brought the six shirts, sir."

"Well, leave them; they shall be examined. Call for your money to-morrow night."

"I should feel extremely obliged, sir, if – if I could be favoured with the amount now, for I confess I am in great want."

"Pshaw! it is your own fault, then. That's the way with you young women. You spend the money on fine clothes as fast as you can get it. Let me see the things."

Mr. Jenkinson looked carefully at the articles, and his scrutiny had reference principally to the quality of the work. While the examination was proceeding, Caroline's eyes fell involuntarily on a little pyramid of shining gold on the desk, one piece of which would have been to her comparative wealth. But her attention was speedily called to the slop-seller, who as he held one of the check shirts closely to his round glistening eyes, frowned a terrible frown.

"Lord help us! what's here? Do you call this *work*, young woman?"

Caroline trembled. It was the last shirt, which she had hurried to complete, and the sewing was less neat than that of the others.

"The thing is not fit for a dog to wear!" cried Mr. Jenkinson, flinging down the garment in a great rage upon the counter. "I pay more than my neighbours by a halfpenny a shirt, on purpose to keep up the respectability of my house; and you dare to bring me home work like this!"

"Indeed, I am very sorry, sir; I have one excuse to plead. I wished to finish the shirt to-night in order to procure a meal for my father, and young brother and sister."

"That's no excuse – none. Now, leave – go back and unpick the work; sew it all over again, or not a copper shall you have."

"It will take me three hours."

"It may take you three days, my dear; I can't help that – now go!"

The inexorable but respectable gentleman pointed his hand towards the door. He then turned with his wonted composure and dignity to his little high desk, and resumed his correspondence.

"Sister is come!" shouted the famishing boy, as Caroline entered the room. "At last, then, we shall have something to eat."

"And what have you brought!?" asked the little girl, peering into the parcel. It contained the rejected work!

"Eat, eat – hungry – starving!" cried the old man, moving uneasily on his stool. But Caroline, who had sustained herself until now, regarded for a few minutes, without speaking, the wretched and helpless ones who depended on her for food. Faint, weary, and heart-broken, her feelings at length gave way; she sank into a chair, and, stooping her face on her little table, burst into a passionate flood of tears.

Our sketch draws to a close. The four went that night supperless to their straw beds. On the following morning the work was completed, the remuneration – a shilling – received, and the wretched family were saved from immediate starvation.

We wish our limits would permit us to trace further the fortunes of Caroline Melford. Still she laboured, still she hoped, and still she struggled on. We do not think we have overcharged the picture, or described what has not happened, or does not almost daily take place, in the eastern districts of our crowded metropolis. No assistance, no mark of approbation from any philanthropic Society – for that alluded to at the commencement of this sketch was not, we repeat, yet established – fell to the lot of the young seamstress. Her unparalleled industry, perseverance, and filial affection, were alike unnoticed and unrewarded. For the sake, however, of our readers, we shall disclose the sequel of her history.

Fate sometimes is kind, when human laws are harsh. Though no Society of good men rewarded the poor girl, heaven did. After some months more of hard struggling, she was driven to extremity, and the woman of the house, as she had threatened, seized her scanty furniture for arrears of rent. The members of this unhappy family were on the threshold, and just issuing as vagrants into the street, when they were met by a young man, the clerk of the lawyer who, some years before, had carried on Mr. Melford's case against the party claiming his property.

"Stop, young woman!" said the attorney's clerk: "I beg pardon. Miss Melford – I remember your face: thank heaven, I have found you at last. Good news, Miss! good news! the case respecting that property down at Norwood, which the old grub Hardflint seized upon, has been again gone into. The former judgement is reversed. Hardflint is ejected and the house and fields are again yours!"

We do not attempt to describe the surprise, the rapture, the tears, which this happy intelligence occasioned. Enough to say, that the sun of prosperity again shone on the late suffering family; and in addition to this, such was the salutary influence of the scene, and sounds familiar to his early days, on the brain of the lunatic, that the mists of idiotcy were gradually dispersed, memory returned, the extinguished torch of reason was again illumined, and old Mr. Melford became as sound in mind, as he was once more happy in circumstances.

The Slave of the Needle (1850)

The world we live in is a bright and glorious one; and kindly feelings, pure desires, and holy passions march with us to our inevitable and inscrutable destiny. Heaven's hallowed sunshine falls on all alike; but there are those with bruised hearts, who walk amidst its beams unmindful of their beauty, and insensible to the warmth they afford. Creatures fashioned after the image of the Great Eternal turn their haggard faces imploringly to the sky, and see only one vast blue depth, in which they can read nothing but the vague hope, the doubtful though half-smiling promise of something better hereafter; and then they look at the stately buildings, the pomp and insignia of wealth, the regal magnificence of power, landscapes glittering in their almost garden beauty, waving fields of God's food, pastures dotted with sleek and stately cattle; and then they gaze at what they see in and around themselves, and with a sigh, oftentimes a groan, they exclaim that there is a world within that which meets the dazzled eye of prosperity, of which no one knows aught save those whom capricious fortune has doomed to be its inhabitants. This world, as typified in the vigorous language of poetry is

> "That frozen continent,
> Dark and wild, beat with perpetual storms
> Of whirlwind and dire hail"

wherein the tossed and troubled soul bewails the hour of its birth in the bitter language of despair. Those born in more genial social climes know nothing of this dreary existence. They never felt the pang that corrodes the heart, or the bitter woe that fires the brain as with a red-hot iron, or had to deplore the loss of a knowledge of the pure or true, or struggle with a life made up of fretful anguish, wounded delicacy, bruised sentiment, and that gnawing and unceasing, though hopeless, craving for those blessings which the human mind, in its lowest degradation, instinctively feels to be its heritage on earth.

There are shadows deep and long on the ground we tread; and the children of success, when they pursue their thousand different ways, are too apt to forget they are treading on the funeral pall of a multitude whose hearts were never made to beat only to the dirge of their own sorrows and miseries – to the wild sad notes breathing eloquent reproach, sent up from every corner of the land. This is a condition of existence as dreadful as the fabled one of Tantalus; and every feature of its wretchedness, every variety of which it is so susceptible, claims from us all that consideration and respectful attention which are based on the best, the warmest, and the holiest feelings.

The participators in the dreadful suffering under which England groans are ranged in classes, and their grievances start up in the gloom like "a forest huge of spears" tipped with dark red fire. Among them is one which flickers dimly in the rear, but the light from it is sufficient to disclose a fair wan face and wasted form, with attenuated hand cramped and stiffened with body-and-mind-destroying toil. That is the slave of the needle; and to leave the language of metaphor, let us introduce her in the garb and under the circumstances which are as common and as well known in this huge wilderness of bricks and mortar as the ebbs and flows of its queenly river.

It was morning, and the old Father Frost and his cousin, the Snow-fiend, had been very busy during the night, for the streets were whitened, and the icicles, like pendant drops, hung from the house-tops, window-sills, and lamp-posts, in a very glistening but by no means comfort-inspiring manner. The air of the streets was "nipping and eager," and every now and then cold blasts swept through them to a very dismal and freezy tune. It was such a morning as makes the nose, ears, fingers, and toes tingle, and produces throughout the frame a chilliness, a sensation of coldness, which leaves an individual in doubt whether he ought much longer to expose himself to its congealing influence. The hour was that singularly unsettled one, nine o'clock; and streams of well-shod and cosily muffled up pedestrians were hurrying down the hill of Holborn to that great centre of the world's commerce, the city of London. Amid the throng was a thinly-clad and delicate-looking girl, who timidly threaded her way, with a package in her hands. Her costume was neat, but scanty. Her cotton frock, fitting tightly across her well-developed bosom, fell in folds around her person; and as the wind drove mercilessly against it, disclosed to the observing eye the whole outline of her slender but elegant figure. The undergarments must have been very limited in number; for as her little feet, encased in fragile, papery-looking slippers, paddled in the snow, her frame shivered, and she hurried on at increased speed. In the crowd she escaped notice, but there was that in her gait and mien which bespoke of poverty and affliction borne with meekness. Her little black bonnet, which only just fitted her head, was faded; it had a melancholy rustiness about it, as if it had frequently been beaded with tears; and the crown was slightly, very slightly indented. It suggested sad thoughts; for no one capable of feeling acutely could look upon that humble little bonnet without sighting and conjuring up in his mind a whole host of grave reflections. It spoke of trials, tribulations and self-denials imposed by cruel depression, and increased in their severity by contrast with those upon whom the demon had not breathed his spell. It told of contention with a degree of adversity too cruel to permit the slightest gratification of female vanity, and forcibly appealed to that keen sympathy which rarely deserts the human breast, however apathetic it may be in its practical appreciation of the distresses of others. Poor girl! she was friendless, and was soon to be alone, with no other support and monitor than her own pure upright heart.

The shop to which she was wending her way was one with a dashing exterior, an imposing array of goods, and half a score of good-looking assistants. It was a noted cheap ready-made shirt mart, and the conductor of the establishment held a kind of levée every morning before the business of the day commenced. His audiences generally consisted of some half-score wretched creatures who had toiled through the previous day and night to earn the scanty pittances doled out for their most killing labour. Annie Lee stood in the crowd, and, like the rest, was exposed to the ribald remarks and bald attempts at wit of the young gentlemen who were dusting the counter, arranging goods for the day's display, and doing a multitude of little things with a vast deal of bustle and noise. Presently the great man arrived, and the trembling slaves of the needle opened their little bundles for his inspection. And now ensued one of those sickening scenes which it is wonderful how any thing in the shape of a man endure. It was a perfect haggling between the women and man who

171

appeared to be responsible for the quality of the work he admitted into the establishment. The women implored to be paid, not an increased sum, but the bare amount previously bargained for and allowed; but the man found so many faults with this collar and that collar, this band and that band – the seams were crooked, the necks awry – and so many faults were pointed out, that many of the poor creatures became frightened, and, to escape from such a place, gladly took what was offered them. Others, more obstinate, insisted upon their lawful demands, and were paid and discharged with a coarse rebuke. Annie was the last to present her package, which consisted of two shirts, the produce of her own and her mother's exertions since the preceding evening, and she did it with fear and trembling.

Now we should mention that Annie was remarkably pretty. Her face, of classic proportions, was as fair as an angel's and her two eyes, of deepest blue, fringed by long lashes, reflected a quiet subdued light that fell upon the gazer as softly as the mild rays of the young moon. Her nostril was delicately chiselled, and her two lips, from which the carnation had not been banished, were slightly parted, and disclosed teeth of dazzling brightness. Her light auburn hair was arranged in braids on each side of her pale cheeks; and as she extended her little hand to receive what might be offered to her, and modestly kept her eyes fixed on the counter, she looked no inapt representation of humility in rags, appealing to insolence and tyranny in tawdry finery.

The fellow, whose name was Watkins, attempted to catch Annie's eye, but in vain; she knew that he was looking at her, and her repugnance at the undisguised assurance of his manner prevented her even attempting to meet his gaze. Her claim was paid without cavil or deduction, and as some more work was handed to her, Watkins in a silky whisper said to her, "To-morrow evening, if you please, Miss Lee. I shall be here; don't fail, my dear."

Annie hurried away; for, although she knew not why, she was afraid of that man. He had ever been civil to her, and paid her death-wages in full; but she was afraid of him, he shocked the extreme purity and delicacy that were interwoven with her nature, and whenever she left his presence she was inexpressibly relieved. On the present occasion she carried with her ninepence; yes, one tiny sixpence, and three heavy ugly penny pieces – the price paid for making two shirts, with showy linen fronts and an elaborate display of wristbands, with their countless stitches, so neat and delicate that the eye could scarcely detect them.

> "O! men, with sisters dear!
> O! men, with mothers and wives!
> It is not linen you're wearing out,
> But human creatures' lives!"

Annie, however, thought not of the hardship of her lot; she had a helpless hungry parent at home, and she traversed the wet pavement of the streets with the lightness of the fawn. Upon arriving in the squalid locality where she resided, the investment of her little stock became to her an object of much concern, and after no small amount of consideration she devised upon the number of purchases she would make. She entered the chandler's shop where she was accustomed to deal, and the following were the items of her expenditure:–

172

	d.
Half-a-quartern loaf	3
Two ounces of butter	1 3/4
Quarter of an ounce of tea	1
Seven pounds of coals	1
One bundle of wood	0
	6 3/4

The balance, being twopence-farthing, was reserved for rent; and here we may observe that the earnings of herself and mother, when in full work, never exceeded six shillings and ninepence per week, and for that they would have between them to make eighteen shirts of the description which the labels in the shop windows term "fine;" Annie did twelve, her ailing parent six, and to accomplish this Annie often worked eighteen hours out of the twenty-four, and her mother, when nature would allow her, sixteen. Out of the six shillings and ninepence they had to pay two shillings for the apartment in which they lived, and thus had only four shillings and ninepence left for their subsistence during one whole week of work sufficient to prostrate the strongest constitution.

With this four shillings and ninepence per week two human beings – women pure as light – copies of that fair and gentle gift placed by Providence under the protection of him whose "fair large front and eye sublime declared absolute rule" – were obliged to provide themselves with food and raiment. Sickness, accident, a diminished demand, a host of casualties might destroy even this miserable supply – but what matter? they were only women; and their complaining cries would be drowned in the roar of the multitude, whose bellowings they could hear like distant thunder in the crow's-nest-like place in which they were perched.

Such worse than pauper allowance made them thin and wan, and they pined like birds in a cage, and starved in the midst of wealth and luxury greater than ever was created before – yes, starved, lacked the bread of life in London, the capital of the world, than which

> "Not Babylon,
> Nor great Alcairo, such magnificence
> Equall'd in all their glories."

But let us describe the habitation of these two poor deserted and friendless creatures. It was situated in the topmost story of a house lying in one of those narrow filthy alleys from which the pure air of heaven is most sedulously excluded. The neighbourhood was rank and foetid with abominations; and the people, who leaned idly from out of some of the windows, seemed scarcely human. The alley itself was a mass of ricketty houses, tenanted by the poorest of the poor. The occupants manifested no absolute depravity, but there was something in their aspect which repelled, instead of attracted, sympathy. It was, in the men, neither ferocity nor brutality, but something of a lean, gin-and-water character, which scowled from out its drunken eyes. In the women it was filth, dishevelled hair, unwashed faces, and disordered garments, that prevented near approach; and when a beholder looked at both sexes, he fancied that he beheld before him wretches whom casual hunger had starved into a reckless indifference to all the decencies of life. The house in which Annie and her mother resided was one of the least inviting in the place; it manifested a decided inclination to embrace its neighbour opposite, but several strong beams interposed, and, as if indignant at being de-barred one of the pleasures it sought, it became sulky, and had departed upwards of a foot from its original upright position.

The room which Annie and her parent occupied was, as we have stated, in the storey next to the sky, and upon entering it, the first object that attracted attention was its cleanliness, but there was a desolation in its aspect which struck a chill to the heart; it looked empty, just like a newly-washed room totally devoid of furniture. There was a coldness about it, a clamminess and dampness, which benumbed and deadened all feeling. The contents were two broken chairs, an old round table, a palliass of slender pretensions, rolled up and placed in a corner, a plate-shelf, on which were a few cups and saucers, two or three knives and forks, a tin tea-pot, and a fragment of looking-glass. The fire-place was more like a hole in the wall than anything else, but it was large enough for the grate, and that kindly accommodated itself to the coals it had to consume. The latter threw out, with no small amount of blowing and puffing, heat just sufficient to boil water in a very ancestral-looking little kettle, and that was the only work it had to do, if we except the occasional bits of heat it afforded to the cramped fingers that were held before it in the "dead waist and middle of the night." The window of this room was very small, but clean; and the panes that were broken were not stuffed with dirty cloths or remnants, like their neighbours', but had their holes neatly pasted over with brown paper. Before it

"A woman sat, in unwomanly rags,
Plying her needle and thread."

Chapter II

No friends, no hope! no kindred weep for me!
Almost no grave allow'd me! like the lily
That once was mistress of the field, and flourish'd,
I'll hang my head, and perish. – *Henry VIII*

We have stated that before the broken but paper-mended window of the almost empty room in which Annie Lee and her mother resided the latter sat stitching. Let us describe the fragile creature upon whom the world had rained its heavy afflictions of rags and destitution, and buried in a living grave of cold and hunger. Traces of former beauty lingered on her features, but they were darkened by the shadows of lines which gathered round her eyes and mouth, and fastened themselves remorselessly on the dead white of cheeks where roses had once bloomed as in a fair garden. Her hair, of mingled auburn and grey, was thin, and hanging in disorder over her sunken brows, imparted to her appearance a wild sorrow, which a pair of dull, glassy, deeply-sunken eyes painfully heightened. Beneath all this sad desolation, a long neck, white as snow, tapered gracefully down to a bosom flat and shrivelled like a crumpled sheet of unstained paper. One of her breasts, once a fountain of life to the babe born to her in her days of prosperity, half-peeped out of a rent in her garment, and although shrunken, looked in that dismal apartment like that early white

174

flower which decks the last days of winter. Yes, it was a snowdrop, glistening amid waste and ruin, and a purer one never reared its modest head. But it told a sad tale; for while a beholder might dream of the beauty of which it formerly made up a portion, he had only to look before him and see its shattered and wasting remnants.

The dress of this victim to our present social arrangements was so scanty, albeit patched with care and neatness, that it disclosed the whole outline of her form. Her fleshless bones were distinctly traced out, and her knees, like two sharp points, almost seemed to be bursting through the frail covering that could not conceal their worn and hungry leanness. Flesh or muscle on her body there was none; and there she sat, with stockingless feet, shivering and shaking in the cold of a winter's morning, without fire, without food, without one ray of hope to warm her frozen sympathies with the world outside.

But she plied the bright and sparkling symbol of her slavery in unrepining silence; and all that was heard in that chilling room was the click of her needle and thimble. Click, click, click, they went, like a watch, keeping time, and wearing itself out; and as the faint shadow of her fast-moving scraggy hand fell on the wall opposite, it looked like a soul darkened by wrong, trembling on the brink of eternity. And the woman, dulled, spell-bound under the curse of her fate never lifted her eyes, but went swiftly on, expending her reel of cotton and her fast ebbing life, until her daughter burst into the room with something like the joyous bound of youth and then a faint smile spread over her haggard face and she whispered, "My child!" It was all she could do, and as her daughter hastily busied herself about the morning meal *their* providence had allotted them, click, click, sounded her needle and thimble.

"Mother," said Annie, putting her arm gently round her parent's neck. Click, click, click, was the only response. "Mother"– the pressure of the rounded arm increased – "come and see how nicely I have made breakfast." Click, click, click. "Mother! dear mother!" exclaimed the alarmed girl, tightly clasping the skeleton frame she embraced, and with tears in her eyes turning her young face up to the one that had withered ere it had looked upon forty years.

Click, click, went the needle and thimble, and then ceased their horrid notes, as with a shriek the mother looked up and clasped her only joy to her prematurely aged bosom.

Her morning dream was over, but its reminiscences swept across her brain like lightning streaks over a dun sky.

"My child – my darling child!" was the stifled, agonising cry, as she wound her bony arms round all that had been left her to love on earth.That grasp was an agonising one; it endured but a few seconds, but to both it was an age.

"I am awake now – oh, yes, awake – but I have been dreaming. Oh, Father in heaven! such a dream!" and she strained her daughter to her heart as if she would hide her there for ever.

Annie, terrified at the unwonted energy displayed by her mother, sobbed, and the more deeply because she knew not why. Poor untutored child of misery! she felt a presentiment – heard a wailing in her soul – but could not recognise the features of a fast approaching evil. She tried to speak, but the grief suddenly excited in her delicate organisation choked her utterance.

"Hush!" said the mother, her eyes brightening as she spoke; "what I should tell you had better be told now. I often thought of it over my work, but this morning it came upon me like memories of the past, and then I slumbered in fancy, and phantoms – things of the earth – slimy creeping things troubled me;

and I saw one – oh! merciful God! hear a mother's prayer and let it be but a dream!" A shudder almost convulsed her emaciated frame, but an idea as frightful as it was bold and vivid seemed to endow her with renewed strength. "Listen, my child," said she; "twenty years ago I was rich, young, and as beautiful, they told me, as you are now. I had home, friends, and all that a happy girl could desire, until I loved, and then I married, and was happy for many many months, until the demon poverty withered the roses that gladdened our sweet cottage, and your father died of a broken heart, and I lived because you nestled at my bosom. A wretch persecuted me with odious offers. I fled from him and came to this great town, and after many vicissitudes came to be a needlewoman. Yes, I have stitched my life away, and the last threads are in my hands. I shall not be here much longer."

Annie screamed with agony as this gloomy anticipation flashed across her mind in all its terrible reality.

"Hush, my darling," said her mother; "all is in the hands of Him who has permitted all this suffering to prepare me for happiness hereafter. But listen. When I am gone, think of me, and pray, when evil men cross your path, and evil thoughts crawl like serpents into your mind, pray, my child, or your beauty will be your curse. Pray – pray!" she wildly exclaimed, "for this is an awful town, and sin stalks unblushingly through every street. Pray, or hush if you must fall. Oh! no, no! You are too good – too pure – too holy to be a victim. Listen! If you should or must – but no – when the temptation comes, whether it be gentle as the lamb or as savage as the tiger, think of me, and," here her voice sunk to a whisper, "*die first*".

She fixed her eyes firmly on the face of her daughter, and in one greedy look saw its beauty and stainless purity; and then as the future and one dark spot came upon the mirror of innocence before her, she uttered a groan, and fell back insensible. She had fainted. This was no novelty to the afflicted daughter; for the poor creature, whose temples she bathed with her trembling hands, had often fallen from her seat through sheer exhaustion. On this occasion she revived but slowly; and when she did, it was only to discover that the last blow had been struck – she was paralysed, and never spoke again. Annie shrieked so loud and piercingly, that an old hag-like figure hobbled into the room, and, in squeaking notes, demanded to know the reason for so great an outcry.

"My mother! – look at my mother, Tibby, and save her!" exclaimed Annie.

"Save her?" said the crone, feeling the pulse of the dying woman with her brown and bony fingers. "She's got her billy-do this time, any how. Yes, young woman, its a clay-box case this; but a drop of something short might bring the tongue back to bless you. Have you any gin?" (Annie shook her head); "nor money? Must call in the parish. But ah!" (here her eye fell on the shirts, in the various stages of preparation) "we can raise something on these. Shall I step over with them to Simkins's? Don't stand shilly-shally, or your mother may die before she opens her mouth!"

Annie, prostrate by the terrible affliction before her, offered no opposition. She neither meditated nor formed the slightest conception of wrong; and the old woman bore off the embryo cheap shirts to that grave of a poor man's independence, the pawn-shop. She soon returned with a bottle of gin in her hand, and the change, but the sacrifice had been a useless one. The mouth of the sufferer was too rigidly closed to admit of any liquid being poured down her throat; and all that could be done for her was to place her tenderly on her humble bed, and send for such assistance as the miserable can obtain. The

176

parish doctor came, but his services were not required – it was too late; and the slave of the needle was left to die under the spell of an awful silence. The old woman crouched at the foot of the bed like a cat, and every now and then raised the bottle to her lips; while Annie, on her knees, prayed as only those who have been smitten by Providence can. Hours passed away, and the potations of the witch-like figure on the floor had so affected her senses, that she began to mutter and indulge in execrations.

"They all goes this way," said she; "they gets thinner and thinner, and then hops away like a light dancing on the wall; and they never says a blessed word again them as brought 'em to it. That cuts me to the heart. If they'd only curse – just leave one curse to them that did it – I'd be satisfied. But no; they gets into the parleyticks, or whimpers about their bright young days, and all is over; and the men that did it all goes on as smiling as ever. May they drink poison, the brutes! And people goes to them – what dirt the fools get for their pains! – and buys cheap shirts; and never thinks of the garret or the attic where God never comes – no, never! No happy face has been here these forty years, that I'll swear to; but there's a rod in pickle for them all."

There appeared to be some consolation in the latter idea, for very soon after indulging in it she dozed off to sleep. Annie kept her position at her parent's head, and when day departed she was the only watcher at that awful death-bed. On the third night, about nine o'clock, Annie, wearied and harassed, slept; and her mother lay looking at her with glazed and watery eyes. We have said that her features were remarkably delicate, but in the state of repose in which they were then, although the cheek was worn, they were enchanting. There was a loveliness in their expression which to the imagination was like a dream of beauty. There was nothing of the earth about them; calm, pure, and holy, they spoke to the heart; and the soul of a beholder who had untainted instincts, as he gazed at them in their classic purity, would have felt elevated – it would have thrilled the presence of so much excellence; and he would have almost deemed it profanity to have left even one soft kiss on that snowy brow. The mother, as she dwelt upon them, was transported to the past, and in fancy she saw herself as in her days of maidenhood with a light heart and a bounding step. She drew from their airy cells sweet memories, and inhaled the perfume of the flowers that grew around her when the world to her wore a smile, and in her own guileless, trusting fondness, she believed it had a heart.

Old associations, like jewels well preserved, nestled at her heart; and worn and withered as she was, she clung to them with a warmth that gave her life, even at the brink of the grave. Wan and wasted, as she lay on the floor of her wretched dwelling, she had still a love for the bright and beautiful; and although her body had been the sport of the fiend Starvation, she could feel that there is an ecstasy in goodness – a delicious reward in the treasured-up reminiscences of an unspotted life – which neither hunger nor oppression can destroy. She was happier in that last hour of thought than the most favoured daughter of fortune; for reproach, with its rankling barb, stood not at the bar of her judgement.

At length a dimness came upon her mental vision, and the voice of the past, in her fond ear, melted away. Her daughter at that moment looked up from her slumber, and her first act was to imprint a kiss on the cold cheek of her now half-blind parent. With the near approach of death came almost renewed strength, and Annie was pressed passionately to her mother's heart.

177

Poor girl! she considered the embrace as a symptom of amendment, and to soothe the sufferer, in a low but distinct and sweet tone, sung that affecting melody, "Home, sweet home." Tears gathered in the mother's eyes, and, with a gentle sigh, she fell asleep, and never awoke more.

The daughter, jaded and worn, nodded her head, and was soon in the land of dreams. The candle, burnt down to its last fragment, flickered and trembled for a moment, and then all was darkness.

"Annie," whispered the old woman, who had crept into the room, "did she curse? – asleep – well, well, the doom is upon you, and will soon put you in the black pit, where the toads hiss and dance their wicked pastimes; so sleep on, and be as rich in fancy as the Queen. I hope she cursed the monster before she died; I do daily, but I want the curse of a good heart to blight them."

And, thus muttering, she kept swaying her body to and fro like a pendulum, and waited for the wakening of the desolate girl, whose soft breathings came and went like the sighing of a summer's wind.

Chapter III

"Nor long did her life for this sphere seem intended,
For pale was her cheek with the spirit-like hue,
Which comes when the day of this world is nigh ended,
And light from another already shines through"

Moore

It is sad to be alone, to be in the world and yet not of it; to think only, to dream with the eyes open, and the senses painfully acute; to be a stranger in the midst of buxom life, and yet have no sympathy with a single one of the myriads of beings who throng the highways and bye-ways of this bustling world. There is a dirge-like melancholy inseparable from an involuntary and undeserved seclusion from the busy scenes of earth, which saddens the heart and brings the tears of sorrow unbidden to the eye. It seems as if the soul in its affliction would, in despite of the assistance of fortitude or the support of pride, mourn over its isolation and in silence reproach the evil fortune that condemned it to a cruel expatriation, while the blossoms of hope and love shed their fragrance over the most favoured children of Providence. Many of the sons and daughters of mankind upon whom Nature has lavishly smiled – who revel in her choice gifts of health and beauty – are condemned to this hopeless solitude, this crushing and sad despair; and the voices of their complaints are never heard amid the din, of the sonorous notes of prosperity. They fall in the thick atmosphere of despair, and are lost ere they reach the roar in the light outside.

Of this class of unfortunates was Annie Lee, after the death of her surviving parent. She had no sooner seen her poor mother's body consigned by rude hands to a pauper grave, than she felt a desolation – an awful sense of loneliness creep upon her, which made her, young and untutored as she was, shudder with an undefinable creeping sensation of terror. As the few clods allowed by the stringent poor-degrading regulations fell on the unsightly plateless coffin, she felt that every one of the hollow sounds made by them had an echo in her own heart. For days afterwards she moped about like one in a

178

hideous dream, and only awoke to a consciousness of the reality of the destitution by which she was surrounded on every side, when assailed by the keen pangs of hunger. Youth struggled with grief, and in a measure triumphed, for she began to think how she could procure a meal. Every thing in her miserable room of any value at all, even the ragged and slender palliass on which her mother had died, had been disposed of; and as she glanced round and saw nothing on which her eye could rest with any degree of promise of realising something, a feeling of callous despair began to wind itself in serpent folds round her heart. Her little hands became clenched, her delicate nostril quivered, and a cold moisture gathered like dew on her almost transparent brows.

She had formed no distinct idea of what she either could or would do, but a dark shadow fell upon her and it only required a sufficiently tempting motive to induce her to plunge into the grave or dishonour. Her gentle impulses were subdued, and her high moral nature so untuned, that she would at that moment have voluntarily sought relief in the excitement most readily at hand. It was in this mood that she was discovered by Watkins, the overseer and junior partner in the firm in whose service her mother had yielded up her life. He had kept her in view ever since she failed to return at the stipulated time with the work given to her previous to her mother's death – had heard all the particulars of that, by him, long expected event – and, with the ingenuity of the most practised police spy, had ascertained the fact of the pawning of the goods entrusted to her to make up into shirts to adorn the stomachs of gentlemen who never dream, when they look clean and respectable, that they do so at the expense of the toil of the most abused and trampled upon portion of that sex to whose favours they aspire most arrogantly.

Annie was sitting on the only chair, or rather apology for one, the room contained; and as it was mid-day, just sufficient light was admitted through the window to disclose the whole of her thinly clad figure with its exquisite proportions and face "wan and thin," but beautiful, surpassingly beautiful in its pale and contracted earnestness of expression.

Watkins approached her with the air and attitude of a ruffian, who intended to intimidate with a threat of exposure and punishment; but he no sooner caught a glimpse of her features, lovely in their deep sorrow, than he hesitated, looked again, paused, and was subdued. There is something touching in female sorrow, it reaches the rudest disposition, and brings up its good from the lowest depths. It was so on this occasion. Watkins was a man of exceedingly coarse tastes, repulsive morals, and habits of the vilest profligacy. He uniformly selected his victims from among the slaves of the needle, over whom he exercised despotic sway, and was frequently truly diabolical in the refined villany with which he treated them. Many familiar with the features of vice, and others hardened into recklessness by horrible privations, had yielded to his solicitations without much resistance, and he formed an estimate of the character of the whole sex from the conduct displayed by the least courageous and resisting. All were poor, and he thought all were alike. Annie he had long before "booked" as an additon to the number of his dark iniquities, and no cat ever watched a mouse-hole with more vigilance than he did for an opportunity to accomplish his object. Now that the mother was dead, and the girl had been reduced to the degradation of subsisting on the charity of her half-starved fellow-lodgers, he deemed, in his awful indifference to the value of chastity, that he would find her ready to embrace any proposal he should make to her.

But, as we have stated, her attitude disarmed the wretch of half his purpose. The demoniac part of his nature was not invincible; but compassion from such a source to a hungry heart-broken girl was more dangerous than brutal violence, and Annie had to undergo the dreadful trial; and surely the angels, who hover round innocence, must have trembled when that man's honeyed sentences fell upon the ear of the solitary mourner of that cold gloomy garret like

"Silvery sounds, so soft, so dear,"

that the listener, charmed out of her repugnance, held up her head, and, while the tears trembled in her eyes, essayed to speak. She was unable; and Watkins, rightly divining the cause of her emotion, had some refreshments, including wine, procured from a neighbouring tavern, and persuaded her to partake heartily of them. A week's dietary of one scanty meal of dry bread and weak tea per day is a wonderful sharpener of the appetite, and Annie ate of the food before her without reluctance, little dreaming that in driving away the famine-fiend, she was giving audience to one of swarthier hue. But so it is, danger ever dogs the steps of poverty, and the removal of one calamity frequently provokes a still harsher one. With women this is especially so; if poor, and fair, and fascinating, she becomes poor indeed, she listens too attentively to the oily phrases that fall seductively upon her flattered ear, or perhaps in a moment of passion yields with ungoverned impulse to the warm prompting of her loving nature.

Watkins, although uniformly successful, was but a coarse wooer; he trusted more to bribes and coercion, and that species of persuasion which prevails with those untrained instincts and inferior moral organisations. Still he was dangerous even to the habitually correct in thought, for there are moments when the appetites, like ravenous beasts of prey, break the laws imposed by religion and social morality, and drag those they torture through the mire, which only deep and earnest repentance can remove, when once it has soiled the human temple. There are moments when the sentinels of the soul sleep, and then evil, with its magic, makes the brain giddy, and the animal within us all fierce in its thirst for gratification.

Annie, sheltered under the wing of a fond parent, knew little of mankind, and, in her simplicity, thought all that glittered was pure gold; but she was soon to be undeceived. The wine she had drank infused warmth into her frame, and imparted a liveliness to her spirits, which induced her to tell her tale of grief to the scoundrel, who was observing her every action with a degree of pleasure perfectly horrible to imagine. He had great faith in the wine and gin bottle, and on this occasion, as the glow deepened on the girl's cheeks, and an animation sparkled in her winning eyes, he anticipated an easier triumph than he had expected upon entering the room. Affecting to be charmed with her candour and the confidence she had reposed in him, he promised her his friendship and countenance whenever it should be required to promote her views. Annie, flushed and excited, answered him in broken accents, and, like a reed, bent to the storm that wicked man had raised in her bosom. She was under a spell, and in the very excess of her innocence stood on the brink of ruin. Had an impure thought ever darkened her mind, she would have had a defence – a monitor to warn her of the outrage that was contemplated by the sensualist who stood gloating over her person with the undisguised effrontery of the terrible temperament to which he belonged. He had drawn closer to her side, and had one of her hands clasped in his large, but soft and greasy one.

"This is no place for you to dwell in, my pretty Annie," said Watkins, peeping into her face with his bold and impudent one; "let us go to where you will be comfortable, and be dressed like a lady."

Annie looked up surprised; she was too guileless to understand the nature of the proposition.

"Yes," continued the fellow – "to where you will be your own mistress, and forget that you ever were in want of a friend."

And so saying, with increasing confidence he began to sing the first verse of the hackneyed song, "Come, dwell with me," and had flung his arm round her waist, and was proceeding to snatch a kiss, when he suddenly started, and, not without some trepidation, kept his eyes fixed in the direction of the doorway. The object that saluted his vision there was the old woman we formerly mentioned, and who, by the way, was held in a species of reverence in the establishment as being a sort of witch, or wise women. Certainly her appearance qualified her for the former title, for her clothes were ragged and dirty, and her flesh had accommodated itself to the dead brown colour that prevailed all over the neighbourhood.

"A! aha!" hissed the woman through her toothless gums, and fastening her cold glittering eyes on the face of the seducer, "come at last, have you, to sing to my pretty bird, eh? and take her away, and ride in a coachey poachey, eh? and have a horsey porsey, and be a *lady*, eh?"

The manner in which the last words were uttered was as powerful as the sneer of an evil spirit, and their effect was not lost on the, when tried, not over-valorous Mr. Watkins.

"Who is this person?" demanded he from Annie, at the same time releasing his hold of her.

"Who am I!" shrieked the old woman, hobbling into the room, and placing herself before Annie; "I'll tell you – poor, weak old woman; but strong enough to drive *you* hence with the curse of a heart turned to stone by wrong and oppression. Begone! I know your purpose – your vile, ungodly thought. Away! or I'll call those as will soon put the everlasting gloom upon you. Away, monster! and leave us one flower in this little hell for us to gaze at, and think of youth and innocence once again before we die. Away! and may your slumbers be haunted by the ghosts of the dead – of the girls with Thames mud dripping from their hairs! Aha! you tremble at the thought of seeing them again; but they'll come and curse you, shake you about, and drive you mad – ay, mad – and you will beg in vain for that which even wealth cannot buy – for any thing that will bring ease to the burning head of the woman slayer. Away! or I'll call those who will hurl you into the street."

Watkins, amazed and half frightened at this attack, requested Annie to call at the shop on the following day, and bidding her a hurried good-bye, left the room, and descending the rotten stairs out-side with marvellous rapidity.

Annie began to feel giddy; the wine and the excitement had been too potent for her reduced frame, and she began to stagger and reel. The old woman watched her attentively, and laying her finger on her shoulder, said, "Do you know what that man wanted with you?"

"Work – work. Kind to me. I mean to work for him," replied Annie confusedly.

"Work!" sneered the old woman; "do you remember what your mother told you on the day she died – what she whispered in your ear, and bade you think of when the dark hour came? That man and the warning go together. Think, and remember your mother."

Slowly, but surely, the truth flashed across the mind of the poor slave of the needle; and, as it broke upon her in all its hideous reality, a shiver crept through her body, and with a piteous sigh she sank senseless to the floor.

"Oh that Heaven in its mercy would take her away, for the worst has yet to come," muttered the old woman, as she sat on the floor and placed Annie's head in her lap.

Chapter IV

The tale that I would unfold to-day
No fiction is, but from the records pure
Of truth has been obtained. – *Renaldo, the Visionary*

The bleak wind of March
Made her tremble and shiver;
But not the dark arch
Or black flowing river
Mad from life's history,
Glad to death's mystery
Swift to be hurled –
Anywhere, anywhere
Out of this world.
In she plunged boldly,
No matter how coldly
The rough river ran;
Over the brink of it,
Picture it - think of it,
Dissolute man!
Lave in it, drink of it,
Then, if you can! – *The Bridge of Sighs*

The sorrows of the poor have not yet found their true chronicler; and when they have, the pen of the writer must have been dipped into the fire that dries up the warm blood of the heart, and worms its destructive way into the system like a flame noiselessly creeping from chamber to chamber in a fair tenement.

And this dreadful chapter, whenever it shall appear, will be sadly defective if it does not portray the anguish and despair, which are the heritage on earth of myriads of forlorn creatures, in colours which shall not only startle and amaze by their vividness, but be everlasting witnesses against the wrongs matured in the bosom of a social dispensation which crush and mangle the dearest feelings, sully the holiest impulses, and hurry the fair, the loving, the manly, and the pure in purpose to one common dark and howling desolation. It is not that people are indifferent to all this that it exists; the magnitude of the calamity, its almost universal presence, prevents its being so striking to the eye as the painful features of individual cases. Nevertheless, the admission has been made that it is not a creature of the imagination, and the acknowledgement gathers force as time rolls on into deep, unfathomable eternity.

A warm, new feeling on the subject has sprung into existence, and its sympathy promises to be as boundless as practical. But while the heart is in training for its holy mission of redemption, thousands are falling into the dreadful sleep of crime and despair. Women fashioned after the most delicate and beautiful models – gentle creatures whom we sing and write about – form a mighty mass of this almost super-human amount of woe; and not the least appalling feature of the misery to which they are so mercilessly subjected is the fiendish cruelty with which they are delivered over to the tiger-passion that seduces man to trample on those he is commanded by his instincts and high intellectual powers to love and cherish. For a woman once fallen there is no hope – the gates of the hell into which she has been coaxed by fraud and artifice are closed upon her for ever, and she never sees the bright sun and pleasant flowers that cheered and gladdened her heart in her days of innocence. Sneered and jeered at by men, and avoided as a contamination by the fallen of her own sex, she falls into the darkness of her own sad despair, and withers away like a weed plucked from a fair garden and flung indignantly away. Oppressed and trampled upon, she sinks deeper and deeper into the mire of her degradation, and society hails her disappearance as a blessing. But the day of retribution, however long it may be postponed, comes at last, and man's inhumanity to woman is sure to be terribly avenged. The wailing of a broken heart *will* find its way into the most obdurate disposition some day or another, and although the whispers of conscience for a season may be broken and divided, retribution, like a shadow, follows the footsteps of guilt, and deepens as age advances. Nature punishes the delinquencies of her children in themselves, and in this life, however careless or reckless the individual may be, the lash, even in the hours of indulgence, falls heavily on his shoulders, and he feels the pang and the agony which bad deeds fix indelibly in the human system. Remorse, aggravated by decayed faculties, bounds him on to the fate he never attempted to avoid, and the wail of the ruined woman is drowned in the shriek of the destroyer as he tumbles headlong over the precipice on the brink of which he has sported with such blind confidence and daring assurance. In the blaze of his noon he was no better than a toad spitting venom "in the blind cave of eternal night," and in his death a miserable compensation to society for the outrages it had sustained at his hands.

It was not within the scope of our intention to have demonstrated how this wonderful compensatory power might have been developed in the instance before us; we rather intended to have aimed at depicting a few scenes in the life of a fragile creature slain in the murderous war of avarice and brutal passion; and the subject of our sketch is no coinage of the brain, or exaggerated creation of a false and sickly sentiment, but the copy of a living being walking daily in the midst of us, having feelings, instincts, and appetites like our own, and above all those

"Dreams treasured up from early days"

which sweeten and breathe a fragrance over the imagination, even in the direst and most wretched hours of poverty.

The girl we have selected to typify the class to which she belonged was not, like the heroines of wire-drawn romances, sheathed in the triple mail of a well-trained and refined sense of virtue. Her sense of delicacy, from long association with the features of misery, was more instinctive than otherwise; she had an innate appreciation of the pure and beautiful, a yearning after the tender and true, but no indomitable power to resist temptation in the shape of honeyed persuasion, supported by the supply of the means of subsistence, and a few articles of luxury to which she had previously been a total stranger. Her instincts revolted at wrong, but her necessities, like so many fiends, tugged at her natural modesty and weakened its power of resistance. She fell, as many others have done, in the maze and whirl of disordered sense, flushed sensibility, and physical obedience to an idea which insult and fierce unscrupulous effrontery had implanted in her jaded and fevered imagination. In the abstract, between herself and her Maker, she was as spotless as a finely polished mirror; but to her fellow-creatures – men careful of their families, and women proud of their unblemished chastity, those prosperous beings who are privileged to be critics in morals by their education and auspicious circumstances – she was fallen and degraded – a lost spirit driven from the paradise of hope to wander as an outcast in a world where every thing to her, of all others, was cold and repelling. Poor defenceless girl; she only knew the priceless value of the jewel she had parted with in a moment of aberration from the dreadful certainty of its loss. The wretch who had marked her out for his prey succeeded in effecting his infamous purpose, and she was soon to learn that there is but one step from honour to the lowest infamy. To use a commercial phrase, she had never been rated very high, even as a slave of the needle; but now that she had, as her betrayer considered, become a burden to him, she began to experience that cold and cutting neglect, that heartless behaviour which, while it repudiates the intimacy, seeks to hold up its victim to the censure of her own judgement and the scoffs and scorns of those who think of her rather as she is than what she might and could have been had she been allowed to have followed the dictates of her unoffending impulses. Her last appearance in the mart of cheap-clothing was painful and harrowing in the last degree.

It was, as before, morning, and Annie, like the rest stood awaiting the high behests of the slave driver. He was, if possible, more stern and insolent than ever, but his eye wandered and there was a restlessness in his manner which did not much flatter his strength of nerve. Hardened as he was, he was not wholly insensible to the reproach which beamed from the mild blue eyes of his latest victim. The shop was beginning to look very gay, for the arrangement of the goods had almost been completed, and the young gentlemen were practising every variety of smile, from the plain simper to the whole bunch of deluding contortions, for the purpose of entering with spirit into the arduous business of the day. Everyone felt himself to be a species of general officer in his own particular way, and thought that when accoutred and ready for action it would be no idle waste of ammunition to bestow a few leering glances upon the youngest and prettiest of the slaves of the needle. Annie, being unquestionably the most attractive in the throng – for she was well and neatly dressed – had the largest share of these equivocal attentions awarded to her, but heeded them not; for with the shirts – every one of them more accursed than that worn by

Hercules – pressed timidly to her bosom she had her eyes fixed firmly on the floor, and tremulously expected the now unkind salutation of the man who had abused her so cruelly.

"Well, now, what for you?" said the fellow, rudely addressing Annie, but looking in another direction.

The work was presented and paid for, but the poor girl was so shocked at the undisguised ruffianism of his manner, that she trembled, and her wages rolled on the floor. Few in that miserable throng knew her story, and she was too beautiful to be pitied, so found little sympathy with any one of them. Their hearts were frozen, and hunger, rags and filth had dried up in them the fountain of feeling.

Hastily picking up the few coins she had dropped, she hurried from the shop to her home. Guilt had made her a little more sagacious, and she saw that her influence with her seducer was at an end.

The circumstance did not cause her any uneasiness, for disgust had already weakened the little attachment she ever bore him, but she felt a sinking of the spirits, a nervous dread of approaching evil, which drew the bitter tears from her eyes. She was stained and sinful she knew but too well, and without hope or promise of something better she hardly dared to pray. A horrible future was before her, and as she toiled on from day to day, and got thinner and thinner, horrid creatures of her own sex poured vile suggestions into her ears, and men, things disguised in the fair proportions of nature's choicest production, mocked and wounded her bruised and broken spirit. At length she became ill, and she could not perform her work as regularly as formerly; the pretext was seized, and she was dismissed from all connection with the establishment in which she had ruined her health and perilled her soul. For weeks she toiled on in vain expectation of winning a crust of bread and a drop of water. Other shops were glad of her devotion to the needle – she worked well and neatly, and accepted the wages of slavery in such meek silence, that she was rather a favourite than otherwise. But all would not do; work as much as possible, she could not earn the means of subsistence, and starved – wanted bread in the spring of her beauty. The temptation came – drink lured her on, and like a mad creature she leaped into the wild abyss of dark and fearful suffering. She struggled through the world in a dream of guilt – it was to her the grave of the good she once possessed; and one night, when the stars shone and the moon showered down its silver light, she took a mute farewell of them all, and without a pang of regret went to her Maker. As she lay in her pauper shroud, without a solitary mourner near her, it was dreadful

> "To see that white face in its stillness there
> Proving how much she suffered ere she slept
> The dreadful sleep of crime and despair."

A reminiscence might sweep across the brain, and a shudder pass over the heart, but the corpse was there in its ghastly reality, and when hurried to the "blind cave of eternal night," would soon be forgotten by the few who had deigned to bestow a glance on the slave of the needle.

The Poor Man's Wrongs   (1839)

Mary Hutton

Welcome! wanderer of the wild,
Sorrow's lone deserted child,–
Welcome, son of misery,
This lone cot can shelter thee;
Though hard of my fortune, scant my fare,
Yet Hunger's child shall with me fare.

'Twas a cold bitter evening in the dreary month of November and slow drizzling rain had been pattering against the windows all day, and the winter winds had been roaring in loud and terrific blasts through the naked branches of the tall elm trees that environed the neat and beautiful cottage of Albert Freeland. Albert was an honest man and a Christian; and he was now occupied in reading aloud, to his attentive and interesting family, a portion of those weather-beaten pages, which have withstood all the cavils and bickerings of the subtle infidelity for a long course of ages, when the cries of a fellow creature in distress struck upon his ear. Instantly, the Sacred Volume was closed with the utmost care, and laid aside with the most profound veneration; for Albert was not without some peculiarities, which fashionable persons, in such an enlightened and adamantine age as this, would style nothing but vulgar absurdities. He had, from his earliest childhood, entertained a holy love for his blessed Bible. It had been his refuge in trouble, and his solace in adversity; and in his days of prosperity, it was his joy, delight, and glory. In it he always found something new, some comfortable and consoling passage, most admirably adapted to present circumstances, whether that they tended to gloom or brightness. It was his friend, director, physician, and guide, and had he had no other company, he would not have considered himself solitary. Yet there were times when Albert Freeland's feeling heart bled over the wrongs of his distressed country. He daily saw around him some hundreds of starving labourers and mechanics, honest, worthy, and respectable men, blasted in prospects and broken in spirits, – fathers of families, toiling hard for a pittance that would barely suffice to lengthen out expiring nature for a few months longer, – and, in the honest indignation of his soul, he would imploringly exclaim, "Oh, Lord, how long wilt though withhold thy vengeance, and sweep with the besom of destruction every proud oppressor from his groaning land, for they cause the naked to lodge without clothing, who have no covering in the cold! They are wet with the showers of the mountains, and embrace the rock for want of a shelter. They pluck the fatherless from the breast, and take a pledge from the poor. They cause him to go naked, without clothes, and they take away the sheaf from the hungry, which make oil within their walls, and tread their wine-presses, and suffer thirst." These exclamations were made by Albert, as he, together with his eldest son, hastened to the spot from whence the calls of distress proceeded. There they found an old man, drenched with rain and benumbed with cold, totally unable to pursue his journey further, whom they kindly bore to their hospitable dwelling, giving him such refreshments as his destitute situation needed, and which, in a great measure, restored his almost suspended faculties.

"I am glad," said the stranger, whom a good supper and a good fire had made communicative, "to find that all humanity and hospitality have not yet entirely left the earth, for, when you found me, I had almost given myself up to despair. Shame on me. How could I despair in the land of the mountain and the flood? – In a land that will ever be blest, and enlightened, and glorified, by the heartcheering and spirit-stirring strains of a Burns, a Scott, and an Ettrick Shepherd. Peace be to your manes, ever blessed spirits, who are smiling now from your bright homes above upon the bounties of the bountiful. When you found me, my friends, although nearly perishing with cold and hunger, I was busy composing a few worthless rhymes, for, in my younger years, I was a bit of ryhmster:–

> 'Tis almost o'er, my life of toil,
> And England's happy glorious soil,
> That blessed spot where I was born
> Has left me wretched and forlorn.
> All earthly happiness from me has fled,
> And England cannot give me back my dead;
> And if she could, I would not have
> My loved ones from their bloody grave,
> For now they rest most tranquilly.
> I long to join them, and to lay
> This aching head beneath the sod,
> Where pain and misery rests with God.
> Oh, I should sleep both sound and sweet,
> Enfolded in my winding sheet;
> No more the ills of life to share,
> No more the wrongs and scorns to bear,
> That always fall on hapless poverty,
> Produced by beings term'd both good and free.
> Oh, wondrous age! when those we style humane
> Delight to view a fellow-creature's pain:
> Oh, wilful wondrous age, when laws neglect
> The helpless beings whom they should protect.
> Why am I thus neglected – why thus left
> Of every stay – of every hope bereft?
> Why must I perish – helpless in the cold?–
> Tell, tell! ye iron men of godless gold.
> Why must I perish? Why! because our laws
> Do not maintain an honest Christian's cause:
> Why must I die – neglected in the cold?
> Cause England's poor have long been bought and sold!
> White slaves, in fact, and falsely named the free –
> Why, men of England, suffer such to be?
>
> Why bow your heads in silence and dismay,
> Whilst petty tyrants mark you for their prey?
> But liberty, though slow, makes glorious way;
> Yet I shall never see that blessed day

When thinking millions rise in power and might,
And peacefully assert an equal right
To eat their daily bread in Christian love.
Such is the holy will of God above,
Whose blessed ear and pitying eye
Has seen and heard his children cry;
And all our burning wrongs he will remove;
Yet I shall never see that day
When liberty makes glorious way:
For I am nearly eighty years of age.
And soon must close this weary pilgrimage;
And yet this fainting, feeble breast,
Can scarcely find a place of rest
To screen me from the howling tempest's rage.

Yet a cover and a shelter for the night I have found, for which I am truly thankful, and in the morning I shall be able to finish my long journey."

"No, no," cried Albert; "you shall rest here with us for a few weeks, or longer, if it suit you. We have always a crust to spare for those in need. 'Tis a pity that your honest rhymes have not been able to procure you a better asylum."

"No man could desire a better," said the stranger; "but there is no room in the world now for a poor rhymer like me. The lordly ones engross all attention; and there are so many of them, that there is not the least chance for a meaner person. I once, indeed, had hopes of brighter days; but that delusion has long, long, passed away, and I have no wish now but to rest in the silent grave from all my toil. I have lost two dearly-beloved grandsons in the accursed and disgraceful contest which has long laid waste the brightest provinces in unhappy Spain; and I am now going to make a home with a nephew of mine, who resides at Edinburgh, and who, I am sure, will very gladly receive me. I had thought to have reached Edinburgh to-night, but was overtaken in the storm. I am from England; and the New Poor Law Bill, – the cruel effects of which you must have heard of, – has sent me a tramping in my old age. There is no relief out of the workhouse, and I could not go in. I do not like imprisonment and water-gruel diet; besides, I have never been stained with crime to be thus punished. I have toiled hard all my life, and no political economist could have been more careful; yet, the whole course of my existence has been a continued and constant struggle for existence. I have had my share of afflictions, and I have had to encounter wrong and injustice; but I always bore in mind that afflictions come from God, and wrongs and injustice from my fellow-men."

"Even so," said Albert; "and that blessed Being, whose arrows of affliction have so wounded us, ever tempers his judgements with mercy. Man – ungrateful tyrant man – may career on in his course of pride, but he will perish sooner than a summer flower before a northern wind, when He, to whom the forest children are as dear and as precious as the children of the palace, lays his hand upon him. What made your grandsons leave you in your declining age, worthy friend, to fight in the detestable and wretched cause of wretched Spain?"

"Their spirits were broken through privation and suffering," replied the old man. "They could get no employment in their native land, consequently they were reduced to this necessity of embracing any measure that promised

188

temporary relief, however they might despise such a measure; and that they both of them heartily despised it at the very time they embraced it, I was well convinced; but there was no alternative. We had no means of existence left for any of us. They were both killed; but death by the sword or the musket is preferable to the lingering one of starvation."

"There is an awful responsibility," said Albert, "resting upon the heads of these incapables, who have brought their country to ruin and disgrace, and who have wantonly and recklessly shed the blood of the people by the sword, and destroyed them by famine. I once entertained some hopes from the Reform Bill, – at least, I thought that the condition of the labouring classes might be ameliorated by that measure, – but the Reform Bill has made the condition of the labouring population ten times worse than it was before; for now the non-electors are the slaves of the ten-pounders, who have little else but impudence and ignorance to bear them through; yet I have often seen that those, accompanied with that very useful article money, will carry a man through the world very respectably."

"Ah!" cried the old man; "genius, talent, worth, and virtue – all sink into insignificance before that adored and idolized article called gold, which, in fact, is the only god that is worshipped now in Christian England; but redemption for enslaved millions is approaching, – the working classes are now capable of thinking and reflecting for themselves, – and they will no longer submit to the petty tyranny of insolent and over-bearing taskmasters who daily brand them as beings too mean and contemptible to exercise the elective franchise with honesty and discretion. I would tell those who thus brand them, that there are men amongst the working classes as honest and as high-souled, and as sensible and intelligent, as any duke, lord, or squire in the kingdom; indeed, I much question whether if the duke of this, or my lord that, or squire what's his name, had had their difficulties and distresses to brave and suffer so long, they would have acted half as honestly or uprightly? Not they, indeed. Neither could they have borne their wrongs and privations with the patience, fortitude, and forbearance with which the working classes have nobly supported themselves under theirs. I have somewhere read, that elevated situations fill the mind with elevated sentiments, but the actions and lives of the greater part of our nobility most grossly contradict the assertion."

"There are worthless, unmanly, ignoble beings," said Albert, "in every grade of society – from the powerful being upon his throne, to the humble peasant in his lowly cottage – and such, I fear, there always will be; yet, in the true and pure religion of the heart, unaffected virtue, innate honesty and simplicity of soul, the humble inhabitant of the lowly cottage is often far superior. Yet, to such men the franchise is denied, whilst it is given to the sordid and the worthless. Yet I look forward to the day when genius, talent, and industry, will be properly requited – when the ascendancy of the purse will no longer overrule all that is good, great, and glorious. Years of misrule and wrong have filled the bosoms of all honest men with bitter heart-burnings, for injustice can never create love. The rights of brotherly fellowship, and the rights of humanity, have been sacrificed at the freezing and cold-blooded shrine of self-interest; and Universal Suffrage alone can redeem the poor man from his thraldom. National enthusiasm is at length awakened – the decree has gone forth – matters are come to a crisis – and Universal Suffrage is the beacon-star that will lead the working classes of England into a haven of rest; and may happiness, contentment, religion, and liberty for ever-more reside in the dwelling of every honest man!"

"Amen," responded the old man. "I shall not live to see that glorious and auspicious day, for I am very old, and getting rather infirm – at least, I am not so strong as I was twenty years ago – but, with my latest breath, I shall pray that it may speedily arrive.

The Charter and the Land (1847)

WILLIAM WRIGHT, and Betsy his wife, lived in Stockport; they had a son and a daughter, Tom and Betsy, two little factory children, and they spent a very fractious and uncomfortable life, since that plaguy Charter, as Betsy termed it, came up. Will would attend all Chartist meetings, and was more than once imprisoned for what is termed, 'sedition, riots, routs, and tumults,' and which, in understandable phraseology, means a 'fair day's wage for a fair day's work,' and cheering those who teach them the method. During his incarceration, his wife had to bear patiently all the insolence, tyranny, and batements, to which the overseer pleased to subject her, always laying them to the account of her rascally Chartist husband. As soon as the Melbourne definition of the law had finished poor Will up; that is, when he was 'RUINED WITH EXPENCES," or, which is the same thing, marked as an outlaw, unworthy of being allowed to slave for a master, as long as a more pliant slave could be procured; he became a constant attendant at the public house, and as soon as his wife returned on Saturday evening with the scanty week's wage, there was invariably a squabble for the "brass," and the poor wife was but too happy if she could secure enough to make ends meet till Saturday came round again. They had led this cat-and-dog life from August 1842, when Will's master turned out his hands, as a means of carrying free trade, till April, 1845, when the Chartist Co-operative Land Company was established, when, to the no small astonishment of his townsmen and his wife, Will renounced the public house, upon the condition, that, when out of work, the wife would allow him a shilling a week for his pocket, and to which arrangement she cheerfully consented, and Will, from being a "waster," became a steady, sober fellow, the wife frequently thanking God for the change, and charming Will with the altered appearance and condition of his family. After a year of his new birth unto righteousness had passed, Will runs into the cellar, one evening, where his wife had been recently confined, and just as she was calculating, with an old crone, as to how soon she might leave the baby and return to the Mill. Will gathered the tenor of the conversation, and ready to leap for joy, he says, "Nay, Betsy, wench, thou shalt never work for no maister no more, thou shalt nurse youngster thyself this time." As Will had been out all day, and as joy had induced him to take a glass with a friend, the poor wife feared lest he had relapsed into his old habits, and replied, "Art daft, Will, why, how dost think we mun live?" "Live," retorted Will, "why look here, lass, I have drawn a prize in Land Company;" adding, "and look here, lass," showing her five sovereigns; "I gave the shilling a week, thou thought I used to drink, to pay up share, and I saved this here when I got a chance job." "Oh Will?" said the overjoyed wife, feebly, and taking her baby from the crone, "and dost say I shall nurse little lass?" "Aye, lass," he replied, "and I'll help thee." "Well, Will," she asked, "why didn't thou tell me thou had put in?" "Oh!" he replied, "thou wast always so bitter agen Charter, I was afeard till prize come up." "That's not Charter," she answered, "Charter was always getting thee into trouble, and Land will put thee in bread?" "Oh, lass," rejoined Will, "but it's Charter all the time, for only for Charter the land would never come up, and I'de never know aught about it; Charter is the means and land is the end; as ould general says,

Charter is spit, and Land is leg of mutton." "Well, Will," observed the wife, "if it does nout else, it has made thee a better man, and a better husband, I'm sure." Betsy went on as well as could be expected, delighted with her future prospects, and her husband's reformation, and both seemed to grudge themselves every morsel they ate, from a desire to have a good start.

The first of May was the day appointed for the weavers to take possession of their allotment, and to enter upon their new vocation; and as the time approached, the women of Betsy's acquaintance, who were enamoured of the splendid misery of a town life, and the gin shop, constantly haunted her with evil forebodings of Will's unfitness for agricultural labour, and had actually turned her dreams of future joy into evil anticipations, and, to her husband's great astonishment and mortification, when he came home one evening, he found his wife an altered being; he asked her the cause of the change, and she replied brusquely, "Why, thour't not used to land, and folk say it'll harrass and kill thee." "Why," replied Will, "faither, and grandfaither and all folk belonging to I worked on land and it didn't kill them, and why should it kill me? I worked too when I was a lad, and I was stronger and heartier then than I am now, and sure I'll work according to my strength, and I'll mend every day." "Well, but," says the wife, "there's the rent." "The rent," he rejoined, "why, lass, the rent of all, land and all, won't be as much as rent of this black hole." "Well, but," says she, "there won't be the work to get there to pay the rent." "Well, now," says Will, "I've been studying it with folk that knows more about it than old crones, and look here, lass, suppose I work March, April, May, and June, September and October on the land, and morning and evenings July and August. Now, wherever we goes, thy labour will always be worth two shillings a day, in hay time and harvest, and mine will be worth three shillings, for, if I'm weakly now, old master Clodpole the farmer said the other day, how it wasn't all the good men that reaped the harvest, and thou know'st lass, when they wants us they must pay; well, if we earn five shillings a day between us in hay time and harvest eight weeks, there's two rents, and then, lass, when land is sleeping, November, December, January, and February, sure my work at anything all day should be worth sixpence, and I'll get something to do and that would be three pounds, and then, lass, thou may'st earn twopence a day all the year round; there's three pounds more, so, lass, there's three rents, and all the produce of the two acres to eat. Tell me then, lass, how do farmers keep their hunters, and pay for education of sons and daughters, and make money without e'er doing a hand's turn? Sure, lass, its by profit on poor folks labour, and we'll have fifteen pounds to begin, and they'll come bidding for us in hay time and harvest if they'de kill us after; so after all we may call ourselves agricultural labourers, with house and land of our own, and fifteen pounds, for less than poor folks pay for rent of a cellar whether they work or not. Come, lass, to-morrow we leave the cellar and start, and thou'lt soon forget parasol and fan and necklace, when you see'st children growing up well and getting good schooling, and when thou won't be afraid of sleeping over factory bell, or going to factory with baby a week old at breast, till thou gets to the gate, and, Betsy, sure thou don't think we could eat all that grows on two acres, or half one acre, even if we didn't get work; but, see here, rich folk never like poor folk to work for themselves, as then rich folk couldn't make so much of their labour, so, lass, I don't mind all Charter cost me, for Land is Charter, and when I go there I'll be one less for tyrants to fall back on to reduce wages. Charter cost me many a pint of beer, and many a lost day, and many a month in prison, and many a sore heart, just, Betsy, as battle costs soldiers many a long march before they win it, but the difference is here, soldiers win battles for others, and I've fought and won it for myself."

Betsy was a reasonable woman and a good wife, and was now reconciled to her long journey, and the weavers left Stockport, with their three children, by the third class train, on the following morning, and arrived at Watford on the evening of the same day, where, to their great delight, they were met by kind and fostering friends who looked upon them as their children, and having joined many new comrades upon the same mission to the Holy Land, heretofore strangers to each other, and while the sun was yet high, the emancipated slaves started, amid the shouts and cheers of welcome of a vast assemblage congregated to witness the novel and pleasing spectacle of the foundation of a Small Proprietary Class; and the travellers being all seated in vans, in readiness for the occasion, the band struck up – "See the conquering heroes come," – the road, for the whole distance, presented the appearance of a Gala Day, and never was such a merry May-day seen in Hertfordshire, or in England, before. At the entrance to Holy Land the first settlers were met by many old friends and well-wishers, and all were conducted to their respective abodes, all anxiously inspecting their castle and their labour-field, and, though tired from a long day's journey, only terminating their research when the sable cloud of night had spread its mantle over their little domains. Will's wife was amongst the most delighted, and the clock struck twelve before she felt inclined for rest. To her, the journey was a long one – from Manchester to Stockport being the extent of her previous travels – and she slept soundly; not so, however, with Will and the youngsters; they watched the breaking twilight, and rose with the sun. Will's cottage was close to the school-house, and just as the loud bell summoned the youngsters to school, Will returned to his home, when he thought he heard his wife call, and as he opened the bed-room door, he heard her call, angrily –" Tom, thou varmint, and Betsy – thou b–h, dus'nt hear factory bell, eh! – thou'lt be fined, and I'll smack thy – for thee; here, suck, wench, or thou mun do without it." Will stood before her, she rubbed her eyes, looked round, and asked – "Where-ever am I?" "In thy own castle lass," responded Will, with a triumphant laugh – " yon is school-bell for youngsters to go to school; turn on t'other side, wench, and take another snooze and I'll wake thee up, for breakfast – what dost say to Charter now? Why, if thou wasn't going to pitch little lass out on floor." "Nay, Will," said she, "I was afeard we mun all be fined and starve – I thought it was factory bell." "DAMN THE FACTORY BELL," roared Will, with all his heart – "sleep! lass, sleep! and I'll call thee." The wife slept till eight, when Tom and Betsy rushed to her bed side, jumping and laughing, and singing out in chorus, "O mammy, such a nice place, I like school maister so much," says Tom. "And I like missus too," says Betsy, "she says she'll give me a sampler to work, and teach me to read pretty good books, and mend and make faither's shirts and stockings, and bake bread, and plait straw; here's posies for baby, Tom and me picked in land; get up, mammy, we's so hungry, and faither has dug, oh so much, and the taties and cabbage and all the things look so nice. Faither says he'll have baby out with him in wheel-barrow while he digs. O mammy, all the little children look so happy. Mammy, sure you won't let us go back to Stockport and factory any more to be whipped." "No lass," replied the mother, "not if thou'rt good." "O, we'll be good, mammy," responded the delighted children, running out of the room to communicate the glad tidings to a little play-mate of whom they had already made an acquaintance. The mother rose, and for the first time paid proper attention to her helpless babe. The happy family sat down for the first time in their lives to a substantial breakfast, in their own house, with good appetite, cheerful spirit, and a light heart; the father, when it was over, observing, that if they ate like that every day they'de break him. "Eh," responded the wife, "but they'll cost thee nout in doctors." "Thank God and ould Charter for that, lass," replied Will, kissing his wife, and telling her not to have dinner for him till three. "Young folk may dine when they come from school, but we are going to attend a vestry about church rates, and guardians, and overseers, and we all have a vote," said he, "and isn't that CHARTER and LAND, and all got for £2.12s., and thou can trust me in public house now that I work of my own to do, and mun turn out if I'm a waster and can't pay rent; so, lass, don't thou mind any beer for my dinner." "Eh! Will", exclaimed the delighted wife, "but thour't a goodun, thanks be to God, and God bless LAND and the CHARTER:" and Will for the first time in his life went to have his word about church-rates, guardians, and parish officers! and strangers in broad cloth shook him by the hand as he stood at the church door, and when he was canvassed for his vote, he said – "I mun see how Dick Pilling will go – as he's THE FATHER OF THE MOVEMENT, and we mun all go with him for CHARTER AND THE LAND."

The London Doorstep (A True Story) (1848)

Ernest Jones

The clouds were overhead – the rain was driving down the streets, and every now and then a cabman came tearing past at the fullest speed of which a worn-out jaded horse was capable, dashing the mud over the wet door-steps of the stately mansions. On that inclement day, not even the comfortable carriages of the aristocracy were to be seen; but from within the rich and curtained windows you might note the ruddy firelight, and well-clad figures moving listlessly along the warm and carpeted floors.

Different was the state of the outcast on the door-step. Oh! those London door-steps – could they speak, what tales could they tell of the feet that tread over them, the forms that rest on them. They would tell of lust prowling to its morning's lair – of dissipation staggering from its midnight orgies. They would tell of the hard speculator returning with a harsh, firm, step from the side of his ruined victim. They would tell of the fluttering footfall of the female gossamer of fashion – the cold tread of the unpitying statesman, the snake-like gliding of the successful lawyer. Of the bloated trader, purse-proud and vulgar, returning from his city shop to his west-end *apery* of menial insolence, and area theft – of greater robberies by greater robbers, – they could unveil the clock-work of that vile machinery, that crushes human nature in its working, and smoothes its wheels with the blood of fellow beings.

On the day to which our narrative alludes, a poor young woman, with a baby on her breast, sat on the door-step of a mansion in Grosvenor Square. Traces of emaciated beauty still lingered on her face – her tattered shawl and ragged gown clung loosely to her form, for famine had shrunk her frame from its natural proportions. Her dress was wretched, but her hair was neat, shewing that poverty, and not idleness, was the source of her raggedness. She pressed the little baby to her breast, but there was no nourishment there – hunger had been beforehand with that baby, and its turned it pretty, thin, little face, up to its mother with a faint cry, and a look of piteous disappointment and reproach.

Sad was the history of that mother. Some weeks back her husband, who had been long out of work, had been promised a job in London, and accordingly left Leicester, his native town, in search of the expected employment. When in London he found that the master who was to employ him, had taken on a supply of fresh hands at lower wages than were promised to him and he found himself hopeless and destitute. In vain he implored for work – in vain he even fawned upon the rich – wistfully he gazed at the full provision shops – at the great mansions, at the splendid equipages and he whispered, as the carriages of the aristocrats rolled by: "Oh! if but one of you would put down *one* of your fat horses, its costs would make happy a whole family of human beings!" and his tears started to his eyes as he thought of his poor wife and little baby. Had it not been for them, he would have stolen bread to satisfy his hunger; but his liberty was necessary for their support – he still *might* get work. Meanwhile, even the Bastiles closed their accursed gates against him – they were overgorged – the door-step, and the park, and the arch of the bridge were forbidden ground; the houseless outcast was not even allowed to lie on the cold bed that God had smoothed – the hard wet ground – the inhospitable stones – for the "move on," of the policemen broke the rest of the exhausted beggar.

Thus days wore on –it was the tenth of April *– and the weary outcast had gazed on the magnificent pageant of Kennington Common – we will not describe his feelings when he saw the hundreds of thousands, with the seal of REVOLUTION, stamped by oppression on their foreheads – we will not say with what feelings he returned towards the bridges – but he returned peaceably, unarmed, and exhausted. While passing Blackfriars Bridge, he saw an assault made by the police on a group of unoffending persons, and a woman struck with a truncheon – as the blow was about to be repeated, he mechanically interposed his feeble arm: "Down with the – rioter!" cried a sergeant of police, and with a fractured skull the helpless victim was dragged to the nearest hospital, where he died three days after.

Meanwhile the wife, buoyed with hope, had been awaiting anxiously, in Leicester, tidings from her husband. Not hearing, she made up her mind, towards the close of April, to follow him to London, and accordingly, without means and with a heavy heart, she took her baby in her arms and set out for the metropolis. Oh! it was a hungry, weary walk. Foot-sore she reached town, and sought the employers who had promised work – after much difficulty and insult she found them – and with scorn and insolence they drove her from the shop, telling her they "knew nothing about the fellow, – lots of vagabonds came seeking work at their place, and they couldn't be answerable for what became of every idle rascal who called there."

Heart-broken she wandered through the streets – and one weary afternoon she sat, as we have described, on the doorstep in Grosvenor Square. A faithful wife, a kind mother, with every virtue that adorns a woman – she sat there and thus – while the man within had £15,000 per annum, a seat in Monmouthshire, and another in Notts, a title and a place under Government. His wife that morning had been busy issuing directions for a nocturnal *féte*, and was at that moment reading one of the most obscene novels of *Paul de Kock!*

There sat the outcast – she had walked all the way from Leicester – for six and thirty hours she had not tasted food or drink, save some draughts of water on the road-side, and one charitable working-man had given her half a pint of ale, as she was crawling through a country village within twelve miles of London.

There sat the outcast – and the faintness of exhaustion came over her – her grasp relaxed, the baby slipped out of her arms, and slowly rolled down the three stone steps on to the pavement, where it lay moaning piteously and feebly, while its mother sank back against the threshold.

"John," said the baronet, to his powdered lackey – for he stood at the window of his library – and had rung for his cab, seeing that the rain had somewhat ceased – "John, do you see that drunken woman on the doorstop – send her about her business – what does she mean by lying there?"

John obeyed the command with a brutality that exceeded even the intention of his master, and seeing a policeman, committed the poor woman to his charge.

The policeman saw in this prisoner nothing but a drunken prostitute – not his the fine feeling to take more than casual notice of her – and, little removed from the brute by nature, he dragged the child up by its arm, and shook his mother

* 1848 [ed.]

till consciousness returned; when the latter, roused at the faint shrieks of her child, snatched it from his arms, and staggered after her captor.

She was classed with the "drunk and disorderlies," and placed for the night with the most unhappy outcasts of creation, who, though sinners, learned their sin at the hands of society.

That night she died! A verdict was returned: "Died of exposure to cold, and exhaustion." The child was sent to a workhouse – where, deprived of the fostering care of a father and a mother, the love of kindred and the hope of youth – of every domestic tie and manly example – society is rearing a young thief, to punish him, when he has well learned the lesson.

Such is the true history from a London door-step. Had the proud aristocrat been a Christian – instead, he would have invited the poor Pariah to his house, he would have shared, ay, even a mere trifle of his ill-gotten wealth with that wretched victim – he would have become the founder of happiness and virtue in an honourable family, instead of being, as now,

A SOCIAL MURDERER!

'The Convention',

from *De Brassier, A Democratic Romance* (1851–2)

Ernest Jones

"What shall I do with the movement?" This was the question that De Brassier ever asked himself, as he sat in his private room, in the midst of the great factory town, and the whirl and roar of popular excitement, clamouring for action smote upward ever and anon.

"What shall I do with the movement?"

Well would it be if the demagogue – aye, and the democrat, too, – were to ask himself this question a little sooner, – were to ask it before he stirred the waters of the mighty sea of agitation! Tears and blood – chains and madness – might be obviated then; a great movement might be nobly conducted, and grandly terminated; or, better than failure, never undertaken.

"What shall I do with the movement?"

There it lay, heaving and tossing to the breath of unguided passion – not a steady breeze, but fresh flaws breaking forth from every passing cloud, diverting the current of its waves, and clashing them against each other in ominous confusion.

Meanwhile, the death of the banker,* construed into a wilful and barbarous murder under most aggravated circumstances, had vastly turned the tide of public feeling. The deed was laid at the door of the democrats, although they were not in the least answerable for it, as the reader knows – it having been the unpremeditated act of thieves and plunderers, led by a maniac wholly unconnected with the movement. The designing caught the leverage thus afforded them, and trumpeted forth this fact as an illustration of the popular spirit, and a sample of what the people would do, if once installed in power.

The effect of this was soon apparent, in an increasing class-hostility. The small shop-keepers, who were rapidly joining the movement, were frightened back, and the richer portion of the middle-class, who had began to spout liberalism, as they always do, when democracy becomes *respectable* – that is, strong and formidable enough to command respect, now placed themselves at once in an attitude of fierce, decided, and almost aggressive hostility. The watchword was given –"we may as well die fighting as be burnt in our own houses!" – and a general run for constables' staves took place throughout the country.

This began to irritate the people – who, on their side, commenced, arming, drilling, and organising with renewed energy, and the turn-out became general and voluntary. This was the state of the movement immediately after the fire at Dorville factory; but this failing had, in reality, given the movement strength. Previously, a temporising compromising spirit towards the middle class had been partially extending; now that feeling was extinguished – and class stood in sharp antagonism against class – *the outline of Revolution!*

* in a riot [ed.]

That was the propitious moment for a decisive blow.

"What shall I do with the movement?"

Gather it up, De Brassier – guide it – hurl it onward! speak the word – the mighty word! so often hovering on thy lips, when there was no danger of its realisation! – speak it! – the great shibboleth of nations – speak it! – the key-word of the future, in whose one note lies the fiat of destiny! – hark! how they are murmuring it abroad –

REBELLION!

The thought flashed across De Brassier's mind – but no! Lord Weather Cock was right – he was not the man for that! No! agitation was his line – and agitation ran his tether out – he was fit for the first step in revolutions – and no more. Then stand back! and let others take the second – hark! how the popular strength frets, and fumes, and champs the bit of indignant delay. Why muffle the spurred heel of the mighty rider, Wrong, who would dash the steed across the brittle bulwark of the law?

"What shall I do with the movement? I am making money by it, by wholesale: that rascally Bludore* certainly watches the turn of the market – and though he makes two pounds to my one, yet I am growing rich. And then, shall I be more powerful through a rebellion? Do I not sway the people now, and terrify the government? A revolution will unseat me – other men with other objects will rise to the top – no – no! what? shall all my toil, my planning, end in this – to see a few hated rivals – men who rose from between my feet – soar up above my head, and I be lost beneath their shadow? No! no! they reckon there without their host. Shall plebeianism rule the day? Am I not De Brassier? Does not the blood of centuries roll across my veins? No! by the race of my fathers! if I lash the rich, and great, and governments, to avenge the injuries inflicted on my house – that house is called De Brassier still – and I punish the titled and powerful because they won't recognise its greatness – shall I sacrifice it to a rabble who will give it still less of recognition. No! if I am to sink into insignificance, let it be beneath St. James's sooner than St. Giles's. I must check this movement without losing my popularity – and I must alter its tone and temper, for *it is growing too democratic for* DE BRASSIER."

How to solve this problem, however, was the difficulty. It has been already stated that De Brassier was a consummate schemer – the problem was difficult, but he worked out a solution.

Issuing forth from his study, he saw at a glance that no speedy change was possible. Nay – that he must humour the movement to retain his popularity. He, therefore, assumed a higher and more decisive tone than ever – pointed to the day of revolution and the hour of battle with no very covert language, merely screened enough to save him from the law – which, however, he pretty well understood the government would not then enforce against him – and, then, saying to himself: "I must amuse these children with some revolutionary toys"– began to organise a mass of processions and demonstrations. There is nothing more useful and impressive at a critical moment than a procession or great demonstrative meeting, – but there is also nothing more injurious than their too great repetition, or inopportune application. They wear a movement out, to no purpose, and resulting in nothing so often, the people at last become accustomed to look upon them as a useless form – the government as a silly parade – and the masses cease to attend them because they do not see any object

* *his lawyer* [ed.]

199

to be achieved by their attendance. These ridiculous parades have destroyed more than one movement in the world.

A great meeting, on Tara, Clontorf, Kersall Moor, or Kennington Common, should never be held, except it is intended that they shall result in immediate action of some kind or other.

Such meetings are intended to show the people their strength, and to intimidate opponents. If they result in nothing, they have just the contrary effect – they make the people believe that, after all, their strength was not as great as was expected, or the convokers of the meeting would have made good their boasts previous to the meeting – and they make the government believe that, whatever the strength of the people may be, the latter have not the courage requisite to wield it.

De Brassier, accordingly, kept amusing and beguiling the people with these idle shows – gathering and increasing his personal popularity. For, at each procession he was the idol – around him was concentrated the halo of torches – on his head rained a perfect grove of laurels – before him pealed a very paean of triumphant music. It is astonishing how prone the people are to worship an idol – merely *because* they have idolised it. As a father loves its own child, so a people love the idol they have made, however wooden it may be!

When De Brassier saw that his position was secure, he looked round him for the means of unseating his rivals – the foremost, eagerest, and most uncompromising abettors of the movement. They were urging the people, and wisely, to immediate action – for things had arrived at that pitch, that they must *go on, or go back* – they could stand still no longer. The question then was, "shall the movement be broken up – or shall we take the only step left consistent with its antecedent guidance, and its present strength?" De Brassier was determined that this step should not be taken – and that, although the popular movement might be destroyed, De Brassier and his party should still remain erect above the ruin.

Accordingly, in order to accomplish the double object of destroying the power of his rivals, and increasing his own – in order to appear the saviour instead of the destroyer of the movement, he hit upon a most notable plan – he summoned a CONVENTION!

Quoth he, "The people themselves must guide their own affairs. That is democracy, I have no business to think and execute for you. I am no dictator. I am your humble servant. Send your delegates, and let them decide what shall be done in the present crisis."

"I'm right," said Lord Weather Cock to Sir Gaffer Grim, when he heard of it – "that fellow can't lead a revolution – he is afraid of his own position – he is calling a council when he should be marshalling a battle. Let us wait quietly."

"Lord Weather Cock was right in the main – but he had still far too good an opinion of De Brassier – he thought this measure was dictated merely by fear and weakness – he did not comprehend that the demagogue was destroying democracy to exalt De Brassier – and serving government merely because it served himself.

The Convention assembled. Two hundred delegates, the choicest, noblest, boldest, aye! perhaps wisest, spirits of democracy assembled – and De Brassier, amid the general plaudits of that gallant band, assumed his place at the head of the people's council.

A general synopsis of the popular strength was given; and most promising, indeed, was the future drawn.

De Brassier immediately began to challenge the correctness of their statements; he began to throw doubt upon their strength; he told them, "no man was more ready to fight the battle of democracy than he – but that he wished to know the forces he had to command before he led them forth. He knew the strength of his opponents – the government – well enough, but he did not yet know theirs."

He next began to *point out their weakness,* and, by dint of telling them they were miserably weak, he actually began to make some of them think they were! "If my blood could gain you the victory – aye! if it could brighten the cheek of one factory-child, it should be poured out like water; but I cannot consent to see husbands, sons, and brothers butchered like defenceless sheep; – I cannot bear to hear the wail of orphans, mothers, sisters – oh, God!" and the tears ran down his manly cheeks, to the astonishment of the assembled delegates.

However, they were moved; some of them began to be frightened. If the tremendous De Brassier could be shaken thus – it was time for them to quail.

The bolder spirits took fire at this water, and stated that revolutions were not to be made with tears any more than with milk of roses; and, asking what all the agitation, procession, turn-outs, threatening, and arming had been for, if it were to end in nothing – urged immediate action.

Then De Brassier rose, with a solemn air: "Gentlemen!" said he – "a horrid conspiracy is afloat – it is concocted by government – a plot to destroy us. They are thirsting for our blood. There" – he continued, throwing down a letter – "there is a warning I have received, by a member of the police itself – that I am to be shot as soon as a movement is made – the leaders are to be picked off – I have the list of names – there is a file of picked marksmen in every battalion, who are to concentrate their fire on given individuals, instead of random volleys; there is no escaping; a member of the detective-police will accompany them, and point out the devoted men. I repeat, I have the list of names; I won't read them, gentlemen! but in now looking round this board, *my eyes rest on several of their number!"*

The effect was electric – as De Brassier moved his glance from face to face, among those whom he knew most timid, and most easily worked upon.

There was great paleness and dead silence. THE FIRST POINT WAS GAINED!

Then Edward, the young mechanic, and Latimer started up (for both were delegates), and asked if the fear of death should keep the soldier from the field – exhorted the convention to courage, and gave a glowing picture of the power of the movement.

De Brassier rose again: "I have told you that a deep plot is at work. I have hitherto kept the movement clear from committing itself. I have prevented all violence. I have not given the government a handle. I have prevented all bloodshed. I will do so still. I will save the movement from fools and traitors. I know them." And again his eyes rested ominously on the board, and lingered on the boldest and most enthusiastic leaders. "I know them. I now tell you, that some of the people's most trusted leaders are in the pay of government – and *some of them are seated in this room!"*

A fearful explosion was the result of these words; but De Brassier sat down unmoved.

"Are seated at this board," he murmured, almost inaudibly.

"Is it I? – or I? – or I?" – cried several, starting up, with a burst of indignation.

"Whom the cap fits. I name no one!"

"I demand that the honour of this board be vindicated. De Brassier has said traitors are at this board. That is an insult to the Convention – he is bound to name them."

"I name no one! I never said at this board."

"You did – we heard you."

A fearful altercation arose; *public business was stopped* – personal abuse began.

THE SECOND POINT WAS GAINED!

At last, since the debate degenerated into vindictive and insulting epithets launched from end to end, and side to side of the board, by the hostile parties – for *the Convention was now divided* – it was split into two – and two most hostile parties, one or two voices cried – "MEASURES, NOT MEN!" "What can we do for the people?"

The discussion, however, was adjourned, nothing but confusion prevailing in the remainder of the sitting; and during the night, instead of getting cooled by reflection, the rival coteries met, concocting the morrow's campaign.

The discussion opened with the best means of directing popular power.

De Brassier again rose, and asserted that there was no such thing as popular power then in existence: that it was all a delusion – the people were weak, timid, and disorganised. This brought on counter-statements, and (*the government reporters being present*) every possible thing that could be raked up to shew the weakness of the cause, was raked up to strengthen the position of the timid faction. The government thus became fully aware of the weak points of the movement, and where to strike it with effect – it became thenceforth at their mercy. This called forth counter-statements on the part of the true and bold, in which they were, perhaps, even driven into exaggeration, with the object of counteracting the injurious impression the disgraceful exposure must make on the government and the privileged classes. This, however, by shewing the "dangerous" character of the movement, but increased the hostility of the latter, while it served the double purpose of compromising a number of good and honest men, and arraying prejudice in the jury-box against them.

THE THIRD POINT WAS GAINED.

De Brassier was destroying his rivals.

In opposition to the assertion of the movement's weakness, and the want of sympathy entertained for it by the working-classes themselves, the delegates appealed to the enthusiastic meetings and demonstrations in the country, and the excitement caused by the assembling of the Convention in the town in which it sat; nay! the crowded state of the hall, and the cheers of the audience.

"SPIES AND TRAITORS paid by government!" cried De Brassier. "Do not let those cheers mislead you. There are men sent into this hall, in the dress of working-men, ordered to applaud and cheer the most violent sentiments. They are detectives. They are marking you, and every one that applauds. Fools! they cheer you just to get you to commit yourselves."

It became dangerous to applaud, since applause itself excited suspicion. Mutual distrust reigned at the board, and among the public without!

THE FOURTH POINT WAS GAINED.

The constituencies that had sent the delegates, saw the time wasted in bickering and in the most disgraceful strife. De Brassier trumpeted to the world that the Convention was full of paid spies and traitors. That, he being the only man to save the movement, was being made the victim of a conspiracy among the delegates; that the public time was dissipated in a personal attack on him, and called on the country to protest against the suicidal policy of its would-be representatives.

The effect may be imagined – funds ceased to flow for the support of the delegates. De Brassier then turned round upon them, and said, "Did I not tell you so? I said public sympathy was not with you. If it is, where is the money? that is the barometer of the movement. Now you see who was right!"

Alas! it was De Brassier who had destroyed the confidence – it was De Brassier who had thus prevented the supplies – it was De Brassier who had destroyed the enthusiasm – it was De Brassier who had divided the movement – it was De Brassier who had sown distrust, and set every man against his neighbour! And now De Brassier called the effect, the cause; he turned the tables, and made the mischief he had created appear to be the result of the incompetency, envy, folly, and *treachery* of those whom he was ruining.

In vain the latter protested – they had no means of access to the people; De Brassier monopolised all the channels of communication; they had none – they had no papers to report them – they had no money to travel about the country, as he did, and reason personally with the people who condemned them.

THE FIFTH POINT WAS GAINED.

Soon the delegates began to get into debt. Money not arriving from the country, the Convention was obliged to break up in disgrace, covered with liabilities, and the delegates hung like paupers about the town, unable even to get back to their homes.

Then De Brassier came forward – offered the money out of his own private purse. Dire necessity forced most of them to accept. The demagogue took good care to publish the fact with stentorian force; and the returning delegates, if they dared to defend their own characters, were accused of being ungrateful wretches, whose base, little envy had tried to destroy the great leader of the people, who, notwithstanding, had extended the noble hand of unexampled generosity to the jaundiced traitors who had tried to sting him.

THE SIXTH POINT WAS GAINED.

They were made innocuous for some time to come.

De Brassier now rushed off into the country. Post, rail, steamer, all was put in requisition to make him almost ubiquitous – everywhere he shrieked forth –

"Spies and traitors! I have saved the movement from a pack of knaves! I have prevented the shedding of torrents of blood. I have taken you out of the hands of villains! Peace – law – and order! what a victory we should have had if it had not been for those spies and traitors! But we have baffled the government.

We have destroyed their plot. I have saved you – I have saved you!" and the tears of grateful exultation streamed down his smiling cheeks.

Everywhere the cry was echoed – "Spies and traitors – spies and traitors!" Everybody suspected every one of everything. In fact there was but one honest man in the universe, and that man was DE BRASSIER!

Thus ended the first act of the great political drama. The stage was now clear – not a rival was in the field – and over it all stalked De Brassier – sole, absolute, self-glorious, and calm.

The first act was ended – but now the second was to begin – with its baptism of tears and anguish.

Notes

For reasons of space it is not possible to supply further details about the periodical and newspaper sources of the stories. For an excellent account of these publications see Royden Harrison, Gillian B. Woolven, and Robert Duncan, (eds), *The Warwick Guide to British Labour Periodicals 1790–1870: A Check List* (Brighton: Harvester Press, 1977).

Will Harper: A Poor-Law Tale

Taken from *Cleave's Gazette of Variety* (1838), vol. 2, no. 6.

The Widow and the Fatherless

Taken from *Cleave's Gazette of Variety* (1838), vol. 2, no. 7.

p. 33 *Can it be in merry England* – Scott
Not located.

p. 33 *Ah! little think the gay, licentious proud* – Pope
Not located.

The Convict

Taken from the *Chartist Circular* (1839), no. 14.

A Simple Story

Taken from the *English Chartist Circular* (1840), vol. 1, no. 16.

p. 41 *well-known fable of the statue*
In one of the Aesop's Fables (6th century BC), a man boasts to a lion of his superior strength. For evidence he points to an image carved on stone of a man throttling a lion. But the lion retorts that if lions could carve, there would be many images of lions on top of humans.

Seth Thompson, the Stockinger

From Thomas Cooper, *Wise Saws and Modern Instances* (1845).

p. 47 *looped and windowed rags*
Shakespeare, *King Lear*, III, 4, 31.

"Merrie England"– No More!

From Thomas Cooper, *Wise Saws and Modern Instances* (1845).

p. 54 *Atheistical Socialists*
The word 'Socialist' at this time referred usually to the ideas of Robert Owen (1771–1858), who believed in communitarianism and co-operation.

p. 54 *Jonathan Edwards*
Jonathan Edwards (1703–58), American revivalist theologian and extreme Calvinist.

p. 54 *Robert Hall*
Robert Hall (1764–1831), popular Baptist clergyman who settled in Leicestershire from 1806.

p. 54 *Arminian sects*
Followers of the doctrine of the Dutch Protestant theologian Arminius d.1609), who disagreed with Calvin about predestination.

p. 54 *Calvinists*
Followers of the Protestant theologian John Calvin (1509–64) who believed in predestination.

p. 56 *Corn Law Repealers*
The Corn Laws, which kept the price of grain high, were eventually repealed in 1846.

p. 58 *Bishop Burnet*
Gilbert Burnet (1643–1715), Scottish churchman and bishop of Salisbury.

p. 59 *Egede and the Moravians among the Greenlanders*
Hans Egede (1686–1758), a Norwegian missionary, who set up a mission in Greenland to convert the Eskimos.
The Moravians were a Protestant sect originally based in Moravia, now part of the Czech Republic.

The Defender: An Irish Tale of 1797

Taken from the *Chartist Circular* (1840), nos 16–19.

p. 64 *General Abercromby*
Based on Sir Ralph Abercromby (1734–1801), Scottish general in the British army. On 26 February 1798 he issued a general order that the militia then terrorizing the Irish people were more dangerous than any insurgents.

The Rebel Chief: A Scene in the Wicklow Mountains, 1803

Taken from the *Chartist Circular* (1840), nos. 20–22.

The Desmonds: A Tale of Landlordism in Ireland

Taken from *Reynolds's Miscellany* (1845), vol. 1, no. 4.

The Meal-Mongers: Or, Food Riots in Ireland

Taken from *The Labourer* (1848), vol. 3, no. 14.

A secret Irish society set up in 1843 to ambush rent collectors. Its male members dressed up in women's clothes, like the 'Rebecca' rioters in Wales.

p. 99 *Captain Rock*
The name adopted by the leader of an Irish uprising in 1822.

p. 101 *Dr Johnson*
Samuel Johnson (1709–84), English man of letters.

p. 101 *Obadiah*
A colloquial term for a Quaker.

p. 104 *Grimaldi*
A famous clown (1779–1837).

Dissuasive Warnings to the People on Street Warfare

p. 106 *Macerone*
Francis Macerone, author of *Defensive Instructions for the People* (1832).

p. 110 *Woolwich*
Woolwich, in south-east London, location of the arsenal of the Royal Artillery.

p. 110 *Congreve*
Sir William Congreve (1772–1828), invented the Congreve rocket in 1808.

p. 111 *Carlists*
Followers of Don Carlos (1788–1855), pretender to the Spanish throne, who led an uprising in Spain against Queen Isabella in 1834–39. The British supported Isabella. Somerville did active service in this war.

p. 115 *Badajoz*
A city in western Spain, centre of numerous battles in the Peninsular wars, finally taken by the British in April 1812.

p. 116 *Busaco*
A ridge in the Portuguese province of Biera Litoral, site of a battle on 27 September 1810, in which the British repelled the French.

p. 117 *Lord Eliot*
Edward Granville Eliot (1798–1877), diplomat. In 1834 he was sent to Spain as a special envoy to negotiate the 'Eliot' convention, in which the two sides fighting the Carlist wars ceased executing prisoners.

p. 118 *O'Connor's head . . . Cleave*
Prominent Chartists.

p. 118 *O'Connor*
Feargus O'Connor (1794–1855), born in Connorville, County Cork, owner of the *Northern Star*, MP for Nottingham (1847).

p. 118 *Vincent*
Henry Vincent (1813–78), orator, jailed 1839–40).

p. 118 *Frost*
John Frost (1784–1877), Welsh leader of the Newport uprising in November 1839, transported to Tasmania 1840–52.

p. 118 *Baillie Craig*
Baillie Hugh Craig, Scottish draper.

p. 118 *Doctor Taylor*
John Taylor (1805–42), fiery Scottish orator.

p. 118 *Fleming*
George Alexander Fleming, who joined the staff of the *Northern Star* in 1844.

p. 118 *McDowall*
Peter Murray McDowall (1815–54), Scottish Chartist, imprisoned 1840–41.

p. 118 *Hetherington*
Henry Hetherington (1792–1849), London radical publisher.

p. 118 *Cleave*
John Cleave (1790–1847), London radical publisher.

p. 119 *Lord Melbourne*
William Lamb (1779–1848), second Viscount Melbourne, British Prime Minister 1835–41.

p. 119 *Van Halen*
Not identified. Presumably a leader in the Carlist wars.

p. 119 *Cabrera*
Don Ramon Cabrera (1810–77), Spanish Carlist leader.

p. 119 *Colonel Prince*
Not identified. Presumably a military commander fighting the Canadian rebels in the uprising of 1837.

p. 119 *a preacher*
Joseph Reyner Stephens (1805–79), fiery Methodist preacher and anti-Poor Law campaigner, jailed in 1839.

p. 122 *Lord John Russell*

John Russell (1792–1878), Whig statesman, British Prime Minister 1846–52.

p. 125 *Oastlerian school*
A reference to Richard Oastler (1789–1861) who earned the nickname the 'Factory King' for his work in favour of the Ten Hours Bill.

p. 125 *Mrs Trollope's 'Factory Boy'*
A reference to Fanny Trollope's novel, *The Life and Adventures of Michael Armstrong, the Factory Boy* (1840). In Chapter 8 Michael is forced by his master to kiss a young female operative.

The Revolutionist

Taken from the *Chartist Circular* (1840), nos 39, 48, 49.

p. 131 *Count de Sembreuil*
The name of the Governor of the Hotel des Invalides, stormed on 14 July 1798.

p. 139 *Count Las Cases' Journal*
A reference to *Memoirs of Emanuel Augustus Dieudonne, Count Las Casas*, translated into English in 1815. Conveniently, the passage cited has been supposedly repressed. The *Memoirs* contain conversations with Napoleon.

The Insurgent Leader

Taken from the *Chartist Circular* (1840), no. 25.

The Maid of Warsaw

Taken from Ernest Jones, *The Romance of a People*. First published in *The Labourer* (1847–48); reissued as a single volume with the title *The Maid of Warsaw* (1855).

Nationalism

Taken from Ernest Jones, *The Romance of a People* (1847–48).

'A Midnight Rising'

Taken from Ernest Jones, *De Brassier: A Democratic Romance*, which appeared in *Notes to the People* (1851–52).

The Outcast

Taken from W. J. Linton, *The National* (1839) no. 6.

p. 158 *Thou rascal beadle, hold thy bloody hand ...*
Shakespeare, *King Lear*, IV, 6, 164.

p. 160 *Magdalen Hospitals*
Convalescence hospitals for prostitutes.

The Free-Servant

Taken from W. J. Linton, *The National* (1839), no. 6.

p. 162 *Next to governesses ...*
Harriet Martineau (1802–76). Quotation not located.

The Young Seamstress

Taken from *Reynolds's Miscellany* (1847), vol. 2.

p. 165 *Society for the Relief of Distressed Needlewomen*
In Henry Mayhew, *London Labour and the London Poor*, (1861–62)
4 vols, vol, 4, p. xxix, there is a mention of two agencies helping
needleworkers: the Association for the Aid and Benefit of Dressmakers
and Milliners; the Needlewomen's Institution.

The Slave of the Needle

Taken from George W. M. Reynolds, *London Journal* (1850), vols. 10–11.

p. 170 *That frozen continent, Dark and wild ...*
Milton, *Paradise Lost*, II, 587– 89.

p. 170 *Tantalus*
A character in Greek mythology, punished in Hades by never being able
to consume food and drink which were placed just beyond his reach.

p. 170 *a forest huge of spears*
Milton, *Paradise Lost*, I, 547.

p. 171 *nipping and eager*
Shakespeare, *Hamlet*, I, 4, 2.

p. 172 *O! men, with sisters dear ...*
Thomas Hood, 'The Song of the Shirt', 25–28, first published in
Punch, Christmas 1843.

p. 173 *fair large front and eye sublime declared absolute rule*
Milton, *Paradise Lost,* IV, 300–01.

p. 173 *Not Babylon, Nor great Alcairo . . .*
Milton, *Paradise Lost*, I, 717–19.

p. 174 *dead waist and middle of the night*
Shakespeare, *Hamlet* (1601), I, 2, 198 ('waist' should read 'vast').

p. 174 *A woman sat, in unwomanly rags, Plying her needle and thread*
Thomas Hood, 'The Song of the Shirt', 3–4.

p. 174 *No friends, no hope! no kindred weep for me . . .*
Shakespeare, *Henry VIII*, III, I, 150–53.

p. 178 *Nor long did her life . . .*
Thomas Moore (not located).

p. 180 *silvery sounds, so soft, so dear*
Compare Shakespeare, *Romeo and Juliet*, II, 2, 158–59.

p. 182 *The tale that I would unfold to-day . . . Renaldo the Visionary*
Not located.

p. 182 *The bleak wind of March . . .*
Thomas Hood, 'The Bridge of Sighs', 63–79.

p. 183 *in the blind cave of eternal night*
Compare Milton, *Paradise Lost*, III, 18.

p. 184 *Dreams treasured up from early days*
Wordsworth, *Yarrow Revisited*, 79.

p. 185 *worn by Hercules*
In Greek mythology, the shirt of Nessus, which Hercules could not remove without tearing his skin.

p. 186 *To see that white face . . .*
Not located.

The Poor Man's Wrongs

Taken from *Cleave's Gazette of Variety* (1839), vol. 2, no. 30.

p. 187 *Ettrick Shepherd*
James Hogg (1770–1835), Scottish novelist, who for much of his life lived in the Ettrick Forest, Selkirkshire.

p. 188 *unhappy Spain*

A reference to the Carlist wars (1834–39), in which Britain supported Queen Isabella.

p. 188 *the New Poor law Bill*
The Poor Law Amendment Act, passed in 1834.

p. 189 *the Reform Bill*
Passed in 1832 by the Whig government, this Act enfranchised the £10 householder, and reformed electoral districts.

The Charter and the Land

Taken from *The Labourer* (1847).

p. 191 *Melbourne*
See p. 119.

p. 194 *Dick Pilling*
Richard Pilling, a Stockport Chartist, arrested for his part in the uprisings of 1842, made a famous defence speech at his trial in 1843 which had the jury in tears and resulted in an acquittal.

The London Doorstep

Taken from *The Labourer* (1848).

p. 196 *Paul de Kock*
Paul de Kock (1794 –1871), French novelist.

'The Convention'

Taken from Ernest Jones, *De Brassier* (1851–52).